PĀLI BUDDHISM

CURZON STUDIES IN ASIAN PHILOSOPHY

Series Editors:

Indira Mahalingam

Lecturer in Law

University of Exeter

Brian Carr

Senior Lecturer in Philosophy

University of Nottingham

The *Curzon Studies in Asian Philosophy* are collections of papers centering on various themes presented in a manner that does not presuppose the specialist linguistic knowledge which has tended to make these traditions closed to the wider philosophical audience. Among the projected volumes, some reflect recent conferences and others are papers specially written for the series. Some have grown out of recent controversies in the Carfax journal *Asian Philosophy.*

MORALS AND SOCIETY IN ASIAN PHILOSOPHY
Edited by Brian Carr

FRIENDSHIP EAST AND WEST
Philosophical Perspectives
Edited by Oliver Leaman

PĀLI BUDDHISM

Edited by

Frank J. HOFFMAN and
DEEGALLE Mahinda

Routledge
Taylor & Francis Group
LONDON AND NEW YORK

First published in 1996
by Curzon Press

Published 2013 by Routledge
2 Park Square, Milton Park, Abingdon, Oxfordshire OX14 4RN
711 Third Avenue, New York, NY, 10017, USA

First issued in paperback 2016

Routledge is an imprint of the Taylor & Francis Group, an informa business

Typeset in Garamond by Excel Books, New Delhi

British Library Cataloguing in Publication Data
A catalogue record of this book is available from the British Library

Library of Congress Cataloguing in Publication Data
A catalogue record for this book has been requested

ISBN 13: 978-1-138-99473-7 (pbk)
ISBN 13: 978-0-7007-0359-3 (hbk)

DEDICATION

To Kunie, Aya Frances, and
Rika India Miyahara Hoffman

and

IN MEMORIAM

Dr. Jan T. Ergardt
Expositor of "this one way"

"*Ekāyano ayaṃ bhikkhave maggo*
sattānaṃ visuddhiyā ...."
Majjhima Nikāya I, 10:
Satipaṭṭhānasutta

All royalties from the sale of this volume are being donated to:
The Buddhist Publication Society, P.O. Box 61, Sangaraja Mawatha,
Kandy, Sri Lanka.

CONTENTS

Dedication v
Acknowledgements ix
Abbreviations xi
Foreword by Ninian SMART xv
Introduction by Frank J. HOFFMAN and DEEGALLE Mahinda 1
PLATE 1: Anurādhapura elephant 14

SECTION I
Philological Foundations

1. *Theravāda* Buddhism's Two Formulations of the *Dasa Sīla* and the Ethics of the Gradual Path
GEORGE D. BOND
Department of Religion
Northwestern University 17

2. A Proposed Model of Early Buddhist Liberation
ANDREW OLENDZKI
Insight Meditation Society
Barre, Massachusetts 43

3. *Dhammapada* and *Tirukkṟaḷ*: A Comparative Study
SUBRAMANIA GOPALAN
Department of Philosophy
National University of Singapore 57

4. *Abhidharma* as Paradigm for Practice
CHRISTOPHER KEY CHAPPLE
Department of Theology
Loyola Marymount University 79

PLATE 2: Anurādhapura guardian 102

SECTION II
Insiders' Understandings

5. The Moral Significance of Buddhist *Nirvāṇa*
DEEGALLE MAHINDA
Department of the History of Religions
University of Chicago 105

6. Suicide and Emotional Ambivalence: An Early Buddhist Perspective
PADMASIRI DE SILVA
Department of Philosophy and Psychology
University of Peradeniya 117

7. The Logical Grammar of the Word "Rebirth" in the Buddhist Paradigm
A.D.P. KALANSURIYA
Department of Philosophy and Psychology
University of Peradeniya 133

8. A Buddhist Critique of *Theravāda*
GUNAPALA DHARMASIRI
Department of Philosophy and Psychology
University of Peradeniya 141

PLATE 3: Anurādhapura moonstone 156

SECTION III
Philosophical Implications

9. Two Dogmas of Buddhism
ARTHUR L. HERMAN
Department of Philosophy
University of Wisconsin, Stevens Point 159

10. What is the Status of the Doctrine of Dependent Origination?
RAMAKRISHNA PULIGANDLA
Department of Philosophy,
University of Toledo 175

11. Process Philosophy and *Theravāda* Buddhism
SHANTA RATNAYAKA
Department of Philosophy
University of Gerorgia 184

12. *Theravāda* and Processes: *Nirvāṇa* as a Meta-process
NINIAN SMART
Department of Religious Studies
University of California, Santa Barbara 196

13. "Orientalism" in Buddhology
FRANK J. HOFFMAN
Department of Philosophy
West Chester University 207

Appendix 227
Index 229

Acknowledgements

The co-editors would like to offer *special thanks* as follows:

- to Professor *Masatoshi Nagatomi* for introducing Prof. Hoffman to Ven. Deegalle on the occasion of the National Endowment for the Humanities Summer 1988 Institute, "Teaching Comparative Courses" (directed by Professors Carman and Graham);
- to Professor *Ninian Smart* for encouraging the compilation of these papers on Pali Buddhism from the outset of our endeavor;
- to series editors, Drs. *Indira Mahalingam* and *Brian Carr*, for their invitation to submit this volume for consideration as part of the Curzon Studies in Asian Philosophy Series;
- and to *Martina and Malcolm Campbell* of Curzon Press and David McCarthy of Laserscript Limited, for their thoughtful effort and resourceful management in matters of production.

Thanks are due to the *State System of Higher Education* of Pennsylvania for a SSHE 1/4 release-time grant with which to do research, writing, and editing pertaining to this anthology during 1991-92. West Chester University College of Arts and Sciences manuscript typist, Anne Raeburn, did the bulk of the typing.

Thanks are due also to the South Asia Regional Studies Department (SARS), *University of Pennsylvania*; especially to South Asia Bibliographer Ms. *Kanta Bhatia* and Dr. *Richard Cohen* for their support and advice, and to *Karen* and *Lavinia* for occasional practical office support. The availability of the Van Pelt Library through a reciprocal agreement between member institutions of the *Greater Philadelphia Philosophy Consortium*, especially access to the W. Norman Brown collection in South Asian Studies, facilitated this work and is much appreciated.

Deegalle Mahinda expresses gratitude to his preceptor, the Venerable Galauḍa Medhaṅkara, and his mentor, Professor Frank E. Reynolds of the University of Chicago, for their far-sighted guidance and support. Thanks are due to Prof. M.A. Dhaky and Mr. R. Sharma for permission to use photographs from the American Institute of Indian Studies, Varanasi, in Plates produced herein. Manvendra Jhala and Thomas Radice, Philosophy students in the 1994-95 Buddhist Texts Discussion Group, contributed to the proofreading effort and helped with the index at the West Chester University.

Any errors which occur despite such excellent support are the full responsibility of the co-editors.

Dr. Frank J. HOFFMAN	Ven. DEEGALLE Mahinda
Department of Philosophy	Department of the History of Religions
West Chester University	University of Chicago

Abbreviations

A	*Aṅguttaranikāya*
A-a	*Aṅguttaranikāya-aṭṭhakathā = Manorathapūraṇī*
As	*Atthasālinī*
D	*Dīghanikāya*
D-a	*Dīghanikāya-aṭṭhakathā = Sumaṅgalavilāsinī*
Dhp	*Dhammapada*
Dhp-a	*Dhammapad'-aṭṭhakathā*
Dhs-a	*Dhammasaṅganī-aṭṭhakathā*
GS	The Book of the Gradual Sayings = *Aṅguttaranikāya*
It	*Itivuttaka*
It-a	*Itivuttaka-aṭṭhakathā*
Khp	*Khuddakapāṭha*
Khp-a	*Khuddakapāṭha-aṭṭhakathā=Paramatthajotikā*
KS	The Book of the Kindred Sayings = *Saṃyuttanikāya*
M	*Majjhimanikāya*
M-a	*Majjhimanikāya-aṭṭhakathā = Papañcasūdanī*
Mil	*Milindapañha*
MLS	Middle Length Sayings = *Majjhimanikāya*
Nett	*Nettipakaraṇa*
PTS	Pali Text Society
S	*Saṃyuttanikāya*
S-a	*Saṃyuttanikaya-aṭṭakathā=Sāratthappakāsinī*
SBB	Sacred Books of the Buddhists
SBE	Sacred Books of the East
Sn	*Suttanipāta*
Vin	*Vinayapiṭaka*
Vism	*Visuddhimagga*

Foreword

Professor Frank Hoffman and the Venerable Deegalle Mahinda have done a fine job in assembling this volume of papers relating to Pāli philosophy. As they observe in their introduction too little notice is taken of Asian and other areas of world philosophy among professional philosophers in the West. Admittedly there are different general conceptions of what philosophy is in differing cultural regions. But then there have been very diverse ideas on the subject in the Western tradition itself. What do Aristotle, Plotinus, Duns Scotus, Leibniz, Schopenhauer, Marx, Sartre, Wittgenstein and Derrida agree upon in this regard? And if definition by family resemblance is all right in many contexts, why be essentialist over "philosophy"?

But a more vital issue is as to whether the ideas of Buddhism and of the Pāli tradition are intrinsically interesting. The answer is that they surely are. Some of the challenges of Theravādin thought are covered by essays in this book. The fact that Buddhism has no creator God and yet a vision of the ultimate as liberation or *nirvāṇa*, the importance of the notion of rebirth, a different basis of ethics from Western versions, a very divergent psychology, a vital set of meditation practices — these are some of the challenging features of this tradition. Any philosopher who takes the philosophy of religion, ethics, or psychology seriously should find the Theravāda interesting. Of all the forms of Buddhism it is perhaps the most different from most Western ideas of religion.

This volume contains a nice mixture of philosophy and philology, but is intelligible to those innocent of Pāli expertise. It also contains a good blend of Western and South Asian writers and a nice balance of Philosophy and Religious Studies papers. It is both descriptive and constructive, as well as having comparative elements. I would hope that many differing sorts of readers would find something to entice them here.

Ninian Smart
J.F. Rowny Professor of Comparative Religions
University of California, Santa Barbara

Introduction

Frank J. Hoffman and Deegalle Mahinda

I. The Significance of Pāli Buddhist Studies and its Historical Background

The origins of Pāli Buddhist studies in European academia may be traced to the establishment of the Pali Text Society in 1881[1] and *Journal of the Pali Text Society* in 1882. In the journal the aim of establishing the Pali Text Society (PTS)[2] is given as: to "render accessible to students the rich stories of the earliest Buddhist literature now lying unedited and practically unused ..."[3] The founder of the PTS, T.W. Rhys Davids, describes the preservation and study of Pāli Buddhism as a matter of practical necessity. C.A.F. Rhys Davids, the spouse and collaborator of T.W., was an independent thinker of her day who also contributed to the study of Pāli Buddhism, particularly in the area of Buddhist psychology. From T.W. Rhys Davids' point of view, the Pāli Canon is valuable since "... the sacred books of the early Buddhists have preserved to us the sole record of the only religious movement in the world's history which bears any close resemblance to early Christianity."[4] Whether this is so or only wishful thinking is debatable; to some extent the early pioneers of Pāli exegesis saw what their experience prepared them to see, and in this seeing "Protestant Buddhism" emerged.

Examining the authenticity of the Pāli Canon and Pāli language K.R. Norman maintains that the Pāli Canon is "a translation from some

1 India Office Library and Records, *Catalogue of the Pāli Printed Books in the India Office Library* edited by TCH Raper; revised by MJC O'Keefe (London: British Library, 1983), p. 1.

2 For weaknesses in the Pali Text Society's editions of Pāli texts see K.R. Norman's "Pāli Philology and the Study of Buddhism," *The Buddhist Forum*, Vol. 1 (London: School of Oriental and African Studies, 1990), p. 32-33.

3 *Journal of the Pali Text Society*, 1882, p. vii.

4 Ibid.

earlier tradition, and cannot be regarded as a primary source.[5] According to him, the qualifier "oldest" can be applied to the Pāli Canon in two ways: First, the Pāli Canon "in its present form" was composed earlier than any other Buddhist canon, for instance, before any other Sanskrit canons (1984, 4). Secondly, irrespective of the date of composition of the texts, one tradition (*i.e.*, Pāli) as a whole goes back further than the others (1984, 4). Since Norman believes that the Pāli tradition depended upon an earlier tradition in another dialect, he maintains that neither Pāli nor Sanskrit is older but the Buddha's words were collected in a dialect or dialects by which the Buddha spoke of his teachings (1984, 5). Norman further says that "any two or more canons may be dependent upon one and the same tradition" and since "no canon in the form in which we have it now, goes back to the time of the Buddha, the tradition upon which each is based may do so" (1984, 7).

In his conclusion, Norman says "the discovery of Sanskrit versions of the canon has increased the authority of other traditions" while reducing "the claim of the Pāli tradition to be the only authority," but since these other versions are for the most part in agreement with the Pāli tradition and present an insight into the form of Buddhist texts before the schisms, "they have reinforced the authority of the Pāli tradition and supported its claim to be authentic" (1984, 9). So although Norman does not wish to call the Pāli Canon "primary texts," it is clear that he supports the standard view that they are the earliest available texts for the study of Buddhism.

In observing the role of the Pāli Canon, Steven Collins suggests that the equation of the Pāli Canon with Early Buddhism should be rejected and we should move away "from an outmoded and quixotic concern with origins" to "a properly focused and realistic historical perspective."[6] From Collins's perspective, the Pāli Canon — in his words "the closed list of scriptures with a special and specific authority as the avowed historical record of the Buddha's teaching" — is a product of the Therāvada school which came into being as part of a strategy of legitimation (1990, 89). According to Collins, "we cannot know the relation between the "the canon" as we now have

5 K.R. Norman, "The Value of the Pāli Tradition," *Jagajoti Buddha Jayanti Annual*, Calcutta, May 1984, p. 4.

6 Steven Collins, "On the Very Idea of the Pāli Canon: In Memory of I.B. Horner," *Journal of the Pāli Text Society* XV (1990): 89.

it and the canon as it was being transmitted at this time" (1990, 95). He assigns the time of Buddhaghoṣa as the earliest date to which the specific and final form of the present Pāli Canon belongs (1990, 96). Collins maintains "the actual importance of what we know as the Pāli Canon has not lain in the specific texts collected in that list, but rather in the idea of such a collection, the idea that one lineage has the definitive list of *Buddha-vacana.* So the Pāli Canon should be seen as just a "canon" (in one sense of that word) in Pāli, one amongst others (1990, 104).

Turning now to Pāli Buddhist studies prior to the establishment of a Pali Text Society school of scriptural interpretation in 1881, it is appropriate to consider the traditional Sri Lankan view of these texts. According to the traditional account, Pāli texts were transmitted to Sri Lanka in the 3rd century BCE along with commentaries. This tradition was preserved in Sri Lanka orally until both texts and commentaries were written down during the (second) reign of King Vaṭṭagāmani, between 29 and 17 BCE.[7] Afterwards the commentaries which were in Sinhalese were put back into Pāli in the 5th century CE by Buddhaghoṣa. Later, during the medieval period (13th C.), Sinhalese writers heavily incorporated Buddhist ideas found in the Pāli Canon into their Sinhalese literary works such as the *Butsaraṇa*, the *Amāvatura*, and the *Pūjāvaliya*.[8]

II. Criteria, Comparisons and Philosophy

In the Foreword to K.R. Norman's translation of the *Sutta Nipāta*, titled *The Group of Discourses*, Richard Gombrich distinguishes two criteria for determining the meaning of Pāli texts: (1) philological scholarship and (2) the testimony of Theravāda tradition.[9] He goes on to point out a difference in emphasis among Pāli Buddhist scholars. Horner and Rahula emphasize (2), while Norman emphasizes (1).

The emphasis upon the two criteria appears in sections I and II of this anthology, "Philological Foundations" and "Insiders' Understandings" respectively. A guiding belief of the editors of this volume,

7 See K.R. Norman, *Pāli Literature* (Wiesbaden: Harrassowitz, 1983), pp. 7-11 and "The Role of Pāli in early Sinhalese Buddhism," (ed., Heinz Bechert) *Buddhism in Ceylon and Religious Syncretism in Buddhist Countries* (Göttingen: Vandenhoeck & Ruprecht, 1978), pp-28-47.

8 See Mahinda Deegalle, *Baṇa: Buddhist Preaching in Sri Lanka (Special Focus on the Two-Pulpit Tradition* (Ph. D. Dissertation, University of Chicago, 1995).

9 K.R. Norman, I.B. Horner, and Walpola Rahula (translators), *The Group of Discourses* (*Sutta Nipāta*) (London: Pāli Text Society, 1984).

however, is that to these two criteria may be added a third criterion, that of philosophical interest. This third one ideally harmonizes and synthesizes the other two criteria — not by imposing something alien from without — but by giving philosophical interpretation its just due. Accordingly our third section is called "Philosophical Implications."

In this third section many of our contributors tacitly follow the late B.K. Matilal's idea of "comparative philosophy in a minimal sense."[10] There Matilal rightly observes that "comparative philosophy" has acquired a bad reputation mainly because of the failures and lack of depth of the early comparativists." (1982, 259) Although these pioneers often lacked training and insight, modern scholarship automatically involves a sort of comparison and contrast between moderns and ancients. Accordingly, the work of several of our contributors (especially those in section III) affords a comparative perspective which, at best, opens Eastern doors to Western readers and *vice versa* without reductionism.

But comparisons require "roots," and as Pāli exegetes our roots are in the Pāli texts. The texts do not simply speak for themselves, however, but require a method of interpretation. This philosophy can provide. As J.N. Mohanty observes "the orthodoxy of returning to the texts themselves is laudable, but the confidence that one can capture the sense of the texts independently of interpreting them is a sign of either dogmatism or naivete."[11]

Affirming with K.N. Jayatilleke and others the critical spirit implicit in Buddhist philosophy itself our philosophical contributors in section III, even those not themselves South Asian, participate in the critical spirit of the indigenous tradition by exegesis and interpretation. Similarly, our insider contributors in section II, primarily philosophers, participate in the philosophical search for meaning and truth. Both the insiders' understandings and the philosophical implications are themselves rooted, to a greater or lesser extent in the case of each contributor, in the nourishing philological approach of writers in section I. From this it should be clear that the divisions between sections are more like permeable membranes than mutually exclusive compartments. In structuring the work the co-editors take into account the authors' own self-articulation as to how their work

10 See B.K. Matilal in Rama Rao Pappu and Ramakrishna Puligandla (eds.), *Indian Philosophy: Past and Future* (Delhi: Motilal Banarsidass, 1982).

11 Ibid., p. 236.

fits into these three-section rubrics. The goal is to offer an interdisciplinary range of papers in creative tension on some particular points but in symbiotic union as a whole.

In surveying the reasons why Western philosophers of the 19th and 20th centuries who made contact with Buddhism did not transform their own discipline of philosophy as a result, Arthur Herman observes the lack of central authority in Buddhism, the tendency of these philosophers to become either apologists or despisers, and the tendency of non-Buddhistic philosophers to regard Buddhism as destructive of reason and common sense. One thing we wish to extrapolate from Herman's discussion and reflect upon in the practice of Buddhist scholarship is the motto "neither an apologist nor a despiser be."

At present some of the branches of traditional Western philosophy are developing in Eastern directions. One example is the philosophy of religion. In this field some thinkers such as John Hick, Ninian Smart, Don Cupitt, and others have taken into serious account Asian ways of thinking in writing on theoretical issues in religious thought.

Thinkers such as Gunapala Dharmasiri and Herman call attention to the importance of a different kind of thinking than either thinking about the niceties of philology or of the internal working out of Buddhist tradition. Philosophical thinking about Buddhism is just as important in its own way as are textual mastery and Buddhist tradition. Philosophical thinking about Buddhism is dependent for its basis on these other two; these two, in turn, become myopic studies without the benefit of philosophical perspective.

III. Why this Collection of Essays?

A number of important collections of critical essays pertaining to Pāli Buddhism have occurred in the last few decades. (See the Select Bibliography at the end of this Introduction.)

What is noteworthy in surveying the works mentioned in the bibliography at the end of this Introduction is that the present work does not duplicate an already existing volume's structure. Its forte is its interdisciplinary range, specifically its inclusion of philological, insider, and philosophical approaches to Pāli Buddhism all in a single volume. Beyond this general description, the specific features of this anthology are as follows.

First, this is not a *festschrift* dedicated to a single person or for a single idea in Pāli Buddhism. Our goal here is to provide something approaching a comprehensive understanding of Pāli Buddhism from an interdisciplinary, holistic perspective.

Secondly, the overall intellectual scaffolding provided for the volume forms a middle way between philology and philosophy which takes Buddhist insiders seriously. Our contributors — scholars from several disciplines and countries — are pleased to address a wide ranging interdisciplinary audience. Even in particular papers, one can often find a willingness to interpret Buddhism across disciplinary boundaries. Indeed, the co-editors attempted to interest contributors who are committed to the idea that achieving a balanced approach to the study of Pāli Buddhism requires looking at the subject from more than a single disciplinary view.

Thirdly, in the West (with few exceptions even now) many students of philosophy think that they should study only Western Philosophy. On that view, so-called "Asian philosophy" is not worthy of serious academic study since it is supposed to lack philosophical argumentation. On the contrary, this anthology attempts to highlight, *inter alia*, how the study of philosophy may be enhanced by taking seriously Asian philosophical texts. The result, hopefully, will be both an enhancement to, and a challenge for, conventional philosophical discourse.

Fourthly, in contrast to scholarship of an earlier era, the present work does not carry the intellectual burden of locating the very words of the Buddha in an 'original' canon or original doctrine.

In the latter part of the nineteenth century, philologists used their philological studies for the discovery of historical connections. For instance, F. Max Müller used comparative philological method for establishing relations between ancient Greek and Sanskrit.[12] It was aimed at finding Aryan origins.[13]

---

12 F. Max Müller writes in *Lectures on the Science of Religions* (New York: Scribners, Armstrong, 1872): "...it is essential that we should know the most ancient forms of every language, before we proceed to any comparisons, it is indispensable that we should have a clear conception of the most primitive form of every religion before we proceed to determine its own value, and to compare it with other forms of religious faith." (p. 17)

13 F. Max Müller writes in *Introduction to the Science of Religion* (New York: Arno Press, 1978): "Those men were the true ancestors of our race; and the Veda is the oldest book we have in which to study the first beginnings of our language, and of all that is embodied in language. We are by nature Aryan, Indo-European, not Semitic: our spiritual kith and kin are to be found in India, Persia, Greece, Italy and Germany; not in Mesopotamia, Egypt or Palestine. This is a fact that ought to be kept clearly in view, in order to understand the importance which the Veda has for us, after the lapse of more than three thousand years, and after so many changes in our language, thought and religion." (p. 1)

The Protestant Reformation was very much concerned with finding an "original doctrine," and "original cannon," or an "Ur-canon." Many Western scholars including philologists had a similar goal. For instance, the scholars of the Pali Text Society were very much concerned with finding an authentic, real, true, original teaching or a canon.[14] Unlike those pioneers of our field, scholars in this volume do not have an agenda to find an original canon. Instead one goal (especially for contributors in the second and third sections) is to examine the philosophical content and philosophical meaning of Pāli Buddhism in order to see possible applications for contemporary life in modern society.

Although it is desirable to represent multiple aspects of Theravāda Buddhism by including several disciplines, limitations of the present work should be acknowledged. Due to the combined impact of editorial space constraints and the need to include only previously unpublished work, some potential contributors could not have their views represented. In addition its was not the intention of the editors to include ethnographic studies dealing with Pāli Buddhism.

IV. Explanation of the Three Sections

The present work divides the examination into three main sections: Philological Foundations, Insiders' Understandings, and Philosophical Implications.

Papers by Bond, Olendzki, Gopalan, and Chapple are in the "Philological Foundations" section. First of all, philology clarifies the correct uses of terms, concepts and doctrines in linguistic context. It also examines the evolution of doctrines. Philological research is the basis and well-spring of the study of Buddhism. Philology has provided raw materials for academic discourse by indigenous Buddhist scholars as well as philosophically inclined interpreters of Buddhism of both Buddhist and non-Buddhist lands.

Philologists plumb the depths of Buddhist texts and enrich the understanding of early forms of religious phenomena. Their study of the evolution of language in classical philology has immensely influenced scholars in understanding religious forms, *e.g.* in the work of F. Max Müller, Erich Frauwallner, and Eugene Burnouf. Philologists take texts seriously. They examine the stages of development in scriptures. Although oral tradition is important in understanding the

14 See *Journal of the Pali Text Society*, 1882.

specific religious practice of chanting, and despite the fact that the "reciters" (*bhāṇakas*) have historically played a crucial role in the transmission of Buddhist texts,[15] the religious texts provide a stable focal point for the study of religious meaning. Without texts the traditional study of philosophical and religious ideas in a religion such as Buddhism would be vastly complicated, if not downright impossible. In order to understand a religio-philosophical tradition such as Buddhism one must attend to what philologists say about relevant texts.

The twin virtues of textual nuance and philosophical interest are salient in the work of George Bond. Bond discusses Theravāda Buddhism's two formulations of the *dasa sīla* (ten precepts) and the ethics of the gradual path. In this he explores the Theravāda "ethics of virtue" which is expressed in a recognition of *kusala mūla* or "skillful roots," virtues which conduce to the attainment of human excellence.

Andrew Olendzki offers a new model of Buddhist liberation in which he attempts to explain the nature of the transformation that is Buddhist enlightenment. In the same section Subramania Gopalan incorporates Tamil perspectives to illuminate Sinhala Buddhist-tamil common ground. In view of the Sinhala-Tamil conflict in Sri Lanka, Gopalan's approach deserves thoughtful consideration. Christopher Key Chapple turns our attention to *Abhidharma*, and serves as a beacon for those interested in *Nikāya* Buddhism so that Theravāda's own *Abhidhamma* tradition is not ignored.

Papers by Deegalle, De Silva, Kalansuriya, and Dharmasiri are in the "Insiders' Understandings" section. Here it may be observed that the distinction "us" versus "them" is pernicious; the duality between subjects and the describers is outmoded. During the last five centuries, the Buddhist tradition of Sri Lanka has faced the threats of Western Colonialism and the proselytization by Christian missionaries. In that context there were missionaries who wrote about various cultures for the purpose of proselytization. But for the benefit of scholarship it is helpful to see the insiders as conversation partners who enhance one's experience of religious traditions, rather than as objects to be manipulated and converted.

---

15 See Frank J. Hoffman, "Oral Tradition in *Nikāya* Buddhism" in Jeffrey Timm (ed.), *Texts in Contexts: Traditional Hermeneutics in South Asia* (Albany: SUNY Press, 1992).

To form a holistic picture of a philosophico-religious belief system, insiders' perspectives are essential. As Wilfred Cantwell Smith observes, we have to see through the eyes of insiders in order to see what Buddhism means for a practicing Buddhist.[16]

Seeing a kernel of truth in W.C. Smith's approach does not mean that one must sacrifice academic integrity by putting scholarship at the service of religious demands, or must take every insider's perspective as equally valid. The point is rather that it is important to let indigenous voices be heard rather than be greeted with sarcasm.

It is not, of course, necessary that everyone should become a native in order to understand, but rather that, as scholars, one should be able to appreciate insiders' perspectives. The insider's perspective is particularly helpful when it enables one to see the connection between *nibbāna* and morality as in the article by Deegalle.

Bhikkhu Deegalle Mahinda discusses the moral significance of *nibbāna* as against nihilistic interpretations of *nibbana (sa-upādisesa)* (*nibbāna* with psycho-physical substrate of five aggregates intact). Padmasiri De Silva's paper is very timely, dealing with the contemporary issue of suicide and emotional ambivalence. A.D.P. Kalansuriya writes on Buddhist rebirth from a Wittgensteinian point of view, interpreting the rebirth doctrine in an ethical rather than an empirical sense. Gunapala Dharmasiri offers a critique of Theravāda Buddhism from an indigenous Sri Lankan perspective; his analysis of Buddhist establishments and Buddhist practices is very provocative and needs serious reflection and examination. Gunapala Dharmasiri exemplifies the importance of philosophical thinking about Buddhism, but Dharmasiri does so from an insider's perspective, not as a matter of external critique. That is what makes his view so provocative and deserving of consideration.

Papers by Herman, Puligandla, Ratnayaka, Smart, and Hoffman occur in the "Philosophical Implications" section. The philosophical implications are rooted in rich philological soil and are supported by stalwart indigenous stalks. Despite the obvious importance of philological and insider perspectives, Buddhist texts are more than just grist for the philologist's mill or validation of the significance of insider's perspectives: they make a demand on the intellect for

16 Wilfred Cantwell Smith, *The Faith of Other Men* (New York: Harper Torchbooks, 1972), p. 17.

rational comprehension, analysis, and acceptance of an ethically based soteriological scheme. All of the contributors to the Philosophical Implications section participate in the interpretation and in so doing attempt to contribute to the clarification of concepts and the analysis of arguments.

Arthur L. Herman discusses "two dogmas of Buddhism," *anityaduḥkha* and *nirvāṇa*, arguing that the two doctrines are false and logically inconsistent. In so doing Herman understands his task as doing a service to his Buddhist philosophical colleagues by subjecting Buddhist doctrines to rational critique. Ramakrishna Puligandla considers the status of the doctrine of dependent origination, arguing that it is one of phenomenological-analytical truth. In Shanta Ratnayaka's paper there is a discussion of process philosophy and Theravāda Buddhism from a Whiteheadian perspective seeking a common ground of peace and harmony between these traditions. Ninian Smart takes Buddhistic ways of thinking seriously into account while writing on theoretical topic of "meta-process" in religious thought. Frank J. Hoffman discusses Said's critique of "Orientalism" in order to pave the way for a philosophy of Buddhist religion which is not subject to critiques like Said's.

The world of scholarship today is replete with new understandings and reappraisals of scholarship, particularly as these turn on issues of gender, race, class and power. Consequently one cannot nowadays easily ignore, for example, the theoretical philosophical (and practical methodological) issues presented by the critique of "Orientalism."

Although focusing on texts is one feature of the Orientalism which Said attacks, scholars cannot do without texts altogether. Considered philosophical reflection on Pāli Buddhist texts shows that Buddhist texts can stand side by side with Western philosophical texts in academic departments of philosophy (such as is already the case in institutions such as the University of Peradeniya and the University of Hawaii).

V. Concluding Remarks

In this volume the co-editors have provided a context for expression of a diversity of views about Pāli Buddhism. The point is to put forward for discussion a variety of views revealing the vitality and range of contemporary thinkers who work against the background of Pāli Buddhist studies. Inclusion of a particular article, therefore, does not necessarily imply that the co-editors are in full agreement with the authors. Indeed, since the contributors sometimes disagree among themselves on important matters, it would be logically inconsistent for the co-editors to agree with them all on each and every point. The co-editors believe that issues of a controversial kind, such as the philosophical ones raised by Dharmasiri and Herman, deserve to be put on the table for discussion.

It should be remembered that Buddha himself may be viewed as a religious philosopher, so that paying philosophically focused attention to Buddhist texts is to take the subject matter with due seriousness. In the early centuries before the Common Era (sometimes called the axial period)[17] there arose diverse religious philosophies all over the world — Aristotle, Plato, and Socrates in Greece; the Buddha and Mahāvīra in India; Confucius and Lao-tzu in China. Śākyamuni Siddhārtha Gotama Buddha emerges as a major figure in this global context.

One hope is that students of philosophy and religion would benefit from a greater awareness of the global nature of, and imaginative possibilities in, philosophico-religious thinking. Ashok Gangadean's works illustrate this important tendency. In taking seriously other worldviews, one understands the importance of conflicting truth claims in religious traditions.[18]

Several institutions have been formative for the work represented in this volume. Among them are the Society for Asian and Comparative Philosophy (SACP) wherein cross-cultural philosophico-religious studies found expression in the pioneering work of Charles Moore, Eliot Deutsch, and others who organized and developed SACP. Notable in cross-cultural studies in the U.S.A. are the NEH Summer institutes and seminars for faculty focusing on Asia, and the inclusive curriculum projects that foster diversity. The University of Peradeniya, Sri Lanka, has nurtured several talented Buddhistically inclined philosophers, such as K.N. Jayatilleke, David J. Kalupahana, and P. D. Premasiri whose work is important for the contributors to

17 For a detailed discussion of the "axial period" and division into finer gradations than the usual *circa* 5th c. B.C. date seen John C. Plott, *Global History of Philosophy* Vol. II (Delhi: Motilal Banarsidass, 1979), pp. 257-264. Plott distinguishes Earlier Axial Period (750-500 B.C.), Middle Axial Period (500-325 B.C.), and Later Axial Period (325-250 B.C.).

18 For a philosophically interesting study of this issue see also Hendrik M. Vroom, *Religions and the Truth* (Amsterdam: Eerdmans, 1989).

our volume. In Britain and associated countries the philosophical dimension of Religious Studies encouraged by Ninian Smart, Stewart R. Sutherland, and others have contributed to a climate of research and pedagogy sympathetic to the reception of a volume such as the present one. The philosophical stimulation provided by Brian Carr and Indira Mahalingam, leaders of The European Society for Asian Philosophy, is also significant. Our collective debt to both past pioneers of the Pali Text Society and its present-day sustainers almost goes without saying.

This work is dedicated in part to the memory of the late Dr. Jan T. Ergardt of Lund University, Sweden, who passed away before his paper for this volume could be completed.

The co-editors hope that this collection of essays will both consolidate Pāli Buddhist research and stimulate further cooperation between Buddhist monks, scholars, and philosophers where there is an overlap of interests. As Richard Gombrich observes: "they (the Buddhists) believe their scriptures to be of human, not divine origin. This makes it possible for those with divergent interpretations to engage in rational discussion and promote mutual understanding."[19]

19 *Op. cit.*, Norman/Horner/Rahula (1984), p. 1.

SELECT BIBLIOGRAPHY

Somaratna Balasooriya *et al.* (eds.), *Buddhist Studies in Honour of Walpola Rahula* (London: Gordon Frazer, 1980).

G.L. Cousins *et al.* (eds.), *Buddhist Studies in Honour of I.B. Horner* (The Hague: D. Reidel, 1974).

Gatare Dhammapala *et al.* (ed.), *Buddhist Studies: In Honour of Hamalava Saddhatissa* (Nugegoda: Sri Lanka, 1984).

David J. Kalupahana *et al.* (eds.), *Buddhist Philosophy and Culture: Essays in Honour of N.A. Jayawickrama* (Colombo: N.A. Jayawickrama Felicitation Volume Committee, 1987).

A.K. Narain *et al.* (eds.), *Studies in Pāli and Buddhism: A Homage Volume to the Memory of Bhikkhu Jagadish Kashyap* (Delhi: B.R. Publishers, 1979).

Anthony K. Warder (ed.), *New Paths in Buddhist Research* (Durham, NC: Acorn Press, 1985).

Anurādhapura (Sri Lanka) Isurumuṇiya Vihāra complex
Relief on rock showing elephant circa 4th century, Stone
Photograph courtesy of the American Institute of Indian Studies, Varanasi, by way of the Archeological Survey of India. Negative number 337.94.

Section I

PHILOLOGICAL FOUNDATIONS

1

Theravāda Buddhism's Two Formulations of the *Dasa Sīla* and the Ethics of the Gradual Path

George D. Bond

When Buddhaghosa edited the Sinhala commentaries to compose the *Visuddhimagga,* he placed *sīla,* ordinarily translated as moral conduct or virtue, as the initial stage of the "path of purification." The path itself included the three stages of training, *sīla, samādhi and paññā.* From that time Theravāda Buddhism has followed Buddhaghoṣa in teaching that *sīla* stands at the head of the Buddhist path. Although *sīla* in this sense constitutes a very comprehensive element of Buddhism, Theravādins have traditionally formulated and practiced *sīla* in terms of the *dasa sīla* or ten precepts. It is in the form of *dasa sīla* that *sīla* has been known and practiced by most Buddhists.

Interestingly, however, Theravāda's texts and commentaries contain two formulations of the *dasa sīla* which differ at important points. This article examines the nature and purpose of these two lists of *dasa sīla* or precepts in order to elucidate the nature and meaning of *sīla* for Theravāda. Among the questions that are important here are the following: why did the Buddhists postulate these two versions of the *dasa sīla* with these particular precepts? What is the relation between the two lists and what do these two formulations tell us about the overall meaning of *sīla* and the system of ethics in Theravāda? How do the lists of precepts relate to the goal or *telos* of Theravāda?

To indicate in advance something about where these questions will lead us, I would note that according to the Theravāda texts and commentaries, these two formulations of *sīla* are neither competing nor arbitrary but are grounded in Theravāda's understanding of the path as a series of soteriological strategies, a gradual path that enables persons at various levels to attain their individual potential. On this gradual path, the role of *sīla* in general may be described as an element in a Buddhist ethics of virtue which both facilitates and is associated with the ultimate goal of the path, the attainment of the "furthest potential of one's being," or Arahantship.[1]

The first and most widely known formulation of *dasa sīla* enumerates the ten precepts, as in the following list.
I undertake the training precepts of abstention from:

1. Killing/*pāṇātipātā (veramaṇī)*
2. taking what is not given/*adinnādānā*
3. unchastity/*abrahmacariyā*
4. speaking falsehood/*musāvādā*
5. intoxication/*surāmerayamajjapamādaṭṭhānā*
6. untimely eating/*vikāla bhojanā*
7. shows of dance, song and music/*naccagītavādi-tavisūkadassanā*
8. adorning the body/*mālāgandhavilepanadhāraṇa...*
9. high beds and large beds/*uccāsayanamahāsayanā*
10. accepting gold and silver/*jātarūparajatapaṭi-ggahanā*

This list of the requirements of *sīla* is found in canonical Pāli texts such as the *Khuddakapāṭha*.[2] In post-canonical Pāli texts such as the *Milinda Pañha* and the *Mahāvaṃsa*, references to the *dasa sīla* or the ten factors of *sīla* almost always mean these training precepts, which are also termed the *sikkhāpadas*. This understanding of *sīla* has continuity down to recent historical time in Sri Lanka where neo-traditional Theravādins have commonly referred to these precepts as *dasa sīla*. For example, a very popular Theravāda devotional manual entitled *The Mirror of the Dhamma* presents these *sikkhāpadas* or training precepts under the heading of *dasa sīla*. Similarly in his book *Buddhist Ethics*, a modern Theravāda *bhikkhu* and scholar, Venerable H. Saddhatissa, defines and explains *dasa sīla* as these ten *sikkhāpadas*.[3]

The second formulation of *dasa sīla* stands in the same canon as the first list; it may indeed be older than the first one, but it is much less well known in the practice of traditional Theravāda. This list of

1. For this description of the goal of an ethics of virtue, see G.C. Meilander, *The Theory and Practice of Virtue* (Notre Dame, Ind.: University of Notre Dame Press. 1984), p.11. I would not wish to overemphasize this analogy between *sīla* and an ethics of virtue in the Western philosophical tradition. However, it seems to provide a way of beginning to understand the meaning of *sīla*.
2. *Khuddakapāṭha* (London: Pali Text Society), Ch.2.
3. H. Saddhatissa, *Buddhist Ethics* (London: Allen and Unwin, 1970).

dasa sīla has not been used traditionally in rituals and is not referred to in popular descriptions of the precepts. Interestingly, however, it has been rediscovered by Buddhist reformers in the Buddhist revival during the last half century. These reformers, rejecting traditional Theravāda, have accepted this formulation of the precepts and claim that it has a more authentic connection to the true meaning of *sīla*. This formulation contains the following abstentions.
One undertakes to abstain from

1. killing/*pāṇātipātā* (*veramaṇī*)
2. taking what is not given/*adinnādānā*
3. wrong sexual conduct/*kāmesu micchācārā*
4. speaking falsely/*musāvādā*
5. slander/*pisuṇā-vācāya*
6. harsh speech/*pharusā-vācāya*
7. frivolous talk/*samphappalāpā*
8. covetousness/*abhijjhāya*
9. malevolence/*byāpādā*
10. wrong view/*micchā-diṭṭhiyā*

Although this list overlaps with the traditional formulation in the first four precepts, the rest of the precepts are considerably different. They point the way to quite different practices and virtues. The first formulation of *dasa sīla* reflects monastic practice and the demands of the life of those who have renounced society. The reformers argue, however, that when *sīla* is understood in terms of the precepts in this second list, it has greater relevance to the spiritual life of lay persons. As a result, it has gained wide acceptance among the middle class laity of Sri Lanka who have been the primary advocates of what may be called the reformist—in contrast to the neo-traditionalist-viewpoint.[4] For example, the leaders of the Saddhamma Friendship Society, a Sri Lankan reformist society of lay persons, have instructed the members of the society to observe only the second list of *sīla*. Indicating their seriousness about the reinterpretation and practice of *sīla*, this society refuses even to recite the first formulation at Buddhist ceremonies as Theravādins traditionally have done.

This dispute over the meaning of these two lists of *sīla* indicates the continuing significance of *sīla* for the Theravāda tradition. I refer to this dispute, however, not because I wish to side with either group and support their position, but because the dispute itself raises some

---

4. These distinctions between factions in the Buddhist revival are explained further in my book, *The Buddhist Revival in Sri Lanka* (Columbia: University of South Carolina Press, 1988).

interesting questions about the meaning of these two formulations of *sīla* and, through them, the meaning of *sīla* in general.

The Gradual Path as Context for *Sīla* and Soteriology

Theravāda developed these two lists of *dasa sīla* and its entire ethical perspective in the context of its notion of the gradual path. Although many texts in the Pāli Canon seem to imply that the ultimate goal of *nibbāna* can be attained in this life, the Theravāda tradition came to regard the path to the soteriological ultimate as a gradual one, spanning many lifetimes of an individual. Early expressions of this gradual path can be found in the Pāli Canon itself in the explanations of *nibbāna* and arahantship. In addition to those texts that tell of hundreds of people attaining arahantship immediately upon hearing the Buddha preach, there are also texts such as the *sutta* in the *Aṅguttara Nikāya* in which the Buddha declares that just as the mighty ocean slopes away gradually to the depths, so in his teaching there is a graduated training, a graduated mode of progress rather than an abrupt leap of penetration.[5] As I have demonstrated in an earlier article, the arahant ideal seems to have developed from an ideal believed to be readily attainable in this life into an ideal considered to be remote and impossible to achieve in one or even several lifetimes.[6] Traditional Theravāda adopted this view and held that arahantship and *nibbāna* were distant and transcendent goals at the end of an immensely long gradual path than an individual had to approach over the course of many lifetimes.

Early or original Buddhism probably, as Poussin, Weber and others have argued, represented a "discipline of salvation" for, according to the Pāli texts, the Buddha taught that life is suffering and that *saṃsāra* in all its forms is unsatisfactory.[7] Nevertheless as Buddhism developed as an institution it had to address the needs of the "people in the world" who even during the lifetime of the Buddha flocked to him for advice and guidance and who were by definition bound to the wheel of *saṃsāra*. The gradual path developed as Theravāda's hermeneutic for balancing the monastic or yogic and the

5. A. IV.200f.
6. The Development and Elaboration of the Arahant Ideal in the Theravāda Buddhist Tradition, *Journal of the American Academy of Religion* L. II/2, pp.227-242.
7. See Max Weber, *The Religion of India* (The Free Press, 1964), and L. de la Vallée Poussin, *The Way to Nirvana* (New York; AMS Press, 1979).

popular or devotional aspects of the tradition. Dumont's observations about the development of Hinduism seem to apply to Buddhism also: "The true historical development of Hinduism is in the sanyasic developments on the one hand and their aggregation to worldly religion on the other."[8] As Theravāda came to see the goals of arahantship and *nibbāna* as remote and difficult even for renouncers, it recognized that the paths and the soteriologies of the renouncers and the people in the world were linked by transmigration. The *Jātakas* clearly taught this in regard to Gautama. Further, the Theravādins recognized that within these two groups or types there actually were tremendous ranges of spiritual abilities and accomplishments. The Pāli Canon contains *suttas* that describe the Buddha as having the ability to discern these differences in the levels of individuals and to adjust his teachings to them. In one *sutta* the *bhikkhus* declare "It is wonderful and amazing how well the Exalted one who knows and sees, arahant, supreme Buddha, ascertains the various inclinations of beings."[9] The commentary to this passage in the *Dīgha Nikāya* explains that "when he had finished his meal the Exalted one would survey the mental dispositions of those who were present. Then he would teach the *dhamma* to them in such a way that some would become established in the refuges, some in the five precepts, some in the fruits of the *ariya magga*... and others in arahantship."[10]

Rather than understanding the path as a single course which led directly to the ultimate goal, Theravāda saw it as a series of soteriological strategies adapted to the needs of people with differing levels of wisdom and spiritual perfection.[11] The tradition worked out the dimensions of this gradual path in texts such as *Netti Pakaraṇa*, the *Paṭisambhidāmagga*, and the *Buddhavaṃsa*, but it was Buddhaghoṣa who gave the gradual path its definitive expression for Theravāda in the *Visuddhimagga*.

The path was gradual and extended, but it led through its various stages to one goal, one *telos*, *nibbāna*. Dividing the path into two levels, mundane, *lokiya*, and supramundane, *lokuttara*, enabled

8. Louis Dumont, *Homo Hierarchicus: The Caste System and Its Implications*. Trans. by Sainsbury, Dumont and Gulati (Chicago: The University of Chicago Press, 1980), p.434, n.21.
9. *Dīgha Nikāya* (London: Pali Text Society) Vol. I, p. 2.
10. *Dīgha Aṭṭhakathā*, I.46.
11. I use the term soteriological strategies in the same sense that it was used by Steve Collins in his book, *Selfless Persons* (Cambridge: Cambridge University Press, 1982).

the tradition to subsume mundane means and goals under the supramundane in order to relate the *dhamma* to all persons. To discuss the various modes of action possible within the mundane and supramundane levels, the commentators classified people into three general types: the ordinary person, *puthujjana;* the learner or trainee, *sekha*; and the adept, *asekha.*[12] Texts such as the *Netti Pakaraṇa* elaborated on this classification scheme by further classifying persons according to their character, *carita*, and abilities. In the beginning the term *puthujjana* probably referred to an ordinary layman who had little familiarity with the Buddha or the dhamma.[13] The term *sekha* or *sāvaka* implied, by contrast, any disciple of the Buddha. As arahantship became a more remote goal, however, *puthujjana* took on the meaning of anyone, whether monk or lay person, who is on the mundane path and *sekha* came to mean those persons who were progressing on the supramundane path, specifically the seven *ariya puggalas* or noble persons. On the matter of *puthujjana bhikkhus*, Frank Reynolds has observed that although they are on the mundane path along with the lay persons, there continues to be a difference between the *puthujjana bhikkhus* and the *puthujjana* lay persons because "the merit-making activities of the *puthujjana bhikkhus* involve a commitment to the meditative and/or Dhammic vocation... and as a consequence they provide the kind of training that leads more or less directly to path attainment."[14] Following the change of lineage from the mundane to the supermundane path, the *ariya magga* of the *sekhas led* on to the ultimate goal of arahantship and liberation which had already been attained by the third classification of beings, the *asekhas*.

The soteriological means and goals of each person were relative to that person's character and stage of development. This relative nature of the path can be seen in the explanation of *sammādiṭṭhi* given in the *Mahācattārīsaka Sutta* (M.III.71-78). *Sammādiṭṭhi*, ordinarily translated as "right view," is a term that has significant soteriological connotations. In many texts the Buddha criticizes the

---

12. *Petakopadesa*, p.42; *Nettipakaraṇa*, p.49.
13. *Majjhima Nikāya* I. p.1: *Saṃyutta Nikāyā* III. p.16
14. Frank E. Reynolds, "Four Modes of Theravada Action," *Journal of Religious Ethics* 7/1, (1979), p.18. In this article Reynolds usefully distinguishes four empirically relevant roles or modes of action for Buddhists on the gradual path: the path winning *bhikkhus*, the *puthujjana bhikkhus*, the path winning lay person, and the *putthujjana* lay person.

micchādiṭṭhis or wrong views of his opponents, and this term often has been misunderstood to indicate wrong doctrine or wrong philosophical viewpoint in a Western sense. Since the Indians assumed that there was a close connection between philosophical outlooks and soteriologies or paths, however, it seems unlikely that the Buddhists would have used *diṭṭhi* to mean merely a philosophical doctrine. Instead, *diṭṭhi* referred to an existential standpoint and an approach to liberation. The *Mahācattārīsaka Sutta* makes it clear that *sammādiṭṭhi* implied more than just doctrine; it indicated a person's orientation on the path toward the appropriate soteriological goal via the appropriate means. The relative nature of *sammādiṭṭhi*—the path — is indicated in two ways in this *sutta*. First, it shows that there are three categories of *diṭṭhis* or views: wrong view, mundane right view and supramundane right view. Mundane right view, which is the opposite of wrong view, has to do with *karma*, merit and rebirth in *saṃsāra*. Supramundane right view involves the *ariya magga*, the destruction of *āsavas*, and wisdom. These forms of *sammādiṭṭhi* clearly apply to the people in the world and the renouncers, respectively. Second, the *sutta* says that whatever right view a person holds, "that is his right view," that is, the meaning of *sammādiṭṭhi* varies with and is appropriate to the level of insight and spiritual development of the person. The *Mahācattārīsaka Sutta* also goes through the other factors of the Noble Eightfold Path to explain that fulfillment of these factors, such as right resolve, right speech, right action and right livelihood, also is relative to the person. The *Sammādiṭṭhi Sutta* (M.I. 46ff.) similarly offers a series of definitions of what right view means for different types of persons. Analyzing the *suttas*, Collins has argued that the Theravāda tradition used *sammādiṭṭhi* in three senses that related to the three types of individuals. For the ordinary person right view meant "a general and pan-Indian pro-attitude to the belief system of *karma* and *saṃsāra*", for the trainer it was a general knowledge of the *dharma* and "the motivation to accept and interject it;" and for the adept right view indicated the attainment of liberating insight.[15]

Theravāda's Formulations of *Sīla*

In the same way, the meaning of *sīla* was understood to be relative to the place and character of the individual on the proctracted gradual

15. Collins, *Selfless Persons: Imagery and Thought in Theravada Buddhism*, p.92.

path. The *suttas* state that the Buddha specifically tailored *sīla* to his hearers so that he "established some in going for refuge, some in the five *sīla*, some in the ten *sīla*. To some he gave recluseship (*samaṇa*) in the fruition of the *ariya magga*, ...to some the eight higher attainments...and to others the threefold knowledge."[16] To relate *sīla* to the gradual path the tradition developed a two-fold classification of *sīla* as *abhisamācārika sīla, sīla* constituting good behavior, and *ādibrahmacariyaka sīla, sīla* of the beginning of the Brahmafaring. In the canon, the term *abhisamācārika-sīla* represents the basic moral conduct that applies to all Buddhists and particularly to *bhikkhus*. For example, the *Dhammapada* uses the term *samacariyā*, "living in calmness," to define etymologically the term *samaṇa*.[17] In the *Majjhima-Nikāya* the term *abhisamācārika* denotes the general standard of proper conduct that is expected of a *bhikkhu* living in a monastery.[18] By contrast, the term *ādibrahmacariyaka* is used to refer to virtuous conduct related to the higher path and the goal. The Buddha counsels the *bhikkhus* not to think unprofitable thoughts because such thoughts are not connected to the goal nor do they lead to "the beginning of Brahma-faring" or to the remaining stages of the path to *nibbāna*.[19] The canonical texts make it clear that *abhisamācārika sīla* is lower and mundane and that *ādibrahmacariyaka-sīla* is higher and supramundane. In the *Aṅguttara Nikāya* the Buddha declares that he has set forth the *ābhisamācārika* training in order to give confidence and faith to those who practice it, but beyond this he has given the *ādibrahmacariyaka* training to lead those who have advanced further to the "complete destruction of all *dukkha*."[20] That the tradition saw a fixed and serial relation between these two technical terms for conduct is demonstrated again a *sutta* that divides *sīla* into three categories to fit the three types of persons on the gradual path: *abhisamācārika* for the *puthujjanas*; *ādibrahmacariyaka* for the *sekhas* or disciples; and *silāni*, virtues, for the *asekhas* or adepts.[21]

Although the canonical texts establish these two categories of conduct or *sīla*, they leave the content of *abhisamācārika* and *ādibrahmacariyaka* largely undefined. Buddhaghoṣa and the Pāli

---

16. *Buddhavaṃsa* ii.190-192.
17. *Dhammapada* V.388.
18. M. I.469.
19. S.V.417. See also D.I.189.
20. A.II.243f. See also A.III.14-15, and A.I.55 which says that *samacariyā* is along with *dhammacariyā* a cause for a good rebirth.
21. See *Visuddhimagga* (P.T.S. edition) p.12, and A.III.14-15.

Commentaries, however, clarify the definitions of these categories by equating *abhisamācārika sila* with the *sikkhāpada*s from the first list of *sīla* (above) and *ādibrahmacariyaka-sīla* with the *kusala kammapatha*s of the second list of *sīla*. In the *Visuddhimagga*, Buddhaghoṣa defines *ādibrahmacariyaka-sīla* as a term for "that virtue or *sīla* that has *ājīva*, livelihood, as the eighth factor." The commentator explains that this form of *sīla* comprises the three precepts on bodily conduct, the four precepts on vocal conduct and right livelihood as the eight precept. Since these three groups of precepts constitute one version of the *kammapatha*s (see below), Buddhaghosa's reference here unmistakably identifies the *kammapatha*s with *ādibrahmacariyaka-sīla*.[22] To clarify further the meaning of these terms, Buddhaghoṣa says that the "lesser and minor training precepts"(*sikkhāpadāni khuddānukhuddakānī*) constitute *abhisamācāriya* and the remainder constitute *ādibrahmacariyaka*.[23]

The *Sikkhāpada*s, Training Precepts

As the primary form of *abhisamācārika-sīla*, the *sikkhāpada*s or training precepts were differentiated not only doctrinally, as the more mundane *sīla* but also ecclesiastically for the tradition applied them to monks, nuns and lay persons in specialized ways.[24] Although the tradition recognized that both those who had renounced society and those who remained within it could tread the mundane path as *puthujjana*s, it continued to distinguish carefully their roles. The *Milinda Pañha* explained that although both the householder and the Buddhist renouncer, *pabbajita*, could practice the *dhamma* rightly and profitably, the renouncer, nevertheless, had great advantages and many special qualities.[25] Accordingly, the *Visuddhimagga* specified four kinds of *sīla* on the *abhisamācārika* or ordinary level: for *bhikkhu*s, for *bhikkhuṇī*s, for novices (*sāmaṇera*s) and for householders.[26]

The basic formulation of the *sikkhāpada*s is that for the novices, *sāmaṇera*s, who represent the beginners on the path. For them the tradition prescribed the ten training precepts, or *dasa sikkhāpada*s.

---

22. *Vism.*, pp. 11-12.
23. *Vism.*, p. 11f.
24. I am employing this distinction in the way that Reynolds has used it in speaking about the Theravāda modes of action. (Reynolds, p.17).
25. Mil., pp. 243-4.
26. Vism., pp. 11, 15.

The *Mahāvagga* attributed these precepts to the Buddha and set them out for novices exactly as in the first list above.[27]
I undertake the training precepts of abstention from:

1. killing/*pāṇātipātā* (*veramaṇī*)
2. taking what is not given/*adinnādānā*
3. unchastity/*abrahmacariyā*
4. speaking falsehood/*musāvādā*
5. intoxication/*surāmerayamajjapamādaṭṭhānā*
6. untimely eating/*vikāla bhojanā*
7. shows of dance, song and music/*naccagītavāditavisūkadassanā*
8. adorning the body/ *mālāgandhavilepanadhāraṇa...*
9. high beds and large beds/*uccāsayanamahāsayanā*
10. accepting gold and silver/*jātarūparajatapaṭiggahanā*

The same standard formulation was given in the *Khuddakapāṭha* immediately after the Three Refuges. The Commentary explained that these precepts were placed there in order to indicate the trainings that those renouncers, *pabbājitas* , as well as lay persons who had entered the tradition (*sāsana*) should follow. This reference to the *sikkhāpadas* in the *Khuddakapāṭha*, a text that seems to represent the common rituals and formulae of the tradition, points up the centrality of these precepts in Theravāda from an early period. Standing next to the Three Refuges in the *Khuddakapāṭha*, the *sikkhāpadas* mark the entrance to the tradition. In commenting on the meaning of *sīla* for novices, Buddhaghoṣa, in the *Visuddhimagga*, did not specify the precepts because it was clearly understood in traditional Theravāda that *dasa sīla* for novitiates meant the ten training precepts, *sikkhāpadas*. Probably because it designated these training precepts for novices as *dasa sīla*, the Theravāda tradition came to refer to these *sikkhāpadas* as *dasa sīla* in general. As I noted above, this identification, which was made fairly consistently in the Pāli *suttas*, became even more invariable as the tradition developed.

Although Theravādins regarded these training precepts for novices as *dasa sīla*, they also adapted them to fit — or actually, to constitute — the ecclesiastical role for lay persons. To make these monastic precepts more suitable for householders, Theravāda abbreviated the training precepts to form the *pañcasīla* or five *sīla*. The *Sutta Nipāta* sets forth these vows or rules of conduct for the householders as (1) not killing living beings, (2) not stealing, (3) if celibacy is not

27. Khp., Ch.2, and Kh-A., p.22f.

possible, not transgressing the bounds of marriage, (4) not lying, and (5) not indulging in intoxicants.[28] Although Buddhaghoṣa mentions that "when possible" or "through strength" the householders could observe all ten precepts, the tradition expected most persons to follow only these five.[29] A *sutta* in the *Aṅguttara Nikāya* expresses this definition of *sīla* by teaching that the answer to the question "In what respect is a lay person endowed with *sīla* (*sīlavant*)?" is "Insofar as he is one who follows these five training precepts."[30] In the most important Pāli text for lay persons, the *Sigālovāda Sutta*, which Buddhaghoṣa described as the *vinaya* for the householder, the Buddha teaches the young Sigāla that the true disciple abandons four defiling acts: killing, taking what is not given, wrong sexual conduct, and false speech.[31] Although the fifth precept is omitted here, the four that are cited constitute the core requirements of *sīla* for the laity as well as for others, as we shall discuss below.

In addition the Theravāda tradition placed the *pañca sīla* at the heart of several formulations of the requirements for the total path of the householders. First, for the *uposatha*, or observance days, the householders were encouraged to undertake the more rigorous practice of following eight of the monastic *sikkhāpadas* rather than just the five. In addition to the five precepts, the *Suttanipāta* instructed the lay Buddhists to abstain from eating after noon, wearing ornaments or perfumes, and sleeping on beds.[32] Some texts even urge that on the *uposatha* day the devout lay person follow all ten of the *sikkhāpadas*.[33] The texts explain that the reason lay persons should undertake these additional precepts for the duration of the *uposatha* day is both to imitate and to venerate the great *arahants* of the *saṅgha*.[34] A second way of explaining the importance of the *pañca sīla* for lay persons incorporated the five precepts as the central step in the tri-partite praxis that included (1) taking the Three Refuges, (2) *pañca sīla*, and (3) giving offerings, *dāna*, to the *saṅgha*.[35] In many *suttas* and texts, such as the *Khuddakapāṭha*, discussed above, the

---

28. Sn., v.393-398.
29. Vism., p.15.
30. A. IV. p.220.
31. D.III.181f.
32. S. 400-401.
33. A. I.211.
34. A. I.210 f.
35. *Petavatthu*, IV.1.76.

refuges and the precepts constitute the two rituals that mark one's entry into the Buddhist way. These two practices formed a paradigm that the *suttas* referred to by such terms as "the four abodes of ease" and the "eight floods of merit."[36] The third item in this summary of the householders' path *dāna*, alms or generosity, is frequently mentioned as an important corollary to *sīla*. In the *Petavatthu*, Sakkha reminds some householders of their duty by saying "Do not neglect to give alms; kept the precepts and observe the *uposatha*."[37] Similarly, the *Suttanipāta* states that after observing the *uposatha* a householder should practice *dāna* by giving food and drink to the *Saṅgha*.[38] Another important summary of the householders' path complements this one by stating that the duties of lay persons are represented by *dāna* or alms, *sīla* or precepts, and *bhāvanā* or (basic) meditation.[39] Whereas the first threefold formula above summarizes the entry requirements for the householder, this one outlines the ongoing duties of a lay person on the mundane path. Here *dāna* seems to supplement *sīla* in enabling householders to achieve their goals, a dynamic that I will examine further in the discussion below of the relation between *sīla* and the goals of the tradition.

Although the requirements of *sīla* for *bhikkhu*s and *bhikkhuṇī*s who were 'fully admitted to the *saṅgha*" were more extensive than the ten *sikkhāpada*s of the *sāmaṇera*s or the *pañca sīla* of the householders, they were closely related in spirit to those precepts. *Bhikkhu*s and *bhikkhuṇī*s on the *puthujjana* level were expected to follow a four-fold *sīla* that included *sīla* of *Pātimokkha* restraint, the restraint of sense faculties, the purification of livelihood, and that pertaining to requisites, *paccaya*.[40] The Commentary to the *Dhammapada* explains that these four kinds of *sīla* constitute the meaning of the verse that says "one who is well established in *sīla*... is worthy of a yellow robe."[41] The primary requirement here is that of the *Pātimokkha*, the disciplinary code for monks and nuns. In other Pāli texts the stock definition of a *bhikkhu* who is endowed with or in accord with *sīla* (*sīlavant*) says that he is "restrained by the

---

36. A. III.211f., and IV. 245.
37. U Ba Kyaw, trans. *Elucidation of the Intrinsic Meaning: the Commentary on the Peta Stories* (London: Pali Text Society), p.69.
38. S. v.403.
39. A. IV. 241-248.
40. Vism. p.15.
41. Dhp. v.10. See J. Carter and M. Palihawadana, *The Dhammapada* (New York: Oxford University Press, 1987), p.100f.

Pātimokkha" and is "perfect in conduct and resort, and seeing fear in the slightest fault, trains in the precepts that he has undertaken."[42] Buddhaghoṣa refers to the *Pātimokkha* as the *sikkhāpadas* or training precepts for *bhikkhus* and *bhikkhunīs*.[43] This disciplinary code for monks was given in the *Suttavibhaṅga* of the *Vinaya Piṭaka* and the corresponding one for nuns was given in the *Bhikkhunīvibhaṅga*. The two codes were specific to each group except that the nuns had to follow not only their own rules but also many of those given in the *bhikkhu Pātimokkha*.

The connection between the *Pātimokkha* and the training precepts that constitute *sīla* for novices and householders can be seen in that the first four rules of each formulation—the *sikkhāpadas*, *pañca sīla*, and the *Pātimokkha*—have to do with the same four offenses. In the *Pātimokkha* these first four rules are called the *Pārājikā* and concern the most serious offenses, the punishment for which was expulsion from the *saṅgha*. As listed in the *vinaya* they require that monks and nuns abstain from (1) sexual intercourse, (2) taking what is not given, (3) killing a human being, and (4) speaking falsely or boasting about one's own attainments on the *ariyan* path. These four *pārājikās* differ from the first four precepts of the *sikkhāpadas* or *pañcasīla* in that the order of the first and third precepts has been inverted and the wording of all four *pārājikās* applies more specifically to the monastic context. Arguing that the entire "code of discipline is but an enlarged edition of the *pañcasīla*," Pachow attempted to show that all 227 *Pātimokkha* rules represented elaborations and supplements to the four *pārājika* rules.[44] As Holt has demonstrated, however, one cannot convincingly account for all of the 227 rules in this way.[45] Nevertheless, it is significant that these four cornerstones of the *Pātimokkha* for *bhikkhus and bhikkhunīs* are essentially the same as the precepts for novices and householders and that a large number of the other *Pātimokkha* rules also bear upon these topics.

Why did these four rules occupy such a central place in Theravada's delineation of the path? Why did the Buddhists consider these acts or abstentions from action to have such importance? The

---

42. *Mahāniddesa*, p.66. A. I.235. Vism.15.
43. Vism.11.
44. W. Pachow, *A Comparative Study of the Pratimoksha* (Shantiniketan: The Sino-Indian Cultural Society, 1955), p.37.
45. John Holt, *Discipline* (Delhi: Motilal Banarsidass, 1981), p.63-65.

answer to both of these questions is to be found in the observation that the these prohibitions were not original to Buddhism but belonged to an ancient Indian tradition concerning the necessary discipline for renouncers. As Pachow and others have shown, the Buddhist *sikkhāpadas*, including *pañcasīla*, represented an adaptation of the Brahmancial code.[46] We can compare the Buddhist precepts with the five Brahmancial precepts:

(1) not harming living beings (*ahiṃsā*), (2) truthfulness, (3) abstaining from appropriating the property of others, (4) continence, and (5) liberality[47]. Although the order is different, the first four precepts of the *sannyāsin* were essentially the same as the Buddhist precepts. Since the Brahmanic precepts existed first, Jacobi and Pachow seems to be correct in regarding them as the probable source of the Buddhist rules. As Pachow wrote, "The practices of ancient Indian sages and sramanas before the emergence of Buddhism had a direct influence on the formulation of the Buddhist moral conduct for the Bhiksus."[48] The same five Brahmanical rules were taken up also by Jainism as the vows of the Jaina ascetics and by the Yoga school as the *yamas* or ethical precepts that prepare one for the higher stages of Yoga. Buddhism, thus, gave these rules a central place and regarded these four acts as cardinal offenses because it too shared the ancient Indian tradition that taught that these abstentions were essential for success in meditation or yoga.

The background of these precepts has significance in two ways for our understanding of the Buddhist path. First, it demonstrates that these ethical formulations — the *sikkhāpadas*, the *pañcasīla* and the *pārājikās* — were not uniquely Buddhist but represented a pan-Indian code for ascetics and renouncers that Buddhism attempted to reinterpret in several ways. In the *pañcasīla* Buddhists reinterpreted this code to apply to householders, but the emphasis still inevitably fell on values that pertained more to renouncers than householders. The *pārājikās* represent the Buddhists' application of this ancient code to renouncers on the Buddhist path. They moved the precept concerning celibacy or *brahmacariya* to the first place on the list, probably because of its importance for a monastic community. The other changes that the Buddhists made for *bhikkhus* might be seen as ratioinalizations of the original Brahmanical precepts. For ex-

46. Pachow, p.61.
47. Jacobi, *Jaina Sutras*, Sacred Books of the East, Vol. 30, p.xxiii-iv.
48. Pachow, p.61.

ample, the *pātimokkha* reinterpreted the precept against killing to mean that one should not kill human beings and the precept on false speech to mean the prohibition of lying or boasting about monastic spiritual attainments.

The second reason that the history of these precepts is significant is that it indicates that the renouncers' code from which the Buddhists derived these precepts was shared by other śramanic or yogic sects that held different goals in meditation from Buddhists. As one author describes these differences in goals, "The meditational methodology as a yogic discipline was originally conceived as a way of achieving freedom and power *in* and *over* the world, whereas the Buddhist Nibbanic goal entails the use of meditation as a means of achieving freedom *from* the world and *all* its values, by detachment from them."[49] Another basic difference between yogic or Brahmanic meditation and Theravāda's meditation tradition is that yoga led ideally to a state of enstatic identification of the soul, whereas Buddhist *vipassanā* led to an ecstatic awareness of no soul. Because of this difference the Buddhists had to reinterpret these precepts and to supplement them with others that were more Buddhistic in their aim.

The Theravādins judged the *abhisamācārika sīla* to be mundane, *lokiya*, because these virtues do not enable individuals to attain their "furthest potential," the ultimate goal of the tradition. Nevertheless, on the scheme of the gradual path, the *abhisamācārika sīla* function as what we might call second-order virtues which have benefits in the present life and make possible the higher virtues. For *puthujjana*s on the mundane path, *sīla* has a direct relation to the attainment of the mundane goals and benefits within the *saṃsāric* realm. Buddhaghoṣa restates the traditional understanding of the relation of *sīla* to the aims of the mundane path when he comments that the *puthujjana*s who undertook *sīla* received five benefits: wealth (*bhogakkhandhaṃ*), good reputation (*kittisadda*), confidence (*visārada*), a peaceful death, and rebirth in a heavenly realm (*saggaṃ*).[50] The Commentary to the *Dīgha Nikāya* expands on this understanding of the value of *sīla*, saying that *sīla* is the basis for joy, security and freedom. One who has virtue, *sīla*, is praised by the wise, does not blame himself and is not blamed by others for anything.

49. Winston King, *Theravada Meditation* (University Park, PA: Pennsylvania State University Press, 1980), p.89.

50. *Vism.*, p.9. See also D.II.86, and D.III.236.

Virtues surpasses beauty because it is not conquered by aging or health. Virtue promotes one's highest welfare and even follows one to the world beyond.[51]

Clearly the most important function of *sīla* on the mundane level of the path, however, is to ensure a favorable rebirth which will make possible further progress toward the ultimate goal. Sigāla, the young Brahmin who is the subject of the *Sigālovāda Sutta*, hears from the Buddha the promise of a happy rebirth in the heavenly realms if he fulfills the basic precepts of *sīla*.[52] Observing the precepts or *sīla* generates merit, *puñña*, which accrues to shape the destiny of the *puthujjana* as the *Dhammapada* states: "One who does merit rejoices here and hereafter, he rejoices in both worlds."[53] Similarly, other *suttas* explain that *sīla* combined with the Three Refuges constitutes the "floods of merit" that lead to happiness, delight and rebirth in heavens.[54] The connection between these mundane goals and the ultimate, supramundane goal is established in texts such as the *Netti Pakaraṇa* and the Pāli Commentaries which relate that it was on the basis of merit accrued during fortunate rebirths that the great disciples were able eventually to encounter the *dhamma* and attain arahantship.

The Pāli Canon contains many *suttas* in which these mundane benefits are postulated for lay persons who fulfill the *sikkhāpadas*. After admonishing householders to observe the *sikkhāpadas* and to honour the *saṅgha*, father and mother, the *Suttanipāta* declares that one who does these duties will enjoy rebirth in the sphere of the "self-luminant beings."[55] Visākha, the famed Buddhist laywoman, was told by the Buddha that those who observe the eight precepts on the *uposatha* will be reborn among the thirty-three gods or on another of the heavenly planes.[56] Other texts spell out the negative results that accrue to householders who violate the *sikkhāpadas*. A series of short *suttas* in the *Aṅguttara* teaches that householders who fail to observe the *pañca sīla* become fearful, live without confidence, and eventually are thrown into hell.[57] In addition to these *suttas* that pertain to the after-life results of the *sikkhāpadas*, the commentary on the proclamation of the ten *sikkhāpadas* in the *Khuddakapāṭha* posits

51. D-a. p.276f.
52. D.III.181.
53. Dhp., verse 18.
54. A.II.56-57.
55. S. v.404.
56. A.I.212-213; also A.IV.255.
57. A.III.203-205.

numerous this-worldly benefits that represent the "fruits" of *sīla*. These "fruits" include such diverse benefits as wealth, protection from dangers, courage, popularity in the society, evenly spaced teeth, and non-confusion.

These mundane benefits of *sīla* apply not only to householders but also to *bhikkhus* who are on the *lokiya* path. As Reynolds notes, "Since *puthujjana bhikkhus* have not achieved the change of lineage that projects them into the practice of the path, their actions remain essentially *kammic*, and therefore bear their fruit within the continuing cycle of birth and rebirth."[58] For example, the Buddha says that *bhikkhus* who fulfill the *sikkhāpadas* and *Pātimokkha* can attain mundane benefits such as the respect of others and sufficient requisites.[59] In another *sutta* the Buddha instructs the *bhikkhus* about the "eight fields of merit," which comprise the Three Refuges and the *pañcasīla*. He tells the monks that these acts generate the blessings of happiness and heavenly rebirth for the noble disciples who perform them.[60]

The *Kammapathas*, Course of Action

Employing the same criterion by which it judged the *abhisāmācārika sīla* to be lower mundane, the Theravāda tradition designated *ādibrahmacariyaka sīla*, defined as the *kammapathas*, to be higher or supramundane: *viz.* these qualities enable persons to attain the 'furthest potential" of existence. The *kusula kammapathas*, or profitable courses of action have integral and essential links to the Buddhist understanding of the path and its ultimate goals. The Pāli texts record two main forms of the *kammapathas*, one version with seven precepts and another with ten. In the seven-fold form, the *kammapathas* prescribe that a Buddhist abstains from (1) killing beings, (2) taking what is not given, (3) wrong sexual conduct, (4) speaking falsely, (5) slander, *pisuṇā vācāya*, (6) harsh speech, *pharusā vācāya* and (7) frivolous speech, *samphappalāpā*.[61] The ten-fold form, which is more common, adds to these precepts the vows to abstain from (8) covetousness, *abhijjhāya*, (9) malevolence, *byāpādā*, and (10) wrong view, *micchādiṭṭhi*.[62] Of these ten precepts, the first

58. Reynolds, p.18. By path here Reynolds means the *ariya magga*.
59. M. I.33. This *sutta* goes on to say that the monk can also go further and attain supramundane goals based on his being established in *sīla*.
60. A. IV.245f.
61. S. II.167f., and A. I.268.
62. S. II.167; A. I.268.

four are the same as the four Brahmanic or ascetic precepts and the first four Buddhist training precepts, *sikkhāpadas*. Beyond these four, however, these precepts differ significantly from the *sikkhāpadas* or training precepts. When stated in the negative, these *sīla* look like prohibitions or rules, but if we convert them to positive forms they express central virtues for Buddhism. For example, not killing becomes compassion or non-violence, not stealing becomes desirelessness, the precepts against speaking harshly or slanderously translate into kindness or *metta*.

The relation between the *kammapathas* and Theravāda soteriology can be seen in the connection that the *suttas* make, both implicitly and explicitly, between these precepts and the Noble Eightfold Path. The authors of the Pāli texts grouped these precepts under the headings of bodily actions (*kāya*), verbal or vocal actions (*vācā*), mental actions (*mana*). The first three precepts pertain to bodily actions, the next four pertain to verbal actions, and the last three to mental actions.[63] Organized in these groups, the precepts relate to the factors of the Noble Eightfold Path as texts such as the *Mahācattārisika Sutta* imply. The *Mahācattārisika Sutta*, discussed above, which explicates the Noble Eightfold Path, defines the factors of the path in terms of the actions or abstentions contained in the *kammapathas*, although this designation is not used in the *sutta*. It explains that right speech, *sammā vācā*, the third actions of speaking falsely, slanderously, frivolously or harshly, which are the same as the precepts grouped under verbal or vocal actions, *vācā*, in the *kammapathas*. Right action, *sammā kammanta*, the fourth factor of the path, involves abstaining from killing living beings, taking what is not given and engaging in wrong sexual conduct, the same injections as the precepts grouped under the heading of bodily actions, *kāya*, in the *kammapathas*. In the explication of the other factors of the path, the *Mahācāttarisika Sutta* mentions at least two more of the precepts contained in the *kammapathas*. Since in the *sutta*'s explanation, three of the factors of the path — right view, right efforts, and right mindfulness — do not constitute separate practices but pertain to the practice of all of the other factors, and since one factor, right concentration (*sammā samādhi*), constitutes the end of the path rather than a stage on the way, these actions or abstentions, which are the *kammapathas*, represent the practical outworking of

63. See A. V.264; Netti., p.43; M. I.286; M. III.46ff.

the path under the factors of right thought, right speech, right action and right livelihood.

That Buddhaghoṣa knew of this correspondence between the *kammapathas* and the Eightfold Path appears from a somewhat cryptic definition of *sīla* in *Visuddhimagga*. As one of the definitions for *abhisamācārīka sīla*, he says that "this is a term for *sīla* other than that which has livelihood as the eighth factor."[64] The commentator suggests that this means the three kinds of bodily action, the four kinds of vocal action, and *ājīva* as the eighth factor. But where does one find this unusual eight-factored list of *sīla*? It does not correspond to the usual formulations of either the five or ten *sikkhāpadas* or the seven or ten *kammapathas*. If one analyzes the Eightfold Path as the *Mahācattārīsaka Sutta* has done, however, the first seven precepts of the *kammapathas* are subsumed under the third and fourth factors of the Eightfold Path, *sammā vācā*, right speech, and *sammā kammanta*, right action. These two factors plus *sammā ājīva*, right livelihood, constitute the section of the Eightfold Path that is said to represent *sīla* (see below). Thus, Buddhaghosa's list of eight precepts comprises the seven precepts that constitute the third and fourth factors of the Eightfold Path with *sammā ājīva*, the fifth factor, included as the eighth precept.

Noble Eightfold Path

1.	*sammā diṭṭhi*/right view	}	*paññā*
2.	*sammā saṅkappa*/right though	}	
3.	*sammā vācā*/right speech	}	*sīla*
4.	*sammā kammanta*/right action	}	
5.	*sammā ājīva*/right livelihood	}	
6.	*sammā vāyāma*/right effort	}	*samādhi*
7.	*sammā sati*/right mindfulness	}	
8.	*sammā samādhi*/right concentration	}	

This correlation between the *kammapathas* and the Eightfold Path establishes both that this formulation of *sīla* is integral to the Theravāda path and that for that reason the *kammapathas* are higher than the *sikkhāpadas*. Other texts, particularly the *Abhidhamma* texts, elaborated upon this correlation and demonstrated in other ways that the *kammapathas* were central to the soteriology of Theravāda. These texts routinely analyzed action or *kamma* into the three modes, bodily, vocal and mental, and regarded the *kammapathas*

64. Vism. p.11.

as the expression of these three.[65] Moreover, when texts such as the *Nettipakaraṇa* and the *Dhammasaṅganī* tabulated what were considered to be the central factors of the *Dhamma* and the path, they included these three forms of action explicitly and the *kammapatha*s implicitly.[66]

In their explanations of the path as a process of mental or spiritual purification, these Theravāda texts clarify the distinctive role of action and virtue in Buddhist soteriology. If *sīla* can be understood somewhat on the analogy of an ethics of virtue, as we suggested earlier, these texts reveal the distinctive nature of the Buddhist ethics of virtue and the role of *sīla* in such a system. The *kammapatha*s are depicted as integral to the path because they constitute crucial links between outward actions and the inner goal of spiritual purification. According to the *Nettipakaraṇa* and other texts, all conduct and consciousness—i.e. existence—can be classified under the two headings, *akusala*, unprofitable, or *kusala*, profitable. These two terms define Buddhist ethics and soteriology. As Mrs. Rhys Davids noted in her introduction to the *Dhammasaṅganī*, *kusala* means good or profitable in the sense of "that which insures soundness, physical and moral, as well as that which is felicific."[67] Profitable action thus is defined in terms of the goal of the path: liberation and the attainment of the human potential, arahantship. Unprofitable action is that which leads in the opposite direction.

Underlying these distinctions and serving as the heart of the entire Theravāda system of ethics and virtue are the root terms, *(mūlā).* Stated in their negative or *akusala* forms the roots are *lobha, dosa and moha*, or greed, hatred and delusion. The *kusala* forms are simply the opposites of these. Nyānaponika describes the essential nature of these roots when he notes that "The three wholesome Roots are the main criteria by which a state of consciousness is determined to be wholesome."[68] In terms of the path, these root terms constitute the basic—or to use the analogy of an ethics of virtue-cardinal virtues. To be sure, the tradition holds many virtues to be important, but according to analysis of action in the *Abhidhamma* and the *Netti's*

65. *Atthasālinī*, p.88.
66. See *Dhammasaṅganī*, p.1f., Netti, p.43 ff. Also see Nyanaponika Thera, *Abhidhamma Studies:Researches in Buddhist Psychology* (Kandy: Buddhist Publication Society, 1976), p.30-33.
67. C.A.F Rhys Davids, *A Buddhist Manual of Psychological Ethics of the Fourth Century B.C.* (London: Royal Asiatic Society, 1900), p.1xxxiii.
68. Nyanaponika Thera, *Abhidhamma Studies, p.78.*

exposition of the elements of the *Dhamma*, these terms constitute the roots of the entire system. The *Netti* indicates the connection between these roots and the other terms for the Buddhistic Virtues or vices when it says, "when one idea is mentioned, all ideas of like characteristic are mentioned also (by implication)."[69] Nyānaponika refers to these roots as "motive powers" in that they "impel the other simultaneously arisen powers to act in the service of that motive."[70]

Theravāda understood the *kammapathas* to be closely related to these roots and to constitute one of the ideas of "like characteristic." In the *Dhammasaṅganī's* list of the factors of *kusala* consciousness the *kusala kammapathas* immediately follow the *kusala mūlā*. In this list the "kusala *kammapathas*" comprise only the last three of the ten *kusala kammapathas* — non-conventousness (*anabhijjhā*), non-ill will (*avyāpāda*), and right understanding (*sammā diṭṭhi*) — because these represent the aspects of "mental action" which are applicable to consciousness. The other *kammapathas* are implied, however, under the supplementary factors. So close is the connection between the roots and the *kammapathas* that these last three factors of mental action are said by Buddhaghoṣa actually to be the roots themselves described under a different aspect.[71]

According to the Theravāda analysis, the ten *akusula kammapathas* or unprofitable, unvirtuous courses of action arise as manifestations of the *akusula mūlā*, but the profitable or virtuous courses of action arise from the *kusula mūlā*. Both the *Netti* and the Commentary to the *Dhammasaṅganī* identify specific roots with specific *kammapathas*. The *Netti* says that hatred (*dosa*) is the root manifested in the actions of killing, slander, and harsh speech. Stealing, misconduct in sensual desire and speaking falsely are generated by the root, greed (*lobha*). And frivolous speech is molded by delusion (*moha*).[72] Buddhaghoṣa adds that in many cases actions motivated by the roots of greed or hatred also have delusion as a root. Thus, killing arises not only from the root of hatred but also from that of delusion.[73]

The connection between these roots, which can be thought of as psychological dispositions, and the actions or *kammapathas* are provided by volition, *cetanā*. The *Abhidhamma* texts cite the saying

69. Netti, p.30 f.
70. *Abhidhamma Studies*, p.80.
71. *Ibid.*, p.81.
72. Netti, p.43.
73. *Dhammasaṅganī Aṭṭhakathā*, p.102 f.

attributed to the Buddha, "It is volition that I call action. For having willed, one performs an action through body, speech or mind."[74] For the Buddhist system, volition is basic to action, so the texts speak of threefold volition paralleling the threefold action.[75]

The overall significance of this system for an understanding of the *kammapathas* as *sīla* is expressed in the *Sevitabbāsevitabba Sutta* which teaches that wrong conduct in the three categories of the *Kammapathas* — body, speech and mind — causes the unwholesome or unprofitable states of mind, *akusala dhammā*, to increase and the profitable states of mind, *kusala dhammā*, to decrease. That is, whenever a person acts according to the *akusula kammapathas*, the unprofitable volitions and roots are reinforced in him. Conversely, when one undertakes the *kusala kammapathas* the roots of the unprofitable, *akusala mūlā*, are diminished and the inclinations toward the profitable are increased. The *kusala kammapathas* thus have a pivotal function this process of Buddhist soteriology. As a modern scholar-monk has written of the *kammapathas* formulated as precepts, "each precept is a tangible expression of a corresponding attitude of mind, a principle which clothes in the form of concrete action a beam of the light of inward purity."[76] This positive reinforcement of profit or virtue begins with the *kammapathas*, continues with the cultivation of positive states of mind through meditation on topics such as the *Brahma vihāras* and ends with the attainment of wisdom. The arahant, who has reached the end of the path, has eliminated the three *akusala mūlā*, and his naturally virtuous actions reflect his purified character. Those who have not yet reached the state of arahantship, however, must strive to purify both their actions and their minds and in this process, *sīla* formulated as the *kusala kammapathas* has great soteriological value.

As a more comprehensive formulation of *sīla*, the *kammapathas* have relevance to persons on both levels of the path, the mundane and the suprramundane. The virtues were regarded as higher not because they applied only to the supramundane path but because they had the potential to lead to the "complete destruction of *dukkha*." If a person were not ready to actualize this potential by attaining the "change of lineage," however, the *kammapathas* would

74. A.III.415.
75. Dhs-a p.88.
76. Bhikkhu Bodhi, *Nourishing the Roots and Other Buddhist Essays*. Wheel Series, No. 259-260 (Kandy: Buddhist Publication Society, 1978), p. 14.

function as the most profitable form of *sīla* on the mundane path. According to the *Aggañña Sutta*, the *kammapathas* represent the essential ethical code followed by people of all castes, from Brahmins to *śudras*.[77] In one discourse the Buddha defined the nature of *dharmic* and *adharmic* conduct for the lay folk of the village of Sālā by explaining the threefold conduct that constitutes the *kammapathas*.[78] In another *sutta* addressed to the layman, Cunda, the Buddha explains the *kammapathas* as the *ariyan* discipline of purification, substituting these ethical practices for the Brahminical rituals that Cunda had previously followed[79] After teaching Cunda about the *kammapathas*, the Buddha tells him that one who fulfills the precepts can be assured of a good rebirth among either the *devas* or human beings. No mention is made in this *sutta* of the supermundane goals of the tradition. Other *suttas*, however, reveal the way in which the *kammapathas* can lead to results on the supermundane as well as the mundane path and thus represent the dynamics of the gradual path. The *Aggañña Sutta*, after relating the mundane rewards of rebirth possible for one who has good conduct in deed, word and thought, adds that if people not only follow these profitable *sīla* but also go on to practice meditation and attain wisdom, they can reach the ultimate goal of liberation in this life.[80] In the *Sāleyyaka Sutta*, mentioned above, after telling the householders of Sala about the heavenly rebirths that are possible for those who follow the *kammapathas*, the Buddha explains that if the householders go further and combine the observance of *sīla* with destruction of the *āsavas*, they can attain the levels of wisdom that signify entry onto the supramundane path.[81] The nature of this higher *sīla* is such that one cannot attain the *lokuttara* path with these virtues alone, but neither can one attain it without them as the base for the higher practices of mental purification.

Conclusion

In his book *The Forest Monks of Sri Lanka*, Carrithers relates his attempt to convince the forest monks that the traditional relationship between *sīla* and meditation should be reversed. "That is, after first meditating, one would realize the significance of living a moral life by

77. D. III.80 ff.
78. M. I.285 ff.
79. A. V.263-268.
80. D. III.96-97.
81. M. I.289 ff.

the Buddhist precepts..." The forest monks, however, found such a reinterpretation impossible. "The impatience and even outrage with which the monks heard it and the unity of view with which it was rejected, left no doubt that the monks place moral purity in the central position I had wished to accord to meditative experience.[82]

To help account for the forest monks' insistence on the central place of *sīla*, I want to explore briefly my earlier suggestion that the Theravāda system of ethics resembles an ethics of virtue. In the Western sense, an ethics of virtue "requires a teleological scheme that links together 'man as he is' with 'man as he might become where his *telos* fulfilled'."[83] In such a system the virtues are "those excellences which enable a human being to attain 'the furthest potentialities of his nature'."[84] Since the Greeks, virtues have been seen as dispositions to act in beneficial ways and as springs to positive action. An ethics of virtue stresses cultivating these dispositions rather than acting out of obligation or duty. Virtues are held to be more basic than actions for they engage the will; virtues have to do with the intentions behind actions. As Hume observed, "The external performance has no merit...all virtuous actions derive their merit only from virtuous motives."[85] Virtues are seen as correcting the human predicament and contributing to the attainment of the human potential. As Yearley says, "Virtues correct some difficulty that is thought to be natural to human beings, some temptation that needs to be resisted or some motivation that needs to be made good."[86] In this sense the virtues stand opposite to the vices which represent the fatal weaknesses of human nature. Each culture thus delineates virtues and vices depending on its underlying theory of human nature and human flourishing.

The Western tradition established four cardinal moral virtues: courage, temperance, justice and wisdom.[87] This list, however, has

82. Michael Carrithers, *The Forest Monks of Sri Lanka* (Delhi: Oxford University Press, 1978), p.14 f.
83. Russell Hittinger, "After MacIntyre: Natural Law Theory, Virtue Ethics and Eudaimonia" *International Philosophical Quarterly* Vol. XXIX, No.4, (Dec.1989), p.453.
84. Gilbert Meilander, *The Theory and Practice of Virtue*. (Notre Dame, Ind.: University of Notre Dame Press, 1984), p.6. In this statement he is partially quoting Josef Pieper.
85. Hume, *Treatise of Human Nature*, Book III, Part II, Sec. 1. Cited by Wm. Frankena, *Ethics* (Englewood Cliffs, N.J.: Prentice Hall, Inc., 1973), p.63.
86. Lee Yearley, "Recent Work on Virtue," *Religious Studies Review*. Vol.16, No.1 (Jan. 1990), p.2. Also Yearley, *Mencius and Aquinas: Theories of Virtue and Conceptions of Courage* (Albany: State University of New York Press, 1991).
87. Philippa Foot, *Virtues and Vices and Other Essays in Moral Philosophy*. (Berkeley: University of California Press, 1978), p.2.

been widely debated. Socrates included piety in the list, and Aristotle and Aquinas regarded wisdom as an intellectual rather than a moral virtue. In addition to the cardinal virtues, most systems of virtue ethics posit a hierarchy of other or second order virtues that depend upon and relate to the cardinal virtues.[88] This hierarchy explains the priorities among the virtues and their relation to the ideal or goal of facilitating the highest potential of human nature.

Theravāda Buddhism may be said to have posited a system of cardinal virtues in its *kusala mūlā* or profitable roots. These root virtues operate at the level of the will and dispose the person to act in positive ways. Their opposites, the *akusala mūlā* or unprofitable roots, name the defects of human character or the vices which the virtues correct.[89]

In this Theravāda ethics of virtue, *sīla* in general and the two formulations of *dasa sīla* in particular are important for two reasons. First, the formulations of *dasa sīla* constitute the hierarchy of virtues that extend outward from the root virtues.[90] In a strict sense, the *sīlas* are not virtues because they are more involved with action or the restraint of action. However, the line between virtue and action becomes very fine at many points and it is difficult to determine in some cases, for example, whether the *kammapathas* are or are not virtues. Buddhaghosa, as noted above, indicated that the final three *kusala kammapathas* — non-covetousness, non-malevolence and right view — actually are the profitable roots themselves "seen under a different aspect." This close connection between the *kusala kammapathas* and virtues becomes evident also if one translates the *kammapathas* not as negative but as positive qualities, i.e. compassion rather than not-killing, contentment rather than not coveting.

The second reason that *sīla* are important in the Theravāda system is that they represent the way that the higher or root virtues are

88. Yearley, p. 3.

89. The Buddhist root virtues resemble the cardinal virtues of the West not only in their role in the system, but to some degree in their content also. For example, in the Western system courage and temperance represent two primary virtues. Their significance is as Foot says "that the man of courage does not fear immoderately nor (does) the man of temperance have immoderate desires for pleasure"(p.8). Similarly for the Buddhist, the two roots of *adosa* and *alobha* counteract aversion and attachment respectively.

90. The *Brahamajāla Sutta* (D.I.1ff.) and each of the first thirteen *suttas* in the *Dīgha Nikāya* contain a stock passage that analyzes the precepts into three divisions or grades: *cūla* or lesser, *majjhima* or middle, and *mahā* or great. These passages demonstrate the elaborate nature of the hierarchy of *sīla*.

acquired. A central question in the West has been whether virtue can be learned or acquired. Socrates was asked for example, "Is virtue something that can be taught? Or does it come by practice? Or is it neither teaching nor practice that gives it to a man but natural appetite or something else?"[91] The Buddhist answer to this question is that virtue is acquired by practice of *sīla*. Thus, *sīla* constitutes the path to the profitable root virtues. But not only is *sīla* a part of the path, *sīla* and the root virtues together are important constituents of the goal of the tradition. The *arahant* is defined as one who has eliminated the unprofitable roots and lives fully in the profitable ones. *Sīla* has a central place here because as Crossin notes about virtue and the goal of flourishing, "The exercise of virtue is a necessary part of such a life not a mere preparatory exercise to secure such a life.''[92] Buddhism has described its ideal in terms of seeing—*vipassanā, vidarśanā*— and would agree with those in the West who have said that "To see rightly, requires that we have the virtues."[93] The practice of virtue is not a mere precondition for following the path, but is an integral component of the path and part of the hierarchy of virtues that constitute the goal. Thus, the forest monks insisted that *sīla* should have primacy because they understood the essential connection between *sīla* and the attainment of human excellence or flourishing.

91. Meilander, p.70.
92. John Crossin, *What Are They Saying About Virtue?* (Fortress Press, 1985), p.5.
93. Meilander, p.17.

2

A Proposed Model of Early Buddhist Liberation

Andrew Olendzki

What is *Nibbāna*?

Often the most simple questions are the most difficult to answer. Such is certainly the case in the study of Buddhism, when one asks: "What is *nibbāna*? What does it mean to become enlightened or liberated? How are we to understand what is said to have happened to Siddhāttha Gotama, prince of the Sākyas, under the Bodhi tree, that transformed him suddenly into the Buddha?"

One is likely to get different answers to these questions from different people, depending on the sort of Buddhists they are or their perspective on Buddhism. Nevertheless both Buddhists and scholars need often to articultate to themselves and each other their understanding of what the phrase "the attainment of *nibbāna*" means. It is not as important in this enterprise that all Buddhists agree, as it is that each can present an explanation that is coherent and meaningful.

Theravāda Buddhists, those who look to the Pāli *Tipiṭaka* as the primary source of traditional lore about the Buddha, have a tendency to view the enlightenment of the Buddha as an episode that can be placed in a particular historical context. That is to say there was a certain moment as which the transformation of Gotama into the enlightened Buddha took place. Before this he was a wandering ascetic not unlike many others populating ancient India, and after this moment he was fully enlightened and a light to the suffering world.

Theravāda Buddhists also tend to portray the nature of the Buddha's enlightenment in psychological terms. The liberation of the Buddha involved a psychological transformation from one mode to another, the change from a mind in bondage to suffering, to one of blissful emancipation from suffering. In the stories told about the Buddha's lifetime, *nibbāna* emerges as an event that happens to a person, a transformation of somebody's mind, and has little if any meaning when considered independently of a being that attains it. The view suggested by the *Nikāyas* is not that *nibbāna* is a place or state or condition that exists somewhere in counterpoint to the world of *saṃsāra*, but is something manifest in this world by a person who becomes liberated. It is not a matter of *nibbāna* existing or not existing, but of occurring or not occurring.

These two tendencies, to regard the Buddha's enlightenment both historically and psychologically, are often at odds with the explanations of various Mahāyāna Buddhists who see Śākyamuni as a minor player in a vast drama. Indeed the entire issue of how the Buddha's enlightenment is understood and described is a significant indicator of sectarian affiliation. But all Buddhists and scholars of Buddhism presumably agree on one thing, even though they might diverge significantly on much else: a person, Siddhārtha Gotama Śākyamuni, is said to have attained *nibbāna* in ancient India, sometime around 483 BCE — this is the essential starting point of Buddhism.

But what might this *mean*? I would like to explore here the nature of liberation from this historical and psychological perspective, and to offer a new, and hopefully coherent and meaningful, model of liberation.

The Inherent Duality of Buddhist Thought

It might help to begin by recognizing some of the philosophical implications of the early Buddhist conception of liberation or enlightenment. There are three aspects to the concept of liberation that emerge upon reflection, and looking at these will reveal the direction in which a new model of liberation might be sought.

The first thing we should acknowledge is that, the doctrine of *anatta* (or non-self) notwithstanding, early Buddhist thought rests on an essential duality implicit in the very concept of liberation. The notion of liberation demands that a distinction be made between two elements — between, first of all, the liberation *of* someone or something, and secondly its liberation *from* someone or something. In Buddhist doctrine it is usually said that a being is liberated *from* suffering, which is to say that a being is one thing and suffering is another.

Now it may be that what is generally regarded as a 'being' is misconstrued and does not in fact constitute any essential personality or imply the existence of a permanent self (*atta*). It may also be that suffering is largely illusory, derived from the constant misperception of experience. Both of these positions are supported by the Buddhist tradition. Yet however ephemeral or inconsequential this duality may be in the final picture (both in terms of the ultimate goal for a Buddhist and in terms of later developments of Buddhist thought), it is nevertheless a ubiquitous feature of early Buddhist doctrine. It plays a significant role in the conceptual models of early Buddhist thought, and greatly influences the way that words are used in early Pāli literature. From the distinction between unwholesome and wholesome thoughts (*akusala/kusala dhamma*), to bad and good destinations (*dugati/sugati*), foolish and wise (*bālo/paṇḍito*) associates, unwise and wise attention (*ayoniso/yoniso manasikāro*) impure and pure (*asubha/subha*) states, and bound or liberated minds (*baddha/vimutta citto*), Buddhism is rife with a functional, if not an ultimate, duality.

The existence of this duality or dichotomy suggests that our grasp of what is meant by *nibbāna* hinges in the first place upon clearly distinguishing and defining two things — the parameters of 'suffering' (*dukkha*), and the characteristics of a 'being' (*satta* or *sattva* in Sanskrit). Since the human condition involves the suffering of beings, and the attainment of enlightenment results in the emancipation of beings from their suffering, then we must be very clear about what is to be considered suffering, to be brought to cessation, and what aspects of a being remain to become liberated. It is a matter of determining which factors a being can do without (and is better off without), and which factors constitute an essential ingredient of what it means to be a person or a being.

What is made evident by careful study of the Pāli texts is that everything that has been characterized as suffering ceases with the attainment of liberation, but it is *only* this that ceases. There are a number of other factors that continue to function after the attainment of liberation. The Buddha's long teaching career following his enlightenment is proof enough of this simple but important fact. Though devoid of craving, aversion and delusion, for example, the Buddha certainly was still in possession of consciousness, volition, perception and feeling. So the first problem is to account doctrinally for this fundamental division between the suffering that ceases with *nibbāna* and the elements of a being that do not cease.

The Two Phases of *Nibbāna*

The second challenge is to explain the difference between the two phases of *nibbāna*. A distinction is made between what happened under the Bodhi tree at Uruvela, when the Buddha attained liberation, and what happened between the Sal tree at Kusinara forty five years later, when the Buddha passed utterly away. The former is described as *nibbāna* with substrate remaining (*sa-upādisesa-nibbāna*), while the latter is called *nibbāna* which leaves no substrate behind (*an-upādisesa-nibbāna*). It has become common to refer to the first phase (at Uruvela) as *nibbāna,* and to call the second phase (at Kusinara) *parinibbāna.* We will conform to this convention here, although in many ways this is a misleading application of the terms.

These two events are profoundly different, and failure to appreciate the difference between the two can lead to great mischief. The first we are told involves the psychological transformation of Gotama into the Buddha, the total cessation of greed, hatred and delusion in his mind, the thorough destruction of the *āsavas*, the final cutting off of craving that so purifies his cognitive process that the conditions for suffering and rebirth are no longer present. The second event involves a metaphysical change, where the Buddha, as an enlightened being in human form, becomes no longer manifest in this world of elements and aggregates.

Most of Buddhist history and tradition has taken place in the years following the final passing of the Buddha, and having a meaningful understanding of the metaphysical change represented by this event has been crucial. Coming to terms with the *parinibbāna* and understanding the "post mortem" ramifications of *nibbāna* would likely have been a pivotal question shortly after his passing away, when the teacher was no longer present to model the teachings. A good explanation of this event might mean the difference between the movement dying out with the first generation of "hearers," or continuing on for 2500 years as a living tradition.

But for those who followed the Buddha during his lifetime, the paradigm they were exposed to was an awakening in this life, such as Gotama experienced under the Bodhi tree. Although final escape from the rounds of rebirth is said to be one of the implications of the attainment of *nibbāna*, the emphasis was placed in his teaching upon working towards liberation of the mind in this lifetime. Very little if anything was said about the fruits of *parinibbāna*; indeed, questions about the fate of a Tathāgata were soundly discouraged. The central thrust of Gotama's teaching for forty five years was about what he had himself discovered at Uruvela, how it had transformed him, and how anybody else can achieve the same transformation by diligent practice and right understanding. One might even say that compared to his enlightenment, the *nibbāna* at Uruvela, the Buddha's passing away, his *parinibbāna* Kusinara, was an anticlimax.

There is also an important different between the sources available for the study of *nibbāna* versus *parinibbāna*. Not only did the Buddha suggest that discussion of what happens to a Tathāgata when he passes away was a waste of time, but there is little or no information on the subject. Anything said about *parinibbāna* must ultimately rest on speculation. By contrast, a great deal is said in the *Tipiṭaka* about how the human mind works, how it is in bondage to suffering, how it can be brought steadily towards liberation, and what are some of the characteristics of an enlightened mind. A careful examination of these sources might still yield much detailed information that could throw light upon the nature and dynamics of the Buddha's own liberation. Perhaps we can try to put the complex technical vocabulary of Buddhist psychology to work in modeling the psychological transformation that is *nibbāna* is this life.

The notion that *nibbāna* occurs in two phases again supposes a dichotomy; it forces the distinction between the factors of a person's constitution that cease with the first phase of *nibbāna* and the factors that do not cease until the second phase. In other words, in order for a two-phased cessation to be possible, there must be an implicit division of a being into two separable groups or units. *Some*thing stop when *nibbāna* is attained, and *some* things do not. It is only with the attainment of the second phase or of *parinibbāna* that *all* the factors making up a particular continuum come to an end. If we find *nibbāna* described in two separate phases, then we must look for a way of conceptually distinquishing two separable sorts of factors in an individual person. The one would appear to require the other. If a being were to constitute one inseparable whole — one indivisible system of interdependent elements — then he would cease entirely with the attainment of *nibbāna*.

If anything ceases, then everything must cease. But if nothing at all ceases with *nibbāna* and cessation only occurs with the advent of *parinibbāna*, then it is difficult to understand in what sense a transformation has indeed taken place. In either case, it does not make sense to distinguish two phases to the process unless there is a corresponding functional dichotomy somewhere in the definition of a person.

Liberation and Cessation (*nibbāna* and *nirodha*)

The third issue, closely bound up with the previous two, has to do with the subtle and often confusing distinction in Buddhist thought between cessation (*nirodha*) and liberation or enlightenment (i.e. *nibbāna*). In many contexts the meaning of these two terms overlap and are even indistinguishable, and yet in some crucial respects they are very differently applied. The most basic meaning of *nibbāna* is simply 'extinction' or 'extinguished' — like a lamp or flame. The word. *nirodha* just means 'cessation' or 'stopping,' and can equally well be applied to the going out of a flame. With such definitions in mind, the two terms are often used side by side, and in some contexts are clearly meant to be taken as simple synonyms. In other situations, however, *nirodha* and *nibbāna* signify entirely different ideas that are fundamentally contradictory. For example, it is common to construe the frequent expression '*nirodha nibbāna*' as 'the cessation that is *nibbāna*' or 'the *nibbāna* that is cessation,' and yet it is imperative to recognize that such an 'extinction' or 'extinguishing' results in the liberation (*vimutti*) of a being rather than in his or her cessation (*nirodha*). If the two terms *nirodha* and *nibbāna* are not handled with extreme care, one can see how some very serious problems can arise.

The worst of these is the specter of annihilationism. It is recorded in the *Alagaddūpama Sutta* (*The Discourse on the Parable of the Water Snake*) [M.1.140] that the Buddha was accused in his own lifetime by rival wandering ascetics of being an annihilationist (*venayika*), because "he teaches that there is the cutting-off (*uccheda*), the annihilation (*vināsa*), the non-existence (*vibhava*) of a being" (the word used here for being is *satta*). The Buddha soundly denies the charge, saying "Indeed monks, this is just what I am not, and just what I do not say." The explanation that he offers in his defense is that "Before, monks and at all times, I teach only suffering and the cessation of suffering."

This is a very revealing exchange, for it shows that from the earliest times there was some confusion between the word cessation (*nirodha*) and the words 'cutting-off' (*uccheda*), 'annihilation' (*vināsa*), and 'non-existence' (*vibhava*). It is not clear whether the Buddha succeeded in mollifying his critics, or whether his explanation was even understood by them. But, as the Buddha's response to the charge of annihilationism makes clear, the key to distinguishing the cessation that is enlightenment from the cessation that is annihilation is to be found in the notion of what it is that ceases. Both cessation and extinction are, like liberation, transitive concepts—i.e. they refer to the cessation or extinction *of* something else. It is not so much that the two ideas themselves are very different (for actually they are not), as it is that they are being applied to quite different things by the Buddha and by his ancient critics. The rival wanderers construe the Buddha's doctrine of cessation as referring to a *being* (*satta*), while the Buddha himself maintains that it is only a being's suffering that is made non-existent. This distinction makes all the difference in the world, for upon it hinges the differentiation of a doctrine of profound spiritual enlightenment from one of inevitable personal oblivion.

This is one possible answer to the objections of someone whose common sense understandably leads to confusion over the application of the Buddhist concept of cessation. It seems, however, that there should be in the prodigious storehouse of Buddhist philosophical doctrines some firm basis for making the all-important distinction between what constitutes a being (*satta*) and what constitutes his suffering (*dukkha*). The boundary between the two, and the grounds for distinguishing where is should be drawn, is of the utmost importance to understanding *nibbāna*.

The Need For A Two Part Model

All three of the features of Buddhist liberation just outlined seem to require a two-part model of liberation capable of representing some of the subtleties of the dynamics of the attainment of *nibbāna*. A model consisting of two distinguishable and separable elements is necessary in order to represent: 1) *what* it is that becomes liberated, and what it is that it becomes liberated *from*; 2) precisely what it is that ceases in the first phase of *nibbāna* and what it is that ceases in the second phase or *parinibbāna*; and 3) what it is that is annihilated with attainment in this lifetime and what it is that is transformed or liberated. In each case what seems to be required is a working model that contains the essential definition of a being, and describes exactly in what way this being is bound to resurgent suffering over a series of lifetimes. What is needed is a simple model that will illustrate the nature of a being before enlightenment, when he is subject to suffering in its numerous manifestations; that will account for the dynamics of the liberation process itself; and that will also give some account of the finished product—a liberated being.

Interdependent Origination (*Paṭiccasamuppāda*)

My suggestion, quite simply, is that we look to the central but enigmatic early Buddhist doctrine of interdependent origination, the *paṭiccasamuppāda*, for a model of early Buddhist liberation. In our modern attempts to reconstruct what the early Buddhists might have meant by *nibbāna*, we are much better off adopting an indigenous model than imposing a modern and inevitably alien one. The virtue of the *paṭiccasamuppāda* as the basis for a model of liberation is that it is already an important early Buddhist articulation of the human situation. We need only to reason out the consequences of liberation, and apply them to the model that already exists. Recognizing that the doctrine is a description of the human predicament before enlightenment, all we need to do is inquire how this model might change as a result of someone attaining enlightenment.

It is not my intention to suggest that the *paṭiccasamuppāda* was originally intended as a model of liberation — as an image meant to portray the psychological characteristics of a person both before and after the attainment of *nibbāna*. To say so would be to imply that many generations of Buddhist scholars have completely misinterpreted the doctrine. As a psychological model, the *paṭiccasamuppāda* describes only a person who is still caught up with suffering in rounds of repeated births.

The *paṭiccasamuppāda* as it is found in the Pāli texts in fact is not a symbol of liberation, but of bondage. It describes the situation in which most people find themselves, and analyzes the elements of their predicament.

It lists the factors that collude for the perpetuation of suffering, and arranges them in a specific order. Together these listed factors constitute a coherent explanation of what defines a being, what that being does to ensnare himself in suffering, and what the consequences of that ensnarement are in the present and the future. Although the *paṭiccasamuppāda* portrays a person bound up with suffering, this in itself is a good foundation upon which to build a model representing his condition after suffering has been stopped.

The *paṭiccasamuppāda* is an ideal basis upon which to develop a model of liberation, partly because it is essentially a psychological model to begin with. Many of the factors named in the classical rendition of the doctrine indicate elements of an individual's 'psyche', such as consciousness, volition, and feeling, other factors suggest symptoms of an unhealthy or pathological mental process, such as ignorance, craving and grasping; and the remaining factors such as birth, ageing and death refer to the consequences of that disease. The doctrine of interdependent origination is a systematic presentation of the essential elements of an unhealthy 'being' (*satta*), coupled with a probing analysis of what is wrong with the patient, and an accurate prognosis of the consequences. It is therefore an ideal basis for representing both the healing process and its results.

Best known by the image of the 'wheel of life' (*bhavacakra*), a twelve-spoked wheel of *saṃsāra* embraced by a demon which is common in later Buddhist iconography, the *paṭiccasamuppāda* doctrine we find presented in the Pāli *Nikāyas* takes a very different form. Variations of construction and sequence abound, but one form, consisting of twelve interdependent factors, dominates above all others and will be referred to here as the 'classical' rendition of the doctrine. In the texts we find the twelve terms simply listed, within a simple statement of conditional relation, but for the sake of our argument we will arrange the terms in the popular circular diagram. A careful study of the variations of the causal series as well as of the nuclear causal formulas used to bind the factors together reveals, I believe, that they all for the most part serve to clarify the classical formula. There are extensive variations of the associated factors, as well as prolific elaborations, additions, and omissions, but these I think should not be taken as expressing different doctrines. There are not as many teachings on causality as there are renditions of the *paṭiccasamuppāda*. Rather, all variations tend to reflect different aspects of the doctrine of interdependent origination, whose subtlety and complexity calls for a wide range of approaches to its explanation.

The *Paṭiccasamuppāda* as a Model of Liberation

The main innovation that I would like to offer in the interpretation of the *paṭiccasamuppāda*, and the one that paves the way for a two-part model of liberation, is that we view the twelve factors of the classical *paṭiccasamuppāda* as belonging to two distinct groups or units. These are normally linked together, but are capable of being separated with the attainment of *nibbāna* or liberation. Though the two parts of the *paṭiccasamuppāda* rise and fall together in a normal person's lifetime, they may be construed as independent of one another because when an exceptional person attains liberation one half stops while the other half remains for some time. One group is made up of those factors which collectively comprise suffering (*dukkha*), namely craving (*taṇhā*), grasping (*upādāna*), existence (*bhava*), birth (*jāti*), ageing and death (*jarāmaraṇa*) and ignorance (*avijjā*). The other group consists of those elements which form the early Buddhist psychological model of a being or person. These include the factors of feeling (*vedanā*), contact (*phassa*), the six spheres (*saḷāyatana*), name and form (*nāmarūpa*), consciousness (*viññāṇa*), and that aggregate known as *saṅkhara* (volition/activities/formations). The determining criterion for making this division is whether a factor stops when *nibbāna* is attained or whether it persists beyond the accomplishment of *nibbāna* in this lifetime.

The *paṭiccasamuppāda* is usually taken to be a single system of mutually related elements, but these two groups of factors that I have identified represent sub-systems which can be distinguished within it. In the majority of beings these two sets of factors function together and are so intimately interwoven that they are indistinguishable as two separate sets. Thus in the early Buddhist view a person is in perpetual bondage to suffering. But the Buddha demonstrated by his own example that it is possible to alter this condition of bondage—to separate the sentient faculties of the mind from the influence of suffering. The Buddha demonstrated that the mind can be liberated from suffering by the cessation of suffering, and this liberation is what *nibbāna* is all about.

Nibbāna is defined in the third of the four noble truths as the cessation of suffering (*dukkha nirodha*), and our two-part model of the *paṭiccasamuppāda* can be used to demonstrate what precisely this means. *Nibbāna* in this present lifetime, the *nibbāna* experienced by the Buddha under the Bodhi tree at Uruvelā, can be accurately described as the cessation of the group of factors which make up suffering, and the persistence of the other groups—the aggregate of factors that make up a model of a person or that constitute the essential elements of a being.

In fact the adoption of this simple two-part model of the *paṭiccasamuppāda* can lead us towards a very detailed definition of *nibbāna*. By this I mean that the model provides a structure for dividing a host of Buddhist vocabulary found in the texts into two basic groups: 1) the factors that have ceased with the attainment of *nibbāna*; and 2) the factors that have not ceased and which persist in one who has attained it. In the first case we have a comprehensive definition of suffering (*dukkha*), and in the second we have an essential definition of a being (*satta*).

To put the matter another way, we can say that the doctrine of interdependent origination can be briefly summarized in two sentences:

> The mind (*citta, viññāṇa*), endowed with the capacity of volition (*cetanā, saṅkhāra*), is mutually conditioned by a body (*rūpa, kāya*) which allows for the faculties of perception (*sañña, saḷāyatana, phassa*) and the experiencing of pleasant, painful or neutral feeling (*vedanā*). This complex of factors, however, is influenced at every moment by craving (*taṇhā*) and ignorance (*avijjā*) to act in such a way that *karmic* substrates are produced (*upādāna, saṅkhāra, upadhi*), which condemns a being to participation in the recurring cycles of existence (*bhava*) characterized by birth, ageing and death (*jāti, jarāmaraṇa*); this entire process is generally called suffering (*dukkha*).

In this synopsis the first part describes the normal operation of the human psychological process, while the second describes a pathological process that involves a being in continual suffering. What the attainment of liberation or of *nibbāna* in this lifetime actually accomplishes is the separation of these two groups of factors or sub-systems of interdependent activities. All the manifestations of suffering cease utterly, as they did for Gotama under the Bodhi tree, but the normal human perceptual process itself continues until its dissolution with the attainment of *parinibbāna*.

The crucial point to recognize here is that when suffering ceases, a being persists. The genius of the Buddha's program of liberation is precisely that the attainment of enlightenment is a process of *selective* cessation. It represents a way, if I may be excused a modern metaphor, of draining off the bathwater without throwing away the baby. And it is the doctrine of interdependent origination, the *paṭiccasamuppāda*, that provides the framework for recognizing this important point.

Can the *Paṭiccasamuppāda* Be Divided?

It is natural to raise the objection, "How is it that the doctrine of interdependent origination can be divided into two parts?" After all, every rendition of the classical formula in the Pāli texts concludes with the phrase: "Such is the arising of this *entire* aggregate of suffering", or "Such is the cessation of this *entire* aggregate of suffering" (*evaṃ etassa kevalassa dukkhakkhandhassa samudayo hoti* or *nirodho hoti*). The use of the terms *kevala* here is significant, because it is strongly suggestive of unity. It stresses that the *entire* system of interrelated factors arises and ceases as a single unit, and suggests that the entire unit is to be referred to as the 'aggregate of suffering' (*dukkhakkhandha*). Indeed it seems that the main point of the doctrine of interdependent origination is precisely that the enumerated factors cannot be separated from one another.

It is my contention, however, that this expression cannot be taken at face value. When we look carefully at the *patterns* of interdependent factors — at what is said to be dependent upon what — we are led to question the inseparability of the system of interrelated factors. Quite simply, maintaining the unity of the *paṭiccasamuppāda* leads to an unacceptable set of contradictions, and is incompatible with the central Buddhist teaching that *nibbāna* is attainable in this life. If the *paṭiccasamuppāda* is conceived as an inseparable whole, then the attainment of *nibbāna* results in either the liberation of all twelve factors or the complete cessation of all twelve. Both of these alternatives have their problems, and indeed it can be shown that they are equally unacceptable. To say that a liberated being has any trace of craving (*tanhā*) or ignorance (*avijjā*) or grasping (*upādāna*) is impossible, for all such things have ceased with the attainment of *nibbāna*. On the other hand, admitting that all twelve factors of the *paṭiccasamuppāda* cease with enlightenment would amount to denying consciousness (*viññāṇa*), feeling (*vedanā*) and perception (*saḷāyatana, phassa*) to the arahants, and even the Buddha himself.

The teaching on *nibbāna* contained in the third of the four noble truths states unequivocally that liberation in this life is possible, and is manifest as the cessation of suffering. The prose and verse literature of the Pāli *Nikāyas* is filled with assertions that for the enlightened ones certain factors are completely stopped, never to rise again. We often hear, for example, that "birth is destroyed" (*khīṇā jāti*), that "craving is completely brought to cessation" (*taṇhāya asesavirāganirodho*), that "now there is no more renewed existence" (*n'atthi dāni punabbhavo*), and so forth. Many of these factors that are said to cease are named in the *paṭiccasamuppāda*, and if it is taken as forming a single, indivisible unit of interdependent factors then we are required to admit that the entire unit ceases with the attainment of *nibbāna*.

This is a big problem, however, because many other of the factors named in the *paṭiccasamuppāda* are such basic constituents of both physical and mental life. It would be difficult to imagine a person operating in the world, as the Buddha did for more than forty years after his enlightenment, without essential factors such as perception, feeling, thought and will. These factors are represented in the *paṭiccasamuppāda* by *saṅkhāra, viññāṇa, nāmarūpa, saḷāyatana, phassa* and *vedanā*. It is clear that in light of the conventional early Buddhist definitions of terms, the Buddha manifested consciousness and several other psycho-physical factors mentioned in the *paṭiccasamuppāda* even after his enlightenment under the Bodhi tree. The only possible exception to this assertion is the condition known as the cessation of perception and feeling (*saññāvedayita-nirodha*), where it appears that the mind does achieve a temporary cessation (although the body remains in a suspended State). This condition, however, is a special case which warrants independent discussion.

The simple fact is that there is a basic incompatibility between 1) the position that all the factors of the *paṭiccasamuppāda* are interdependent and thus arise and cease as a single unit, and 2) the position that with the attainment of *nibbāna* some of the factors cease utterly while some continue to function for the duration of this life. The only apparent way to reconcile this dilemma is to allow the bifurcation of the *paṭiccasamuppāda*.

Conclusion

Once this is done, we are left with a simple model which is nevertheless capable of expressing matters of great complexity. It resolves all three of the problems raised earlier simply by coming up with a specific delineation, using the doctrinal details of the *paṭiccasamuppāda*, of what suffering is and what a being is. It shows what is liberated from what: a being is liberated from suffering. It shows what ceases in the first phase of *nibbāna* and what ceases in the second phase: only suffering ceases in the first phase, as for the Buddha under the Bodhi tree, while in the second phase the other psycho-physical aggregates that constitute a being finally pass away. It also shows the difference between annihilation and illumination: annihilation is the cessation of a being (*sattassa nirodho*), something suggested perhaps by certain *ucchedavādin*s who did not accept rebirth, but never by the Buddha, who regarded illumination as the cessation only of a being's suffering (*dukkhassa nirodho*).

In conclusion, we have suggested that a functional model for conceptualizing the attainment of *nibbāna* as a phased process of psychological transformation might be found in the indigenous Buddhist doctrine of *paṭiccasamuppāda*, if we envision the possibility of its bifurcation. The two-part model of interdependent origination outlined here yields a two-part model of interdependent cessation. This may be of some value in helping us understand the simple but baffling question of what happens to a person when he or she becomes enlightened.

3

Dhammapada and *Tirukkuraḷ* : A Comparative Study

Subramania Gopalan

I

The present paper is aimed at studying the parallel perspectives on the concept of the *good life* discernible in two Indian classics,[1] *Dhammapada* and *Tirukkuraḷ*,[2] known as much for their literary value as for the deep philosophical insights into religion they throw. The interesting feature of both pieces is that though they incorporate within themselves the essentials of a serious philosophy of man and are highly suggestive of the need for cross-cultural philosophizing,

1 The term *classic* which is used to refer to the Greek writings in the context of the western world is applied to *Dhammapada* and *Tirukkuraḷ* here. It is interesting to note that at least two important aspects of the notions of a classic are significant in regard to both the works. They are: (i) possession of deep thought which are of enduring interest to humankind and (ii) presence of literary value of the first rank. As classics, both the works have universal relevance, addressed as they are to man as man and have been translated into a number of Asian and European languages.

2 It is well-known that early Buddhistic thought is to be found in 'three baskets of tradition' (*Tripiṭaka*), the *Suttapiṭaka*, the *Vinayapiṭaka* and the *Abhidhammapiṭaka*. Our interest in *Dhammapada is in its* forming part of the *Suttapiṭaka* and reflecting the essentials of the teachings of the Buddha. Though *Dhammapada* was not written by the Buddha himself and in this respect different from *Tirukkural* in that the Tamil work was authored by Tiruvalluvar and intended as quintessential work on the philosophy of good life, it seems to us that the value of the Buddhist work does not get diminished. For, it is accepted by critical scholarship that the First council settled the *Suttapiṭaka* and *Vinayapiṭaka* held at Rajagṛha immediately after the *parinirvāṇa* of the Buddha. (See. B. Jinanada, "Four Buddhist Councils" in P.V. Bapat, ed. *Two Thousand Five Hundred Years of Buddhism* (New Delhi: The Publications Division, Government of India, 1956), p. 35 Furthermore, as M.E. Spiro *Buddhism and Society* (New York: Harper and Row), 1970, pp. 6-7, while defining his term *normative Theravāda Buddhism* (as the doctrines contained in the Theravāda canon, which may or may not correspond with the teachings of the historical Buddha), observes: "The question of the historical Buddha is 'irrelevant' because the distinction itself is foreign to

they are comprehensible by the common man. Even while they arrest the attention of the technical philosopher to ponder over the ideas presented in them, they have proved attractive enough for the man-in-the-street to think about the ideals exhorted. Though they both abound in common-place maxims, they leave a deep imprint in the minds of those who have become *acquainted* with them even, whatever might be their religious persuasion and cultural background.

Dhammapada is undoubtedly a Buddhist classic and is reflective of the essentials of the teachings of Buddhism and also of the Indian tradition within which it was born. *Tirukkuraḷ* was certainly post-Buddhistic but it is difficult to give it the nomenclature of a Buddhist text. Buddhist ideas, it certainly reflects but it is also a blend of ideas current in the Indian scene — Brahmanical and Jaina[3] — and is acceptable to non-Indian religious traditions too.[4]

II

The Buddha and Tiruvaḷḷuvar whose thoughts the two classics

believing Buddhists, for to them *all* the words which the canon attributes to the Buddha, are indeed his words and *all* doctrines contained in the canon represent the teachings of the Buddha." We might add that although determining the precise dates of the two classics is not important for our purposes too, it is worth remembering that of the two works, *Dhammapada* perhaps predated *Tirukkuraḷ* which is established, by reputed scholars of Indian history, to have belonged to the period 100B.C. - 100 A.D. (See V.R. Ramachandra Dikshitar, *Studies in Tamil Literature and History* (London: Luzac & Co., 1930), p. 132; See also his *Pandyan Kingdom* (London: Luzac & Co., 1939), p. 24 and *History of India* (Oxford, 1955), p. 110; and Vincent A. Smith, *Early History of India* (Oxford, 1957), p. 445.

3. In this connection it should be noted that what we today refer to as Hinduism, Jainism and Buddhism were all inextricably woven together in the earliest phase of Indian thought. This perhaps accounts for the co-existence of the three traditions and also throws some light on the commanality-elements found in them. (See Wilfred Cantwell Smith, *The Meaning and End of Religion* (New York: The New American Liberary of World Literature, 1964), pp. 61, 62 and 249-251).

4 It is interesting to note that G.U. Pope, a devout and pious Christian unfailingly spotted the sayings of Lord Christ in *Tirukkuraḷ*. The ten couplets constituting the fourth chapter entitled 'Commendation of Virtue' fascinated him most and he wrote:"I translate the ten couplets of which it is to be noted that they are perhaps on the whole the most polished in the book; absolutely perfect, flawless gems in Tamil. The teachings of this chapter are obviously to some extent that of the eighteenth chapter of the *Gīta*: action is not to be forsaken; great as are ascetics, it is in the performance of virtuous deeds that men are to partake of the highest enjoyments and merit the greatest rewards. And since the writer: (1) was an avowed eclectic; (2) was unfettered by caste; (3) was an inhabitant of San Thome and so in the midst of Christians, it seems to me a natural supposition that he had heard the Sermon on the Mount. To such a man the lives and words of our blessed

capture in all their distinct details, impress upon us the picture of two serious thinkers who wanted to transform the lives of people by their transparent openness of heart and a mind which was receptive to worthwhile ideas from any quarter.[5]

Since the details of the Buddha's life are fairly well-known we may gloss over them here. Suffice it to reiterate, however, that the life of the Buddha reveals two sides — personal and social. The former gives us the picture of a sage absorbed in meditation and drawn unto himself and enjoying inner peace and tranquillity. The latter throws into bold relief his abiding concern for men with compassion filling his heart and kindness for all emanating from his gentle personality. While they represent two among many forms that Buddhism itself took, they also reveal an essential unity in terms of the aim of philosophy and religion, viz. transforming the quality of human life.

Tiruvaḷḷuvar was probably born during the *Śangam* age[6] (coinciding with the pre-Christian and early Christian era) when Tamil civilization was at its peak. The picture of Tiruvaḷḷuvar that emerges from his work is that of a man of universal vision and understanding who defies identification merely in terms of caste obligations and religious affiliation. It is quite possible that he was a man involved in and committed to action, a contemplative who could identify himself with the 'low' and the poor, and was not prepared to accord distinction for *mere* learning unaccompanied by virtue. He was perhaps a man who was well aware of his *duties* without unduly asserting his rights, a warm person and above all a wise man who was not without a word of advice alike to the ascetic and to the man of the world.

Lord and of his holy Apostles, especially St. Paul, would have a peculiar charm." (Cited in K.C. Kamaliah, *Preface in the Kural* (Madras: M. Seshachalam & Co., 1973), pp. 3-4) Kamaliah also refers (ibid., p. 6) to Pope's seeing in the *Kuraḷ Mohammendan* influences as well and remarks: "It is patent that the Kural is acceptable to all strata of people in the community of mankind, irrespective of their religious persuasions, social status and even political affiliations. But verily can it be said that the *Kuṛaḷ* is forthright in appeal, never compromises on fundamentals, with its affirmation of truth and negation of evil."

5 See *Tirukkuraḷ*, 43.3.

6 Though a precise date for the *Sangam* period of Tamil literature is difficult to fix, it is possible to indicate a wide period within which the literature was produced. Historians writing on South India generally agree that the *Sangam* literature may be placed between the fifth century B.C. and fifth century. See Sastry, *The Cholas* (Madras: University of Madras, 1937), Vol. I, p.3. In terms of these, *Tirukkuraḷ* may be considered to have belonged to the mid-*Sangam* period.

What is generally conceded in the case of great men of history — that they are both creators and also the creatures of their times — may be said both about the Buddha and Tiruvaḷḷuvar. The Buddha, as it is said, "was born a Hindu, grew up a Hindu and died a Hindu." But what was characteristic of him was that he tried to reform the church by removing the sloth the tradition had gathered during its long history, and rekindle the spirit which had not been put out due to the basic vitality it possessed. Though sometimes Buddhism has been referred to as a philosophy and protest, it did not break away completely from the mainstream of Indian tradition - by rejecting all the earlier ideas. The Buddha's critical approach was with a view to constructively enhancing the value of the message that was sought to be conveyed rather than cynically marring its transmission to the masses for whom it was intended.

Tiruvaḷḷuvar was simultaneously labeled as a Hindu, a Jaina and a Buddhist. While differing with the three traditions in a number of respects, he did not fail to accept the best in them all.[7] While the basic philosophy of transformation of man presented in all the three traditions current during his time in India was accepted wholeheartedly by him, some details in regard to the methodology adopted by them and also the categories employed while attempting to transmit the ideals were set aside by him as inconsequential.[8] Just as from his acceptance of certain ideas one could make out their sources, from the mild but effective critical observations he makes,[9] one could visualize the tradition which drew his attention.

III

Looking first at the two classics as literary peices, we find interesting and striking parallels. But what is significant is that the literary worth which has elevated them both to the status of world-classics does not displace nor delete their value as deep philosophical works with a clear message to mankind at large. A reference to some

7 For instance, the ethics of non-violence and the ideal of disinterested performance of duty propounded in Hinduism, Jainism and Buddhism was accepted by him wholeheartedly.

8 He was critical of the metaphysical system-building characteristic of Hinduism and non-acceptance if God in Jainism and Buddhism and some schools of Hindu thought.

9 *Tirukkuraḷ*, 26.6 is a case in point. The critical comment that if no one would eat meat, no one would sell meat for money is obviously a mild criticism levelled against Buddhism.

of the comparable ideas here in regard to style and content would indicate how they themselves have made for the richness of the philosophical contents of the two works.

The gentle but effective art-poetry employed cannot fail to attract the attention of even a casual reader of the two classics. Telling phrases, apt similes and comparisons found in abundance in the two works lend a realistic touch to the analysis of the human situation.

Let us first cite some examples from the *Dhammapada.* A man who reads an enormous amount of literature but who seldom is influenced by the reading is compared to a cowherd who only counts the number of cows that he grazes, but has no proprietary rights over any of them.[10] What is important to notice here is that the analogy itself is a clear pointer to the need for appropriating the ideas contained in one's reading in order to derive real and lasting benefit out of it. In the absence of being 'processed' by the ideas gathered, the time and energy spent would be a waste. Also, the value of literature itself is indicated as consisting in influencing the thinking and eventually effecting a change in the life of the reader.[11] Similarly, while describing how the monks may enter villages only to take their food but not to interfere with the life of the village or in the affairs of the people dwelling in them, the analogy of a bee reaching a flower, sucking the honey and doing no damage either to the colour or to the smell of the flower is employed.[12] Once again, the attitude that should characterize the monks is, without any ambiguity portrayed through the simile.

To make the point that craving (*taṇhā*) and ignorance (*avijjā*) are the potent causes of life and suffering, the analogy of the speedy growth of grass may be utilized. We read: "Whomsoever thirst holds in subjection, that thirst, that contemptible thing which pours its venom throught the world, his suffering grows as the grass grows. Whosoever holds it in subjection...suffering falls off from him as the water drops from the lotus flowers."[13] Again: "As, if the root be uninjured, even as a hewn tree grows up anew mightily, so, if the excitement of thirst be not wholly dead, suffering even and anon breaks out again."[14] An important idea of Buddhistic philosophy is conveyed by means of an easily understandable analogy. The

10. *Dhammapada,* I. 19.
11. Ibid., VI. 82.
12. Ibid., IV. 49.
13. Ibid., XXIV. 335 and 336.
14 Ibid., XXIV. 38.

individual's own responsibility in getting caught up in the round of births and deaths is pointed out with emphasis by comparing the situation to a spider finding itself being enmeshed in its own web.[15]

Tirukkuraḷ is replete with analogies which just describe a person, portray a situation or point to an attitude. "Her frame tender shoot, her teeth pearls, her smell fragrance, her eyes darts, her shoulders the bent of bamboo."[16] is an instance of a simple description of a tender girl. To illustrate the loss of status, the analogy made use of is this: "Like the hairs from off the head that fall to the earth."[17] The conduct in the presence of a king, is explained by stating: "Like those that warm themselves at the fire."[18] To point to slanderous rumour, the analogy of the moon being seized by the dragon is employed.[19] 'Inconsistent' conduct is portrayed by likening it to the cow wearing a tiger's skin.[20] To picturize the ruin-chasing sinful deeds, the telling analogy found useful is this: "As a man's shadow dogs his steps wherever he wends."[21]

Constructing analogies and making use of them to convey an idea may be construed sometimes as not necessarily a sound philosophical method of arguing for a position. For one thing, analogies have their own limitations and cannot be relied upon to precisely 'convey the meaning', and for another, the idea that is sought to be expressed does not necessarily follow as a logical sequel to the analogy employed. The limitations of the method of analogical reasoning referred to above may be conceded, but what is important to notice is that the Buddha and Tiruvaḷḷuvar were not as much concerned with logically demonstrating that an idea followed from a given idea as with making an imprint on the minds of the 'audience' to bring about a change in attitudes and viewpoints. Not that the logical side of the issue was totally ignored but that while employing analogies, conveying an important idea in such a way that it would sink into the mind of the listener, was accorded prime importance by both the thinkers. Perhaps the phenomenal success registered by both the classical philosophers was due to their making audiences get absorbed in the world of ideas presented and enable interiorization.

15 Ibid., XXIV. 347.
16 *Tirukkuraḷ*, 112.3.
17 Ibid., 97.4.
18 Ibid., 70.1.
19 Ibid., 115.6.
20 Ibid., 28.3.
21 Ibid., 21.8.

Such an interiorization of ideas — in the case of the Buddha and Tiruvalluvar these ideas themselves are regarding ideals — are, in the ultimate analysis, responsible for the inner transformation of man and is the *sine que non* of true religion.[22] Religion in this sense is intimately tied up with and infuse meaning and significance into life. It will be equally true to state that leading a good life itself constitutes the essence of religion.

IV

The good life has always been a theme of serious discussion in the Indian tradition as a whole. In spite of the divergences characterizing the viewpoints of the religio-philosophical traditions within the Indian scene,[23] there has been a significantly unique area of agreement regarding the core-idea of what constitutes the ultimate Good. The ultimate Good in human life has been visualized by them to have the significance of inspiring man to aim at and achieve a state which is an epitome of spiritual perfection. They seem to agree that man is basically possessed of an amphibious nature, living on 'the good earth' and looking forward to entering a 'brave new world' of experience which is, at the moment it is thought about, a *concept merely* but which begins to haunt him sooner or later and creates a state of restlessness and discontentment with the existent state. They thus seem to point to two phases of human life which are distinct but not discontinuous and are clearly apparent for a person of discernment:[24] one, the stage in which the individual complacently acquiesces in the ordinary, unreflective mode of living and the other, the

22 The clear implication here is that religion is not to be understood in terms of ritualistic practices, ceremonies and sacraments. The Buddha's definition of a brahmin in terms of qualities characterizing him than in terms of officiating in sacrifices is an important point to be considered in this context. (See *Dhammapada*, XXVI. 386, 388, 393, 396, 399-403) and cf. the mild criticism that *Tirukkuraḷ* levels against rituals (See 26.9 and 30.5) The type of criticism of caste found in the *Kural* (14.4 and 98.2) seems also to be intended to make the point that mere birth-criteria without the high ethical qualities ought not be played up in religion.

23 It is common knowledge that philosophy and religion are found intertwined in the Indian tradition. This intimate and reciprocal relationship has had an effect on both the disciplines. Philosophy supplies the intellectual content to religion and religion in turn is responsible for the practical orientation of philosophy. Hinduism, Jainism and Buddhism are hence as much philosophies as they are religions.

24 Tiruvaḷḷuvar devotes two chapters to the subject of knowledge and wisdom. Chapter 42 which is entitled "Learning" and chapter 43 with the title "Possession

state of 'ultimate concern' which brings with it, a tremendous attitudinal transformation.

In the two works we are considering, these ideas find articulation. The term *good life* is used in them to indicate the *ultimate ideal* in human life as also the *ideals* to be pursued in the 'immediate present.' As long as man is content with the 'immediate' and the 'actual,' he may not be motivated at all to consider 'what lies beyond.' The good life in the ultimate sense indicated cannot then be understood. Paradoxically however, for this very reason, the good life in the 'less ultimate sense' too gets to be ignored and hence leads to the situation of its now being comprehended.

The paradox may be explained thus. The sole concern with the immediate may itself be responsible for the purely egoistic and self-regarding tendencies and activities. This might prevent an idealistic attitude to life setting in. In it's absence, the need to become 'other-regarding' will not be recognized. But since realizing fully this ideal 'expansiveness' itself constitutes the ultimate good, by not leading a good life, the Good in life cannot be attained. The difficulty in comprehending the idea of the good life is attributable to the difficulties inherent in the human predicament itself.[25]

The Buddhistic and the Tamil concept of the good life as briefly paraphrased above are found reflected in the concepts of *nirvāṇa* and *vīdu* respectively. Both the concepts are interpreted to have a positive meaning, notwithstanding the negative overtones they may seem to possess.[26] The implication of both the concepts is that there is, in the sense indicated already, a subtle but significant distinction between

---

of Wisdom" impress upon his readers that discernment, the very object of education can be achieved only if the inquiring habit is infused into the mind. The implication is that in the absence of the ability to 'absorb' and 'analyze,' knowledge regarding the ultimate purpose of life cannot dawn at all. Chapters III and VI of *Dhammapada*, respectively entitled, 'Thought' and 'The Wise Man' also seem to be concerned with this deeper implication of learning as transformation of human life.

25 Both the classics incorporate deep reflections on man and his predicament. It will not be an exaggeration to suggest that even while they provide guidelines on true ethical living, they reveal thoughtful analysis of human nature. Perhaps this is one reason why ideas found in the two works have both universal applicability and wide acceptance from people belonging to diverse religious and cultural traditions.

26 From its literal meaning viz., 'blowing out,' the term *nirvāṇa* has been misunderstood in some quarters to have negative significance. The idea that the ultimate ideal is extinction is also put forth. This does not quite explain why, after the

the good life conceived of as an *ideal life* and the *ideals in life* (as means). Whereas the one is the goal set, the other is the means of reaching the goal. Whereas the means are to be adopted 'now', the 'end' can be attained only 'later,' i.e. after leading a life dedicated to the pursuit of the ideal.

All the same, the ideal of the Good and the ideals of good life need not be construed to be discontinuous. The deeper significance attached to the ideals to be pursued in the immediate workaday world is that they help the individual in realizing his ultimate goal. In fact, without the pursuit of the latter, the former cannot be realized, it is maintained in both the classics.[27] For the purposes of this paper however, the details regarding the means to be adopted for achieving

---

attainment of *bodhi* at the age of thirty-five, the Buddha spent the remaining forty-five years of his life in actively preaching the *dhamma* and doing good. It is hence obvious, *nirvāṇa* has a positive significance. Dr. S. Radhakrishnan, *Indian Philosophy* (Madras: Blackie & Son Publishers Pvt. Ltd., 1985), Vol. I, p. 447) prefers 'cooling,' the other meaning of *nirvana* and writes: "Blowing out suggests extinction. Cooling suggests not complete annihilation, but only the dying out hot passion...That Buddha means only the extinction of false desire and not all existence comes out from a large number of passages. *Nirvāṇa* is only destruction of fires of lust, hatred and ignorance." In regard to the Tamil term *vīdu*, it is etymologically derived from *vidu* which 'leave.' Even though such a derivation imports the sense of 'giving up,' the term vidu enjoys in actual, popular and literary usage, the highest positivity of meaning. 'Realizing *vīdu*' is therefore like home-coming. Just as in one's home one is free from any sense of constraint, 'realising *vīdu*' in the religious sense becomes a synonym for the ideal of real freedom.

27 The importance of taking the path of *dhamma* represents in one sense, the quintessence of the Buddha's teachings and this is reflected in the whole of *Dhammapada*. *Nirvāṇa* is not a mere concept, it is a state of being to be attained by the striving man who is caught up in the wheel of birth and death. Only by adopting the *dhamma*, only by disciplined living that treading the path of *dhamma* involves can the ultimate ideal be realized. The idea is conveyed through the *Dhammapada* in a crystal-clear fashion. Likewise supreme importance is accorded to aram in *Tirukkuraḷ*. Tiruvalluvar exclaims: "There is no greater good than aram nor a greater source of evil than forgetting it." (*Tirukkuraḷ*, 4.2) The same idea is slightly differently presented by him in the tenth couplet of the fourth chapter: "That is *aṟam* which one ought to do and that is not aram which ought to be shunned." The significance of aram is further highlighted by suggesting that the attitude of procrastination in regard to aram is to be completely avoided: "Do virtuous deeds now, defer it not to a future date for it will be never-failing friend at the dying hour" (*Ibid.*, 4.6). The idea is driven home more forcefully by the observation that the individual's passing days without doing virtue is tantamount to his placing a block of stone to the passage to other birth" (*Ibid.*, 408). "True joy of living flows only from virtue, all else is sorrow and deserve no praise," Tirucalluvar empatically points out (*Ibid.*, 4.9).

the end envisaged in the two classics need not be gone into. However, the general layout of the good life found in the two works requires to be indicated with a view to substantiating the statements we have made above regarding the *Weltanschauung* discernible in them.

V

Turning our attention first to *Dhammapada*, the exhortation to lead a good life found in it is in terms of its insisting that man leads a life of *dharma*.[28] Realizing the Good that is promised by adhering to *dharma* is referred to as *nirvāṇa*.[29] One way of appreciating the spirit of the Buddhist classic's approach to the whole question of achieving *nirvāṇa*, the Transcendent state of the Good by adopting the path of *dharma* (by choosing to lead a good life) is to note that neither the means-end dichotomy model nor considering *nirvāṇa* as a negative state is helpful. The text evidences the idea that *nirvāṇa* is a Transcendent state of experience to be attained in human life.[30] This state is attained when the individual leads a dharmic life in the full sense of the term.[31]

The exhortation to develop attitudinal changes by following the path of *dharma* indicates that the ultimate Good can be achieved *not by negating life* but by *positively considering how best life can be made use of.* The two expressions have to be carefully understood. 'Not negating life' does not signify 'clinging to life.' This fundamental tenet of Buddhism is driven home in the *Dhammapada*[32] without any ambiguity. 'Positively making use of life' does not refer to enjoying life in order to overcome suffering. Rather, it is an exhortation to lead a disciplined life, a good life, so that the Good in life will be realized. The context of the exhortation is *life* and *not death*, the discipline to be introduced is into life rather than abandonment of life in order to embrace death.

Hence by electing to adhere to the principle of *dharma* in its prestine purity, the potentiality for spiritual perfection can be actualised.[33] The ideal life-style can itself be described as ideal-

28 I.16; IV.44; VI.79; XIII.169; XV.208; XX.274.
29 XV.204.
30 II.23; VII.93; IX.126.
31 II.21, 25 and 27; IV. 45; VI.86.
32 XXIV.334 and 338.
33 XX.273.

realization. Needless to add in this connection that the idea of *dharma*, the importance of adopting the way[34] is reiterated. By so doing, ending the pain, overcoming suffering and transcending the cycle of birth and death (what is referred to also as transcending the effects of *karma*) is assured.[35] That the way of *dharma* consists in dynamically taking the necessary steps[36] is also indicated positively as well as negatively. By keeping the three roads of action, (those of the body, mind and speech) clear[37], the individual will be able to practice the way (of *dharma*); and one who is full of sloth will never be able to do so, it is emphasised.[38] By following the *path of dharma* in this way, getting over the shackles imposed by *dharma* is possible. This is a state of freedom which can be attained in this world itself[39], in this life itself.[40]

The deeper implication of law of the *karma* for the good life becomes evident when we pause to analyze the idea of 'overcoming karma'. First and foremost, the law of *karma* points to the responsibility of the individual himself.[41] **But what is not so evident but which is emphasized by the Buddha is that the cycle can be ended,[42] though with difficulty and after a good deal of discipline infused into life.[43]**

In brief, the idea underlying the Buddha's teaching here is one of emphasizing the inescapability from *karma*, on the one hand, and the need to overcome it through transmutation, on the other. *Karma* has its sway in strict proportion to the sense of agency and possession with which one acts. If one does good and abstains from evil, one surely creates for himself a 'good fate'[44] just as by doing the opposite, he is only sowing the seeds for an evil destiny.[45] This is the doctrine of rewards (for good actions) and punishment (for evil doings) constitutive of the very essence of the law of *karma*. The problem with which the Buddha was faced, life the generality of his forevears,

34 The whole of Chapter XX is significant in this context.
35 XX.275.
36 XVIII.236; XX.280.
37 XX.281.
38 XX.280.
39 XIII.168.
40 XXIV.351.
41 XII.160 and 165; XX.276; XXIII.323.
42 IX.120, 121, 125, 127 and 137.
43 See VI.85, XIII.174; XXIV.347 and 348.
44 IX.118 and 122.
45 IX.117 and 121; X.136.

was one of the resolution of *karma*, for it was only be rendering *karma* ineffective that one could realize the ultimate Good. In the context of the present paper it is important to note that the solution suggested by the Buddha bears a remarkable resemblance with that suggested by Tiruvaḷḷuvar as will become evident in the sequel.

The Buddha's solution consisted in affirming the need for a progressive striving towards overcoming the innate sense of the ego by man. Even though the other-regarding attitude characteristic of a altruistic approach would considerably mitigate the evil-effects of the ego-play and certainly widen the areas of human concern, it cannot by itself help man to transcend the cycle of birth and death. For, expanding the area of concern from the smaller to the larger groups does not by itself help one to efface the ego since basically the narrower as well as the wider groups are all alike hedged in by 'ties' — biological, social and cultural. Furthermore, the concern and love exemplified even at the level of general humanity may not be of the most spontaneous kind and as such the operation of the ego-motive cannot be transcended.[46]

Such a state which sees the individual transcending the 'I' feeling and 'feeling of mine', when attained, is truly the state of *nirvāṇa*. This shift from a life of 'I' and 'mine' to a life which is characterized by a totally context-free disposition of compassion is what effects total freedom, *nirvāṇa*. Since the 'shift' brings with it a total transformation of personality, the Buddhist ideal of *nirvāṇa* could also be interpreted as pointing to the individual having attained the full stature of human perfectibility. Since the ideal is admittedly a difficult one to achieve,[47] it is not surprising that various stages are envisaged in the gradual progress registered in this regard.

It is obvious too that since eradicating the ego involves a cleansing act of removing the sloth of self-centredness, achieving mental purity is vitally important.[48] This seems to be the idea behind the exhortation that one should treat others as one would like to be treated by them, for that is the way the ideal of compassion can be cultivated. Wisdom and the truth[49] are in this context considered foundationally important for they both help the individual in attaining the Transcendent goal of *nirvāṇa*. The right kind of knowledge

46 See IV.14.
47 VI.85; XIII.174.
48 See XVII.223, 225 and 233; XVIII.238, 248-251.
49 See III.38 and 39; VI.82.

is basic since in the absence of it, the need for getting over the 'present' state will not even be thought about. True knowledge is getting over ignorance which is the cause of birth.[50] Thus it is that leading a good life and achieving the Transcendent ideal of the Good are considered by the *Dhammapada* to offer us a continuum. They can, only for purposes of analysis, be distinguished from one another.

VI

Passing on to consider the ideas that can be gleaned from *Tirukkuraḷ*, we note that the Tamil work refers to the ultimate Good as *Vīdu* and the mean of realizing it as *aram*. In our terms, *vīdu* may be referred to as the state of ultimate spiritual perfection attainable (and hence exhorted to be attained) by man. *Aram* may be considered the prerequisite, the disciplined life that needs to be led, as the indispensable requirement. Since the conceptualisation of *vīdu* is in terms of visualizing the perfectibility of man achievable even in this life, the continuity between leading a life of *aram* (good life) and achieving *vīdu* (realizing the Good in Life) is quite apparent and is indeed seen to run parallel to the Buddhistic analysis.

In *Tirukkuraḷ* we find the idea of continuity worked out in great detail by elaborately treating the various values to be pursued in human life. These are referred to as *aram, poruḷ, inbam*, and *vīdu*.[51] While *vīdu* could be referred to as the ultimate value, the other three could be referred to as instrumental values. Among the instrumental values a distinction is drawn between *aram* on the one hand, and the other two values constituting the group. This is to the effect that *aram* is an ethical-regulative value and the other two, *poruḷ* and *inbam* are the secular values. Suffice it to note here that the unique features of *Tirukkuraḷ* is that it lays its emphasis on the idea that the ultimate value, *vīdu*, requires the instrumentality of the other three values, and as the end to be actualized, they be realized as well.[52] *Aram* as the

---

50 XVIII.243.

51 *Aram* stands for the ethical value, *poruḷ* refers to the economic value, *inbam* represents the psychological value of desire and *vīdu* is the ultimate spiritual ideal to be aspired for. The idealistic scheme of values here is to the effect that if the secular values of *poruḷ* and *inbam* are regulated properly by observing the ethical principle of *aram*, the spiritual ideal of life vīdu can be realized even while living.

52 The means-end continuum suggested here is that ultimate end, to be realized requires that the ethical means of satisfying the demands of secular living ought not to be disregarded or underplayed. The end to be realized, *vīdu* as well as the means to be employed, living a life of *aram*, both ensure that the economic and the psychological aspects of secular life are realized as well.

ethical-regulative value is considered to have a pervasive influence on the pursuit of the secular as well as spiritual value.

Though this reflective of the general Indian philosophy of values, the author of the Tamil classic conceives this relationship in a unique way. While certainly he treats of the ethical and secular values which concern man in the immediate context of life in answer to the different aspects of his personality make-up, he does not speak of the ultimate ideal as entirely different from the non-ultimate ones. The structure of the text itself evidences this fact in two important respects: (i) no separate section is allotted for a consideration for the ultimate ideal[53] and (ii) even when the immediate ideals are spoken of, there is a clear suggestion that pursued in an ethical way, they themselves 'constitute' the realization of the ultimate ideal.[54] The pervasive significance of *aram* is conceived to consist in making the realization of *vīdu* possible by ethically regulating the pursuit of the secular values.

It seems to me that understanding *aram* in such terms would be helpful in appreciating the fact that Vaḷḷuvar (another name for Tiruvaḷḷuvar) is not thinking merely in terms of the importance of the ethical life (which certainly is a necessary ingredient in his philosophy of good life), but goes beyond it and conceives of the good life neither merely humanistically nor as a state which can be realized only in the hereafter. The Good is thus not just an ethical principle which regulates inter-personal relationships nor is it a 'given virtue' — 'given' by an external authority totally different from, and outside of man, but a principle which helps transcending the idealized social level even. The transcendence (which is as difficult to achieve as it is to visualize) may be referred to both as *vīdu* and as actualizing the potentiality that man in inherently capable of. In this sense, realizing *vīdu* may be visualized as 'becoming truly human.'

It is important in this context to highlight an idea which has not been mentioned yet in regard to the Tamil classic. This refers to the

53 Tiruvaḷḷuvar deliberately designed his work in such a way that he developed the theme of good life without even allotting a separate section for *vīdu*. The message is that *vīdu* gets realized by living a life dedicated to the pursuit of secular life with the regulating rod of *aram*. Hence he treated the theme of good life by discussed elaborately in the three different sections of his work with the Sectional title, *Arattuppal* (Section on Ethics), *Porutpāl* (Section on the Economic value) and *Kāmattuppāl* (Section on Kāmam or Inbam or desire).

54 The message reiterated here is that this world itself is the preparing ground for spiritual realization. The secular and the spiritual realms of human existence need not and should not be considered antithetical to one another.

context of the discussion of *aram* as well as *vīdu*. The concern of the Tamil classic, like that of the generality of the Indian philosophical classics (of which *Dhammapada* is an example) is with analyzing how the human predicament of being tossed about from birth to death and again from birth to death and again from death to birth could be ultimately understood and tackled. The idea that man himself is responsible for his plight is wholly accepted,[55] and by the same count, the idea that freeing himself from the round of births is also 'his own responsibility.' Good acts leading to good consequences and bad deeds bringing in bad experiences as their after-effects[56], was seen to suggest that transcending the cycle of birth and death could not be achieved by merely adding to one's merits rather than indulging in evil deeds, but by bringing in an attitudinal change even towards doing good. The binding effect of action (*karma*) was considered to be due to the ego-play due to a sense of agency felt innately. Hence, getting out of the cycle of birth and death would be possible only by leading a good life not in the usually accepted sense of doing good to others with a sense of agency (however mild it might be) but in the more difficult and deep sense of doing good for its own sake.[57] Thus, like the Buddha, Tiruvaḷḷuvar is seen to accept the inexorable law of *karma*, both in the sense of 'casual law' and in the sense of facing the consequences of the two-fold deeds accruing to the agent (the doer of the deeds).

What the author of the *Kuraḷ* seems to suggest then is that if one lives a life of *aram* in its comprehensive sense and exemplifies this sense of *aram* in the form of compassion and concern for fellowmen and fellowcreatures, and achieves complete conquest over the sense of 'I' and 'mine' the deeds of such a person mean the Good and that he is no longer under the control of *karma*, i.e. he is also one who has realized *vīdu*.[58]

The upshot of the whole argument regarding the difficult idea of transcending the cycle of birth and death in order to realize the ultimate Good can be expressed in terms of two propositions: one, the need for mental purity[59], the idea which was just explained in

55 *Tirukkuraḷ*, 38.1 and 60.8.

56 Ibid., 4.1, 2, 7, 8; 14.5, 7; 32.10.

57 Ibid., 36.1.

58 Ibid., 35.6, 8 and 10.

59 The importance accorded to mental purity can be gauged from the author devoting three chapters (28, 30 and 31) to this theme. In addition in several other couplets, too numerous to indicate here, he reiterates the point.

terms of the importance of bringing in attitudinal changes to such an extent that the tendency to project one's ego is completely eliminated; and two, the idea which needs some explication here, *viz.* that the individual is personally responsible for his spiritual evolution.

The idea is made clear by Tiruvaḷḷuvar by offering us the concept of *ūl* which is sometimes mistaken as *fate*. The exact scope of this complex concept and its place in the sceme of good life is difficult to determine and has been a subject of considerable debate. But what can be said categorically is that the deterministic element (in the sense of an action leading to its consequences) is fully accepted by him.[60] Even at the risk of his being misunderstood here he categorically states that one can never escape from his *karma*. If the idea of personal responsibility which is sought to be driven home here (while insisting that one has to accept responsibility for happenings in his life) is not understood properly, it might wrongly be construed as accepting the iron hands of *fate*. No wonder, therefore, the concept of *ūl* used by Tiruvaḷḷuvar has been misinterpreted as fate. The term *fate* gives us the meaning that the individual is utterly helpless before it, that he is himself not responsible for his own experiences.[61] But since the term is used to drive home the deterministic nature of *karma* and since *ūl* and *karma* have not been used as

60 The whole of chapter 38 is devoted to this difficult task of explaining the cause-effect relationship between human actions and their consequences.

61 The following couplets deserve to be cited in full to reinforce the idea that the *Kuṟaḷ's* author was a great believer in the initiative of the individual in doing good. These may be contemplated in answer to a possible misgiving (that the author subscribes to fatalism) that may arise if chapter 38 is not properly understood:
"The strong-hearted will not faint, even in case they fail just as the elephant stands majestically even wounded by deadly arrows." (60-7)
"Exuberance of spirit alone is strength; those who are devoid of it are only trees having the form of men." (60.10)
"Let die laziness, the death of effort if you wish the esteem of your household". (61.2)
"Shirk not from any work saying 'it is impossible for me', for, strenuous effort yields prevailing power." (62.1)
"Do not give up your task in the middle; for the world will abandon those who leave their task unfinished. (61.2)
"Before a man who is like a bullock pushing its way through uneven tracks, obstacles meet with obstruction." (63.4)
"If those who plan (an undertaking) possess steadfastness of will, they will achieve what they want to achieve." (67.6)
"Deliberation ends with the resolution (to act) but delay in executing it is wrong." (68.1)
Cf. also 61.5; 63.3; 63.5; 66.1 and 67.1.

synonyms, the responsibility-idea espoused gets strengthened and more pronounced.

VII

Before concluding this brief review of the philosophical implications of the idea of good life discernible in the *Dhammapada* and *Tirukkural* we would like to reiterate that the concern of this paper has been with the basic argument found into he two classics and as such an exhaustive treatment of the parallel ideas was not attempted. More importantly, the points of divergence between the two works were not mentioned at all up to this point. I will conclude by emphasizing the differences between their two works.

I shall refer to some Buddhist scholars who have claimed that the religion of the Buddha is unique in many respects. These features themselves may be helpful both in highlighting the dissimilarities between early Buddhism as reflected in the *Dhammapada* and the philosophy of *Tirukkural*. I shall refer to four of the features delineated by J.H. Bateson[62] and one referred to by M.E. Spiro.[63]

The first of the unique features listed by Bateson is **materialism**. This refers to the doctrine of non-soul. Man is an aggregate of five material factors which disintegrate at death, leaving no residue.[64] Edward Conze offers us an analysis of the implications of this doctrine for the transformation of the life of the Buddhist. Only the last part of his analysis needs to be referred to here to prevent any misunderstanding of the serious Buddhist philosophical teaching: "Those who look to Buddhism for startlingly new and unheard of ideas on the problem of self, will find little. Those who look to it on how to lead a selfless life may learn a great deal. The great contribution of Buddhist philosophy lies in the methods it worked out to impress the truth of not-self on our reluctant minds, it lies in the discipline which the Buddhists imposed upon themselves in order to make this truth into a part of their own being."[65] It is obvious that, thought the term 'materialism' is used here, it does not have the same connotation as

62 J.H. Bateson "Creed" (Buddhist), in *Encyclopaedia of Religion and Ethics*, Vol. IV, pp. 234-237.
63 M.E. Spiro, *Buddhism and Society*.
64 Dh P. XI. 147, 148; XX 279.
65 *Buddhism, Its Essence and Development* (New York: Harper & Row, 1959), pp. 10-21.

it has for instance in the Cārvāka materialist thought of India.[66] The *Kuraḷ* does to at all enter into a discussion regarding the soul, and offers a clear contrast to Buddhism in this respect. The existence of a soul, however is clearly presupposed in the Tamil classic.[67]

The second feature of normative Buddhism, according to Bateson is **atheism**. Buddhism does not believe in the existence of God as the Creator of the universe.[68] In *Tirukkuraḷ*, however, God as Creator is assumed and, in fact clearly referred to in some couplets.[69] The *Kuraḷ* also avoids (though in this respect it resembles Buddhism) detailed discussions regarding the origin and creation of the universe, but this does not seem to be because of preoccupation with 'deliverance'.

Bateson mentions **nihilism** as the third feature of normative Buddhism. Everything in the universe, including the universe itself is impermanent.[70] There can be no Supreme Reality since anything that is 'real', anything that exists, is in a perpetual flux, in a constant state of creation and dissolution, of coming into and passing out of existence. In the *Kuraḷ* we do not find any trace of nihilism. Just as the nihilistic doctrine in Buddhism is attributed to its not accepting a (permanent) soul, we maintain that the acceptance of an enduring soul, but the *Kuraḷ* was responsible for its not contributing to the nihilistic position.

Pessimism is referred to as the fourth characteristic of normative Buddhism. This aspect of Buddhism points out that even the happiest man is not free from painful experiences. Suffering is ingrained in the very texture of life.[71] In the *Kuraḷ* we do not find a description of the world of human life in comparable language.

---

66 *Cārvāka*, the only materialist system of thought in India was hedonistically oriented and offered indeed a contrast with the serious view of life that Buddhism presented.

67 Couplets 2.1 and 36.4 are particularly significant here.

68 Conze (op. cit., p. 39) maintains that the Buddhistic tradition does not exactly deny the existence of the Creator but that it is not interested to know who created the universe.

69 See 1.1; and 107.2.

70 *Dhp.*, XI. 146.

71 Ibid., III. 41; IV.85; V.72; XI.146; XIII.174; XVIII.234-238; XX.278, 286-289 and XXV.369 Conze (op. cit., p. 21) concedes that according to Buddhism this world is wholly evil, is wholly 'saturated' with suffering, is something to be rejected totally, abandoned totally, for the one goal of *nirvāṇa* though he disagrees with the usage of the term *pessimism* on the count that if the world is a vale of tears, there is a joy in shedding its burden."

Certainly the *Kuraḷ* exhorts man to do good deeds and avoid evil ones. The exhortation to do the good is on the count that alone begits man and the discouragement to do evil is on the ground that the evil man has to suffer that consequences himself. The *Kuraḷ*'s view that the ultimate value of vīdu (release) is automatically realized when the individual leads a life of virtue and pursues *poruḷ* and *inbam* in an ethical way would go to show that there is no suggestion at all that this world is evil. The *Kuraḷ*'s view seems to be that man's uniqueness and duty consists in leading a virtuous life and giving no room for evil.[72]

Spiro adds **renunciation** as the fifth characteristic of Buddhism. It consists in rejecting the world since worldly life is major obstacle to the attainment of the goal of salvation. Viewing attachment to the world as the cause of suffering, Buddhism emphatically maintains that suffering can only be got over through detachment from and renunciation of the world.[73] We should not, however overlook the fact that the Buddha, while referring to renunciation, was insisting on cultivating the inner springs of it rather than merely conforming to its outward forms, and this is evident from the *Dhammapada*[74] But the institution of the *Saṇgha* and the insistence that one should take refuge in it just as one should take refuge in the Buddha and in the Dhamma show that actual (in the sense of physically renouncing everything) renunciation formed the core of the Buddha's philosophy of renunciation.[75]

In the *Kuraḷ* we see an entirely different approach to renunciation. May be, the implicit critique of renunciation as an institution that the *Kuraḷ* contains was itself born out of the observa-

72 This would also explain the general thrust of the *Kuraḷ's* philosophy, viz., its insistence on man's doing virtuous deeds in this world. In a significant couplet Vaḷḷuvar says: "If men acquire ample glory in this world by doing virtuous deeds, the world of the gods will cease to laud the sage who has attained that world. (24.4).

73 *Dhp.*, V.75; XIV.81 XVI. 211-214 provide the basis for this interpretation.

74 I.9; X.141 and 142, XIV.184 and XXII.312.

75 Explaining this aspect of the Buddhist philosophy, Conze (op. cit., p. 53) writes: "The core of the Buddhist movement consisted of monks. A monastic life alone will normally provide the conditions favourable to a spiritual life bent on the highest goal...The monks...are the only Buddhists in the proper sense of the word...The life of a householder is almost incompatible with the higher levels of the spiritual at all times. This has been a conviction common to all Buddhists at all times. They differed only in the strictness with which they adhered to it. The Hīnayāna was, on the whole, disinclined to grant any exceptions."

tion for the spirit behind the institution being lost sight of. One of the most outstanding characteristics of the treatment of the subject of renunciation in the Tamil classic is its not considering renunciation as a definite 'stage' (in the sense of the individual giving up his status as a householder). Renunciatory spirit,[76] as against renunciation as a formal 'stage', (involving the abandonment of home) makes for a totally different kind of philosophy of renunciation.

In spite of this difference in the treatment of renunciation in the *Dhammapada* and *Tirukkuraḷ*, it is amazing to find more or less identical couplets in both: *Dhammapada's* couplet: "Not by a shaven head does an undisciplined man, who utters lies, become an ascetic. How will one be an ascetic who is full of desire and greed?"[77] is more or less identical with the Kuṟaḷ couplet which reads: "There is no need of a shaven head nor of long hairs if a person abstains from the deeds condemned by the wise."[78]

Similarly the *Dhammapada* couplet: "What is the use of your matted hair, o witless man! What is the use of your antelope garment? Within, you are full (of passions), without, you embellish,"[79] reads like a couplet of *Tirukkuraḷ*: "There are many men who bathe in holy waters but leading defiled lives; they are of masked conduct and 'appear' great."[80]

Likewise, there is a close similarity between *Dhammapada* and *Tirukkuraḷ*[81] in regard to their views on desire. In this case more or less the whole chapter of the one shows a parallel to almost a full chapter in the other. The keynote of the *Dhammapada* is that desire is the springboard for all suffering. Grief and fear, the symptoms of suffering, can be got over only by cutting at the root of desire. The parallel chapter in the *Kuṟaḷ* entitled 'The Extirpation of Desire'[82] points out that desire is responsible for the round of births and deaths. The most significant point about the chapters in the two classics referred to just now is that it provides additional strength to the thesis of parallel perspectives espoused in the present paper.

The philosophical implications of the concept of good life found in the Pāli and the Tamil classics briefly reviewed are now easy

76 3.1; 28.6 and 7; 35.6-10.

77 Dhp., XIX.264.

78 *Tirukkuraḷ*, 28.10.

79 Dhp., XXVI.394.

80 Tirukkuraḷ, 28.8.

81 Chapter XVI of *Dhammapada* and Chapter 37 of *Tirukkuraḷ* are remarkably similar to each other.

82 The very little of the parallel chapter in *Tirukkuraḷ* (chapter 37) indicates the importance accorded by Tiruvaḷḷuvar to the theme of hankering after those which do not conduce to good life.

to recapitulate. Within the limited confines of this study, we have seen that when the two classics address themselves to the problem of human existence without the tone of dogmatism seeping in, the basic philosophy of man formulated in them holds out a meaningful analysis and reflection on the human situation. The firm conviction with which the ideas are expressed, coupled with the exhortation that mere learning without its having an effect on life is of no use (found in both the works) enhance their value as documents of human thought which are worth preserving and referring to by man everywhere. Philosophy and religion as instruments of transformation of human life, as the two classics have interpreted them, indeed offer great promise in the area of cross-cultural philosophising.

4

Abhidharma as Paradigm for Practice

Christopher Key Chapple

Introduction

The *Abhidharma* (Pāli *Abhidhamma*) provides a general world view for the practitioner of Buddhist meditation. Its enumeration of various factors of existence (*dharmas*) may be seen as an elaboration on the *skandha* schematic contained in the *Sūtra* literature, serving as a detailed road map of human faculties, behavior, and potential. The ultimate intent of this modeling of reality is to provide a means for transcending all conditioned existence. In the final analysis, the view of self becomes a realization of no-self which, for the Buddhist, is the culmination of the religious quest. A paradigm shift is required of the practitioner, not only as a movement within history, but more fundamentally as a radical transformation of self-identity.

In the nineteenth century, Henry Clark Warren, the prominent Pali scholar, commented that "The works comprising the third and last Piṭaka are, of all the Buddhist scriptures, the dreariest and most forbidding reading.... However, like the desert of Sahara, they are to be respected for their immensity; and when they are all printed, no doubt something can be made of them."[1] Since the time of Warren, some translations of texts have been made, though the tradition certainly merits closer and more detailed attention on the part of contemporary scholars.[2] The *Abhidharma* tradition, despite the disdain of some early scholars is of particular importance for understand-

1. Henry Clark Warren, *Buddhism in Translations* (Cambridge:Harvard University Press, 1922), p. xviii.
2. Translations of *Abhidharma* materials are found in the Pali Text Society translations series. Louis de la Valle Poussin's remarkable French translation of Vasubandhu's *Abhidharmakośa* summarizes and critiques earlier *Abhidharma* traditions; it has been summarized in Stcherbatsky's *The Central Conception of Buddhism and the Meaning of the Word "Dharma"* and in Chauduri's *Analytical*

ing the philosophical and psychological foundations of Buddhism. It includes what Christians would call the "anthropology of the human person," categorizing all facets of experience. Its purpose, as we will see, is to provide a framework for understanding the human condition in a manner consonant with the fundamental teachings of the Buddha. Of particular interest to this study is the *Abhidharma* elaboration on the *skandha* schematic in *Abhidharma* and its relationship to the concept of impermanence, specifically of the notions of self.

Historically, the *Abhidharma* texts are of critical importance to the Theravāda tradition and are foundational to the development of later Mahāyāna schools. They represent the heights of speculative thought in early Buddhism, staying closer to the actual philosophy of Buddha than the later Mahāyāna and Tantric innovations. Nonetheless, although largely anonymous, they represent the original thinking of early Buddhist philosophers. Furthermore, the *Abhidharma* teachings continue to exert a profound influence on Buddhist training in Southeast Asian traditions, as indicated by the ready familiarity with *Abhidharma* categories exhibited by modern-day members of monastic orders.

The key word in understanding *Abhidharma* is the word *dharma*, derived from the Sanskrit root *dhṛ*, which means hold, support, or sustain. In general usage it refers to duty, law, or religious teaching. For the *Abhidharmins*, it is a technical term which Ruegg renders as "factor of existence.[3] Conze translates *dharma* as "factual event;"[4] Stcherbatsky, "element;" Kalupahana generally leaves the term untranslated, though, following the Geigers' German translation "*die emphirischen Dinge*," he sometimes substitutes the English word "thing."[5]

After the death of Buddha, various sects enumerated different lists of *dharmas*. The earliest, found in the Pāli canon, counts 82

Study of the Abhidharmakośa. The French version has been translated into English by Leo Pruden (Berkeley, California: Asian Humanities Press, 1989). A Sanskrit manuscript of the text was discovered in the 1950s and has been edited by Prahlad Pradhan. A draft English translation from the Tibetan by Artemus Engle is available on microfiche through the Institute for Advanced Studies of World Religions in Carmel, New York.

3. Class lecture notes, Stony Brook, 1975.
4. Edward Conze, *Buddhist Thought in India* (Ann Arbor: The University of Michigan Press, 1973), p.5.
5. David J. Kalupahana, *Causality: The Central Philosophy of Buddhism* (Honolulu: The University Press of Hawaii, 1975), p. 69.

dharmas. Around 250 B.C. a schism in the *Sthavira* school at the Council of Pāṭalīputra gave rise to the Sarvāstivāda or Vaibhāsika school, which posited 75 *dharmas*. Vasubandhu recorded the Sarvāstivāda position in the *Abhidharmakośa* almost five centuries later. The Yogācāra *Abhidharma*, developed sometime after 200 A.D., lists 100 *dharmas*. Each of these lists of *dharmas* can be subsumed within the general *skandha* schematic that the Buddha taught to account for the intricacy of human life; when the *dharmas* are studied in this light, their function as tools for liberation becomes clear. Before we enter into *Abhidharma* elaboration of *dharmas* it will be beneficial to review the function of the five *skandhas* in explaining the no-self theory and the enlightenment experience.

The Five *Skandhas*

The Buddha delineated five *skandhas* (*groups* or aggregates) which account for all the various permutations of human experience. The five can be translated as form or body (*rūpa*), feeling (*vedanā*), perception (*saṃjñā*), conditioning (*saṃskara*), and consciousness (*vijñāna*). The requisite activity of the practicing Buddhist is to clearly comprehend the pervasiveness of the *skandhas* and then directly experience (not merely think) that one's authentic "identity" is other than these five. "It is by the destruction of these, the not lusting for these, it is by the cessation of, the giving up, the utter surrender of these things that the heart is called 'fully freed'."[6] Before the *skandhas* can be "given up" or somehow transcended, however, they must be fully understood; this is the task undertaken by the *Abhidharmists* which, as we will see, is no easy affair. The Buddha proclaimed that "by thoroughly knowing, by understanding, by being detached from, by renouncing (the five *skandhas*) one is fit for the destruction of suffering."[7]

In order to cultivate detachment, the Buddha exhorts his students not to lay claim to the changes inherent in the five *skandhas*. Quoting Woodward's translation, the process of non-identification is illustrated as follows:

> '... if, brethren, a man should gather, burn, or do what he please with all the grass, all the sticks, branches and stalks

6. F.L. Woodward, translator, *The Book of the Kindred Sayings (Saṃyutta-Nikāya) or Grouped Suttas, Part III: The Khandha Book* (London: published for the Pali Text Society by Luzac & Company, 1925), p.14.
7. *Ibid.*, p. 26.

> in this Jeta Grove, — pray, would ye say "this man is gathering, burning *us*, doing what he please with *us*?"'
> 'Surely not, lord.'
> 'Why so?'
> 'Because, lord, this is not our self, nor of the nature of self.'
> 'Even so, brethren, body (*rūpa*) is not of you. Put it away. Putting it away will be for your profit and welfare. Feeling is not of you perception, the activities (*saṃskāra*) are not of you, nor consciousness. Put it away. Putting it away will be for your profit and welfare.[8]

The Buddha further describes this process to Suradha, who subsequently becomes an arhat:

> Whatsoever material object, Suradha, be it past, future or present... far or near, one regards thus: "This is not mine; this am not I; this is not the Self of me" — so seeing things as they really are, by right insight, one is liberated, without grasping.[9]

Here, as in the *Sāṃkhya Kārikā*, we find that identification is the crux of the Buddhist experience. If one is attached to the activities of form or feeling or consciousness, etc., one is governed by the law of *saṃsāra*, bound to further action, and hence committed to and sedimented in a fixed identity. When one realizes the non-lasting nature of both object and self, freedom is attained. If self is "invested" in any particularity, one is bound. By renunciation of identity, one becomes free and the compulsive desire for continued existence ceases.

Given this basic orientation, it can be seen that two modes of "selfness" are evinced by the Buddha. One, an inauthentic self, is characterized by identity with suffering and change: this would be the young prince Siddhārtha Gautama before he undertakes the ascetic quest. The other, authentic self has been purified, made free, enlightened: this is the state of Buddhahood later described as the uncovering of the *tathāgatagarbha*, the womb of suchness or emptiness. Various devices are used by the Buddha to lead his pupils to an understanding of the authentic, empty nature of self and things. Most of these proceed from a form of negative analysis, a seeing clearly of what one *is not*. This didactic technique is immensely practical, for nowhere does the Buddha allow for a positive statement which might

8. *Ibid.*, pp. 31-32.
9. *Ibid.*, pp. 67-68.

engender attachment. However, later Buddhists, perhaps as a reaction against being left speechless in regard to what one authentically is, went to great lengths to explicate what one *is not*. This concern for cataloging the inauthentic gave rise to the *Abhidharma* teachings.

Pāli and Sanskrit Categories of *Dharmas*

Both the early Pāli *Abhidhamma* and the later pre-Mahāyāna *Abhidharma* group their listings of *dharmas* in a similar fashion, distinguishing between mental states, physicality, and transcendence. The two systems are more similar than dissimilar; their major difference is over the issue of the reality of momentariness, and is not the topic of this paper. Both systems will be described briefly, with special emphasis on the *dharmas* of mind. We will then turn to a discussion of the implication of the system for meditation.

In both the *Tripiṭaka Abhidhamma* texts and in the later *Abhidharmakoṣa*, the *dharmas* or factors of existence can be interpreted in a number of ways, depending upon how they are grouped. In one reading of the traditions, all *dharmas* can be seen in terms of being either conditioned (*saṃskṛta*) *dharmas*, which promote and perpetuate attachment to *saṃsāra* or they can be unconditioned (*asaṃskrta*) *dharmas*, which for the Sarvāstivādins include space, non-arising due to meditation, and non-arising due to natural extinction. *Dharmas* can be in full, *saṃsāric* operation, influenced by the passions (*sāśrava*) or they can be uninfluenced by the passions (*anāśrava*) through the practice of meditation. They also can be read according to the Four Noble truths; pain (*duḥkha*) and the cause of pain are associated with the *dharmas* that are influenced by the passions (*saṃskṛta* and *sāśrava*): release from pain (*nirodha*) and the path to release (*mārga*) are found in the unconditioned *dharmas* and in the conditioned *dharmas* when uninfluenced by the passions.[10]

In regard to its descriptions of physical processes, the *Abhidharma* systems list twelve "abodes" (*āyatana*) that account for the various modes of perception. These twelve are the six senses (*indriya*) of sight, hearing, smelling, taste, touch, and mind (*manas*), and their respective objects (*viṣaya*). The six faculties count as one *dharma* each, as do the objects of the first five senses. The mind, however, has numerous *dharmas* as its object, which reflects the great importance

---

10. Th. Stcherbatsky, *The Central Conception of Buddhism and the Meaning of the Word "Dharma"* (London: Royal Asiatic Society of Great Britain, 1923), p. 96.

give by Buddhism to the processes of the mind. The Pāli version differs slightly from the later account given in the *Abhidharmakośa*, as we will see.

In both forms, the *Abhidharma* lists in outline the basic thrust of the Buddhist path: that the human condition is fraught with suffering; this suffering can be overcome; mental processes hold the key to this achievement. An understanding of mental processes is essential for effective meditation. It explicitly prescinds from the Buddha's teachings in regard to the *skandha* schematic and comes closest to explaining the Buddhist conception of self. In the next section, both the Pāli and Sanskrit delineations of mental factors will be explicated.

The *Cetasika* or *Citta Dharmas*

Within the Theravāda *Abhidhamma*, as summarized in the Anuruddhācariya,[11] the mental states (*cetasika*) are divided into seven universals (*sabbacittasādhāraṇa*), six particulars (*pakiṇṇaka*), fourteen immorals (*akusala*), nineteen "beautifuls" (*sobhanasādhāraṇa*), three abstinences (*viratiyo*), two illimitables (*appamañña*), and one wisdom (*paññindriya*). This grouping begins with two categories that are essentially neutral and potentially present in any experience. It then turns to a listing of negative mental modes, followed by a listing of positive mind states. The last three groupings represent the transcendence of both of these, and are associated with aspects of Buddhist practice. Consequently, this organizational scheme not only lists *dharmas* but also sequences them in light of stages on the Buddhist path.

The universal mental states are said to be present in every instant of consciousness. The first four directly correspond to aspects of both the *skandhas* and the Buddha's listing of the twelve *nidāna*, links in the chain of dependent origination (*pratītya samutpāda*): contact (*phasso*), feeling (*vedanā*), perception (*saññā*), and volition (*cetanā*). The next three are one-pointedness, psychic life, and attention, which constitute aspects of one's ability to focus. This give the "hard-wiring" for mental experience. The next six speak of more specific aspects of mind, though each could be applied either negatively or positively: discursive thought (*vitakko*), reflection (*vicāro*), decisiveness (*adhimokkho*), strong effort (*viriyaṃ*), joy (*pīti*), and desire or inclination (*chando*).

---

11. This information is contained in Narada Thera, tr., *Anuruddhācariya: A Manual of Abhidharma* (Colombo: Vajirārāma Publications, 1957), chapter II, pp. 76-117.

The categories of immorality, many of which are replicated in the *Abhidharmakośa* and will be discussed in greater detail below, include delusion (*moha*), shamelessness (*ahirika*), lack of respect for opinions of others (*anottappa*), restlessness, attachment, misbelief, conceit, hatred, jealousy, avariciousness, worry, sloth, torpor, doubt. Each of these is considered an obstacle.

At the reverse of these, several positive mental aspects are listed: confidence, mindfulness, shame, moral dread, non-attachment, good-will, equanimity, and tranquillity, lightness, flexibility, adaptability proficiency, and rectitude of both body (*kāya*) and mind (*citta*). Each of these first four categories of mind generally are associated with entrenchment within the cycle of life and death prompted by desire. It is only the last three categories, which comprise a total of six *dharmas* that are conducive to liberation: the abstinences, which involve right speech, action, and livelihood as specified in the Eight-fold Path, friendliness (*mettā*), compassion (*karuṇā*), sympathetic joy (*muditā*), equanimity (*upekkhā*), and wisdom (*paññindriya*).

Within the *Abhidharmakośa*,[12] Vasubandhu delineates 46 mental (*citta*) *dharmas* and 14 "linking state" *dharmas*. This latter group includes the exposition of philosophical positions peculiar to the Sarvāstivādin school and are not in the scope of the present discussion. Similar to the system discussed above, the *citta dharmas* are divided into ten general mental faculties (*cittamahābhūmika*); ten universally good (*kusala*) *dharmas*; six impure (*klesa*) *dharmas*; two universally bad (*akusala*) *dharmas*, ten vicious elements (*upakleśa bhūmika*) and eight miscellaneous (*aniyata*) *dharmas*. An understanding of these 46 *citta dharmas* is, at least for *Abhidharmakośa* tradition, important for the proper practice of meditation: without knowing one's transient nature, the tools of transcendence would be of no avail. These 46 *dharmas* will be explicated in the following sections, primarily for those not already familiar with the admittedly tedious *Abhidharma* schematic. Again, it is important to bear in mind that this grouping of *dharmas* deals with what must be transcended; the independent reality of each of these pieces has already been disclaimed. (See the Appendix for a detailed schema.)

12. This material is summarized from Th. Stcherbatsky, *The Central Conception of Buddhism and the Meaning of the Word "Dharma"* (London: Royal Asiatic Society of Great Britain, 1923), pp. 101-107.

The Neutral Mind: Ten Bases of Functioning

The first of the ten general mental faculties in feeling (*vedanā*), which also is designated as a separate *skandha*. It occurs in three forms: "pleasurable, unpleasurable, and neutral."[13] The second *citta dharma*, conception (*saṃjñā*), similarly occupies its own *skandha*. Through *saṃjñā*, specific ideas or notions are formed, "ce qui saisit les marques (male, female, etc.) de 1'objet."[14] Critical distinctions are made, particularities are ascertained through the power of conception. The question is raised in the *Abhidharmakośa* as to why these first two mental factors are assigned separate *skandhas*. This response follows:

> The *cettasikas* of sensation (*vedanā*) and conception (*saṃjñā*) were classed into different *skandhas* because they are the root of disputation, the cause of *saṃsāra* ... inclination for sensations (*vedanā*) and distorted views (*saṃjnā*) are what produce the continuance of existence.[15]

It is through these two that the world presents itself to us and, from the Buddhist perspective, involves us in the wheel of life:

> In the beginningless *saṃsāra* men and women delight in each other's form because they are attached to experiencing sensation (*vedanā*). That attachment leads to distorted conceptions (*saṃjñā*) and those distortions are in turn produced by the afflictions. Since the unconscious too is caused to become afflicted by it, [the order of the *skandhas* is according to the manner in which the mental afflictions arise.[16]

This passage emphasizes the psychological dimension to the continuance of suffering; attachment causes all other *dharmas* to become operative.

Volition (*cetanā*) is the next and the first of the 44 *dharmas* contained in the *saṃskāra skandha*. The *Abhidharmakośa* states that *cetana* "*karma* of the mind, generates the *karma* of body and speech."[17] The fourth general mental faculty is contact (*sparśa*). For experience to take place, contact must be made through the convergence of object (*viṣaya*), sense (*indriya*), and consciousness (*vijñāna*).

---

13. Vasubandhu, *Abhidharmakoṣabhāṣya,* translated by Aretemus B. Engle, manuscript volume I, p.29. Quoted with permission of the translator.
14. Vasubandhu, *Abhidharmakośa,* translated by Louis de la Vallee Poussin (Paris: Paul Geuthner, 1925) I, p. 125.
15. Engle, I, pp. 41-42.
16. *Ibid.*, I, p.44.
17. *Ibid.*, IV, pp. 2-3.

This *dharma* serves and all-important linking function, through which the world may be apprehended.

The fifth *dharma*, desire (*chanda*), divided into three hierarchical categories, reinforcing the ethical intentionality of the *Abhidharma* system. The first is an "immoral" sensual craving (*kāmacchanda*), an obvious impediment to spiritual development. The second is a-moral, the "mere wish to do" (*kattukamyatāchanda*). The third constitutes the highest form of desire, the resolve to religious pursuit (*dharmachanda*).[18]

Insight (*prajñā*) is the sixth *dharma* and is the key to Buddhist enlightenment. Through the application of *prajñā*, one is able to overcome ignorance. This capacity is latent in each person and requires practice to be made fully operational The seventh and eighth general mental functions are memory (*smṛti*) and attention (*manasikāra*). The ninth, inclination (*adhimokṣa*), decides upon an object of attention. Once the mind is fully absorbed, the tenth stage, concentration (*samādhi*) arises. The Pāli rendering of this term (*ekaggatā*) is described by Narada Thera as:

> One pointedness, or concentration on one object, or focussing the mind on one object. It is like a steady flame in a windless place. It is like a firmly fixed pillar that cannot be shaken by the mind ... it is the germ of all attentive, focussed, or concentrated consciousness.[19]

The cultivation of concentration, the last of the *citta mahābhūmikas*, plays a vital role in the practice of meditation.

The ten factors which have been discussed above represent the forces which, in the most general sense, string together the operations of the mind, beginning with feeling and ending with powerful concentration. In keeping with the Buddhist philosophy of no-self, each of these processes represents a functioning mode or instrumentality. No notion of agency is allowed which might be construed as an abiding presence around which reality is oriented.

Ten Aspects of Goodness

The second classification of *citta dharmas* includes ten "universally 'good' moral forces, present in every favorable moment of consciousness" (*kusala mahābhūmika*). The first is *śraddhā*, generally translated

---

18. Narada Thera, translator, *Anurudhācariya: A Manual of Abhidharma*, p. 82.
19. *Ibid.*, p. 86.

as faith but described more specifically as clarity of mind (*cittasya prasādaḥ*).[20] The second is *vīrya*, cognate with English virile, meaning strength and courage in action. This *dharma* overcomes idleness, serving to support, uphold, and sustain.[21] The third, *upekṣā*, is equanimity, a state comparable to that of a calm lake.

The next two moral goods are self-respect (*hrī*) and proper bearing due to concern about the judgements of others (*apatrapā*). C.A.F. Rhys Davids describes the difference between the two as follows:

> *Hri* has its source from within; *apatrapa* springs from without. *Hri* is autonomous; *apatrapa* is heteronomous, influenced by society. The former is established on shame, the latter on dread.[22]

The next three "goodnesses" are not positive qualities in the usual sense, being in negative terms: absence of love or cupidity (*alobha*), absence of hatred (*adveṣa*), and non-violence (*ahiṃsā*). The last two universally good forces are mental dexterity (*praśrabdhi*) and acquiring and preserving good qualities (*apramāda*). The latter emphasizes the need for continual reinforcement of positive qualities.

The cultivation of each of these "goodnesses" serves to purify the practitioner and erode the influence of past *karma*. However, the presence of goodness might also breed attachment in the form of self-righteousness or pride, which would result in further suffering. Hence, these *dharmas* remain on the "constructed" side of the *Abhidharma* scheme. As we will see, the meditation practices listed in the *Abhidharmakośa* do not fall into any of the *dharma* categories.

Eighteen Evils

The next three groups, totalling 18 *dharmas*, are negative states of mind that impede happiness. The first six are referred to as "stages of impurity (*kleśa mahābhūmika*)."[23] The first, ignorance (*moha* or *avidyā*) is the most important and corresponds to the first precondition of dependent origination (*pratītya samutpāda*). Ignorance leads to suffering and causes *saṃsāra* to continue. The five other impure elements of this class are carelessness (*pramāda*), mental heaviness

20. Th. Stcherbatsky, *The Central Conception of Buddhism and the Meaning of the Word "Dharma"* (London: Royal Asiatic Society of Great Britain, 1923; reprinted in Delhi by Motilal Banarsidas, 1970), p. 101.
21. Narada Thera, p.91.
22. C.A.F. Rhys Davids, *Buddhist Psychology*, as quoted in Narada Thera, p. 94.
23. Stcherbatsky, p. 87.

(*kausīdya*), mental disturbances (*aśraddhā*, litterally "lack of faith"), sloth (*styāna*), and arrogance (*auddhatya*).

Vasubandhu next lists two universally bad elements, *ahrikya* and *anapatrapya*. These two are the antithesis of the previously mentioned goods, *hrī* and *apatrapā*. Hence, *ahrikya* would be an utter lack of self-respect, *anapatrapya* disregarded for others. In the last group of evil *citta dharmas*, we find "ten vicious elements of limited occurrence" which are listed as follows: anger (*krodha*), deceit (*mrakṣa*), envy (*mātsarya*), jealousy (*īrṣyā*), approving objectionable things (*pradāsa*), violence (*vihiṃsā*), breaking friendship (*upanāha*), deceit (*māyā*), trickery (*śātya*), and vanity (*mada*).[24]

It is clear that these 18 *dharmas* must be both overcome and transcended; the goodnesses need to be transcended but not necessarily overcome. Each evil overtly perpetuates suffering for both self and others and reinforces attachment to a negative personality type.

Eight Miscellaneous Mind States

The final grouping of *citta dharmas* begins with two factors which are humanly universal without any specific moral purport: mental change or repentance (*kaukṛtya*) and absent mindedness (*middha*). The next two, *vitarka* and *vicāra*, constitute the internal dialogue. *Vitarka* is the wandering of the mind which eventually takes hold of an object. *Vicāra* is the examination of that object. The *Abhidharmakośa* states "*Vitarka* is a coarseness of mind and *vicara* is subtlety of mind."[25] The control and balance of these two forces lead to concentration. The remaining miscellaneous states of mind are love (*rāga*), hate (*dveṣa*), pride (*māna*), and doubting (*vicikitsā*).

Each of these states may be used either for the purpose of enlightenment or deepened ignorance. For instance, hatred, purposefully directed, can be used to suppress an unwanted thought pattern on attitude; pride, properly understood, is important in the establishment of a meditative way of life. Similarly, doubting can prove useful, as seen in the story of the Buddha's great renunciation; without doubting the validity of kingdom, power, and comfort, Siddhartha Gautama would never have experienced *nirvāṇa* or taught the Eightfold Path.

In summary, the bulk of the Sarvāstivādin *Abhidharma* deals with the conditioned realm, that which binds a person to *saṃsāra*,

24. *Ibid.*, p. 102.
25. Engle, II, p. 72

seen primarily as a mental construction. The mind is attributed with sixty constituent *dharmas*; these *dharmas* constitute the psychological world of man, the world of attitudes, the world caused by ignorance. These sixty are divided into two groups, 46 concerned with specific mental states (*citta dharma*) and 14 serving as linking states, which we did not discuss. The group of 46 *citta dharmas*, as we have seen, is further broken up into ten general mind functions, ten good moral forces, six impure forces, two unfavorable elements, ten vicious elements, and eight miscellaneous mental conditions (see appendix).

Early Buddhist scholars attempted to classify the above list of *dharmas* as metaphysics or ontology or cosmology. However, in Buddhism, such categories are problematic: any ontology or cosmology is seen in terms of suffering. The first of the Four Noble Truths states that "all existence is suffering." Worldly reality has no redeeming character; it is painful and must be transcended. Thus, the *Abhidharma*, rather than positing real and lasting things, seeks to outline those things which must be made extinct. The *Abhidharma* is not a cosmology in the classical sense; rather, it is a psychological and religious construct which delineates the attitudes and conditions that bind a person to ignorance.

A problem often raised with *Abhidharma* is that it seems to defeat the very cause it espouses. The Buddha in his teachings continually simplified things; when asked to elaborate, he generally refused. In the "Questions Which Tend Not To Edification", Māluṅkyaputta and Vaccha come to the Buddha on different occasions to ask if the world is eternal, if the body and soul are identical, and if the saint exists after death. The Buddha rebuffs these questions and declares that they do not pertain to enlightenment; the only way to enlightenment is to uproot the five *skandhas*. The Buddha declares, "the *Tathāgata* is free from all theories."[26] By contrast, the *Abhidharma*, with all its categories and technical terms, seems to obscure the enlightenment process rather than elucidate it or bring it about.

This problem of seemingly endless classification schemes that seem more tedious than inspirational finds resolution if the *Abhidharma* is seen as prescriptive rather than descriptive. *Abhidharma*, at least for the early Buddhists, provided a viable explanation of the constitution of the human person and the causes of human suffering. The *Abhidharma* served as an auxiliary to meditation, providing the theoretical framework for practice.

26. Warren, p. 125.

Along with Sānkhya, the *Abhidharma* presents one of the most detailed constructs of the human psychological and emotional condition which has arisen out of the meditative traditions of Asia. One major criticism of the *Abhidharma* is its preoccupation with numerology and lists. Yet the intention of these lists is not merely to itemize facts about the mind, but rather to discern the very functions which underly human awareness. The telos of the system is not found in objectifying reality, but rather in interiorizing reality. Herbert Guenther points out that the purpose of the *Abhidharma* is "applicable within reality, not to reality as a whole."[27] The *Abhidharma* does not offer a permanent, fixed, or absolute point of view, but rather looks at those elements which do cause a person to absolutize existence and thereby miss the enlightenment experience. The *Abhidharma*, when viewed in light of the Buddha's basic teachings, offers a psychology of enlightenment, a road map to the end of suffering. The implications of this system lie beyond speculation, in the realm of practice.

Practice

The *Abhidharma* literature is not solely devoted to psychological and ethical enumerations. All texts of this tradition discuss practices for overcoming all the attachments that have been so carefully delineated. Buddhaghosa's *Visuddhimagga*, a Theravāda text that "systematically summarizes and interprets the teachings of the Buddha contained in the Pāli *Tipiṭaka*,"[28] discusses numerous practices prescribed by the Buddha, including the cultivation of virtue, concentration, and understanding, all of which are accomplished through a process of purification. In the sixth chapter of the *Abhidharmakośabhāṣya*, "The Exposition of the Noble Paths and Noble Souls," Vasubandhu outlines three principal practices that are also found in the Pāli tradition: meditation on the unattractive (*aśubhabhāvanā*), concentration on the inhalation and exhalation (*ānāpānasmṛti*), and the remembrance that all constructed phenomena are impermanent (*anitya*), fraught with suffering (*duḥkha*), impure (*aśuci*), and without self (*anātma*). The breath meditation is also known as *śamatha* and the last process is part of *vipaśyanā* meditation.

27. Herbert Guenther, *Philosophy and Psychology in the Abhidharma* (Lucknow: Buddha Vihara, 1957), p. 25.
28. Bhadantacariya Buddhaghosa, *The Path of Purification (Visuddhimagga)*, translated from the Pali by Bhikkhu Nyanamoli (Boulder, Colorado: Shambhala, 1976), p.ix.

The successful meditator is said to be one who has overcome discontent and great desires. This state of nonattachment (*alobha*) is accompanied by "turning one's back upon the desire for sensual pleasures (*kāmarāga*) and the desire for existence (*bhavarāga*)."[29] These are also referred to by Vasubandhu as an "antidote for the arising of craving (*tṛṣṇotpādavipakṣataḥ*)" and are said to "quell temporarily and permanently the desire for those things held to be 'mine' and 'me.'"[30] In our earlier discussion of the *skandhas* it was seen that enlightenment is contingent on the transcendence of personally possessive consciousness.

The meditations on the unattractive and on the breath are widespread in Buddhism and find direct parallels in Hindu and Jain yogic practice. The first involves a Skinnerian endeavor at behavior and thought modification, and is recommended for those who are overwhelmed with passion (*rāga*). The second is designed to placate the mind and pacify compulsive thought activity (*vitarka*).[31]

Within the dependent origination process (*pratītya samutpāda*), craving or thirst (*tṛṣṇā*) is said to be the cause of continued existence. In order to reverse this pathology of attraction, an opposite thought is cultivated which works at breaking down the blinding influence of the original desire. Referred to as *pratipakṣa* meditation in both Buddhism and Pantajali's *Yoga Sūtra* (II:33-34), it conditions a visceral response to counteract intentions which cause suffering. Perhaps the most graphic example of this practice is "concentration on foulness," popularly referred to as the Buddhist graveyard meditation. It is designed to overcome the influences of physical attraction, and recommends that one reflect on the following aspects of a human corpse in the process of decay: "the bloated, the livid, the festering, the cut up, the gnawed, the scattered, the hacked and scattered, the bleeding, the worm infested, [and] the skeleton."[32] By witnessing or visualizing these aspects of the ultimate putrification of all human corporeality, one will undoubtedly think twice before entering into an inauspicious liason. Buddhaghoṣa writes that "a living body is just as foul as a dead one, only the characteristic of foulness is not evident in a living body, being hidden by adventitious embellishments."[33]

29. Engle, VI, p.32.
30. *Ibid.* Sanskrit: *ātmabuddhi* and *mamatvabuddhi*
31. *Ibid*, p. 34.
32. *Visuddhimagga*, op. cit., VI:1, p. 185.
33. *Ibid.*, VI:88, p. 201.

Vasubandhu advocates this concentration technique as an antidote for overcoming four types of desire. To remedy the first desire, attraction to color (*varṇarāga*), one should conjure up images of a corpse which has turned blue. To counteract the second desire, attachment to a particular form (*saṃsthānarāga*), one should visualize a corpse which has been partly eaten or dismembered. For the third, desire for contact (*sparśarāga*), one should dwell on a dead body partly eaten by insects; and for the fourth, desire for special treatment (*upacararāga*), one should reflect on an immobile corpse.[34] Each of these practices functions to restructure one's psychological orientation toward the world, which in actuality determines how the world is perceived. Ultimately, when all attachments are reversed, the world and self are both revealed as empty of abiding essence. The corpse meditation, however, is a preliminary step and can only serve to suppress unfavourable impressions from past experience; it alone cannot uproot the fundamental causes of attachment.[35]

It is recommended that the skeleton meditation be applied to oneself and then expanded to include all beings, thus circumventing all possible forms of attachment:

> The Yogi who wishes to practice meditation upon the unattractive begins by fixing his mind upon some member of his body such as the toe of his foot or the middle of his forehead or any area desired. He should imagine that the flesh in that area rots and then falls away and gradually continue the practice until the entire body is regarded as skeleton. Similarly, in order to enlarge this conception he should apply the same process to a second person and continue until he has conceived of the temple and compound, the town, the outlying regions and finally the limitless ocean as being filled with skeletons. Then, in withdrawing this image in order to collect the mind, it is reduced until only the yogi himself is conceived as being a skeleton.[36]

This meditation works by a process of elimination to redefine radically one's conception of identity and foster a state of higher awareness, culminating in nonattachment. This process is an inversion of the Hindu and Confucian concepts of the cosmic person. Rather than

34. Prahlad Pradhan, editor, *Abhidharmakośabhāṣyam of Vasubandu* (Patna: K.P. Jayasawal Research Institute, 1975), p. 336.
35. *Ibid.*, p. 337.
36. Engle, VI, pp. 36-37; Pradhan, p. 337.

seeing the macrocosm in the microcosm, as found in the *Purusa sukta*, the Buddhist progressively eliminates any trace of reality in any sphere. For Confucius, a similar progression is outlined in the *Great Learning*, but for the cultivation of social propriety and identification with an ever-expanding community, from self to family to village to province to world.

Meditation on the skeleton helps one to overcome attachment to physical attractions. For those perturbed by mental distractions, attention to the breath is advised, a practice which has been widely promoted in America in the form of *zazen*. Buddhaghosa, quoting the Buddha as recorded in the *Saṃyutta Nikāya*, advocates a sixteen-fold practice wherein the breath is used as the foundation for a sequence of concentrations, beginning with awareness of first a long breath, then a short breath, then a breath that recognizes and fills the whole body and then makes the body tranquil; a breath that brings happiness, then bliss, then awareness of *saṃskāra*, followed with a pacification of *saṃskāra*; a breath that is used to experience consciousness and then gladden consciousness, following with a concentration on the consciousness and a breath that liberates consciousness. The last four breaths involve the contemplation of impermanence, fading away, and cessation, culminating in relinquishment.[37]

Vasubandhu outlines six aspects of meditation on the breadth that focus more directly as a concentration on the physical process of breathing:

> Counting (*gaṇanā*) is to fix the mind upon the inhalation and exhalation of the breath without .. [giving] consideration to the state of one's body or mind. Then with the memory alone count the breaths from one up to ten...
> Following (*anugama*) means to follow the motion of the inhalation and exhalation without wondering what is the proper distance or if the breath is supposed to pervade the entire body or move through certain parts of it. When inhaling, follow it successively from the throat, to the heart, navel, waist, thighs, calves, as far as the feet...
> Fixing (*sthāna*) means to regard the breath as being situated in the area ranging from the tip of the nose to the toes of the feet like a string of precious gems and to examine whether it is beneficial or injurious, cold or warm.

37. *Visuddhimagga*, VIII:146, p. 286.

> Observation (*upalakshanā*) is to consider that the breath does not consist exclusively of wind but rather to observe all five *skandhas*...
> Change (*vivartanā*) refers to the transformation undergone by the mind which focuses upon the air...
> Purification (*pariśuddhi*) means to enter the path of vision, etc.[38]

These six stages are progressively more subtle, giving the practitioner increasing control over his or her mental faculties. Counting serves to focus the mind of the practitioner; following and fixing involve the imaginative faculties and strengthen the powers of concentration. Observation helps one to realize the all-pervasive nature of breath and see its intimacy with all activities, including both form and mental processes. With change, one begins an ascent to virtuous states of conduct, and in the phase of purification, the impressions of past activities are attenuated.

The pacification of mind (*śamatha*) through control of the breath paves the way for application of mindfulness or insight (*vipaśyanā*). Vasubandhu writes that:

> after having attained *Samādhi* (concentration) by means of these two practices [skeleton meditation and concentration on the breath], the following is pursued for the purpose of attaining *Vipaśyanā*: one who has achieved *śamatha* should meditate upon the *smṛtyupasthānas*...[39]

The *smṛtyupasthānas* are a memory-process wherein all conditioned phenomena are seen as impure, suffering, impermanent, and not-self. This fourfold formula, also found in Patanjali's *Yoga Sūtra*, undoes the fundamental misconception (*avidyā*) that one's self and world are fixed and immutable. Vasubandhu specifies that

> All *saṃskṛta* dharmas are impermanent (*anitya*);
> All *sāshrava* dharmas are suffering (*duḥkha*);
> All dharmas are empty (*śūnya*)
> and without self (*anātma*).[40]

The *saṃskṛta dharmas* are the factors of mind (*citta*) and form (*rūpa*); the *sāśrava dharmas* are those that are involved in worldly activity; the totality of *dharmas* includes the unconditioned *dharmas* as well. This form of remembrance allows the practitioner to apply

38. Engle, VI, pp. 42-44.
39. Engle, VI, p. 46; Pradhan, 341.
40. Engle, VI, p. 47.

meditation in all circumstances, not merely at times when one can meditate on the breath or on a skeleton.

Having outlined these basic forms of practice, Vasubandhu then goes into great detail about the specific applications of mindfulness, the corresponding stages which are achieved, the classes of beings who achieve various insights and the regions wherein they dwell, and so forth. These various details would be an interesting topic for a more extended study, but for our purposes we have explained the basic Abhidharma paradigm for meditation: because attachment results in suffering, meditation must be practiced in three phases to achieve nonattachment. The first phase works at wearing away attachment to externals by cultivating contradictory images. That which seems beautiful is reduced mentally through its inevitable changes to its ultimate decay and demise. The second phase deals with overcoming attachment to thoughts, the great confirmers of self-perspective, by mastering the breath and generating states of equipoise. This pacification of mind (*śamatha*), common to virtually all schools of Buddhist practice, is preliminary to the third phase (*vipaśyanā*), a radical world view that all things are impure, suffering, impermanent, without self. Unlike the skeleton meditation, which removes physical attraction, this final method works at erasing the hidden tendencies which give rise to attachment.

Concluding Remarks

Two types of paradigm shift can be seen operating in our discussion of *Abhidharma*. The first is historical: the *Abhidharma* is an elaboration on the Buddha's original teachings of *skandhas*, no-self, dependent origination, *etc.* This shift to increased emphasis on detail evolved because the early Buddhist community perceived a need for more sophisticated analyses of psychological states. At a later phase in Buddhist history, Nāgārjuna saw the need for resimplification and enacted another paradigm shift through his Mādhyamika philosophy. Similarly, the Yogācāra doctrine of *citta-mātra* may be interpreted as a paradigm shift emphasizing the need for meditation.

For the historian, each of the above movements or shifts radically altered the development of Buddhist philosophy. None of the above paradigms fundamentally disagrees with the original teaching of the Buddha. Regardless of the historical context, the basic Buddhist teachings remain constant: there is suffering; release can be had; the practice of meditation is the means for release. This realization requires a shift in perspective which does not necessarily depend upon historical period (although it might be argued from a sociological perspective that times of strife are accompanied by a upsurge of interest in religious practice). Regardless of the circumstance, the Buddhist path requires that one become radically ahistorical and divorce oneself from all conditioned notions which give rise to attachment and its consequent suffering. From the time of the historical Buddha to the modern day Buddhist, the paradigm of practice involves restructuring the concepts and notions one holds regarding oneself, as indicated by Gunapala Dharmasiri elsewhere in this volume. Pain is caused by imputing real, lasting, and pure self-nature to both self and things. Through the process of meditation, one purifies the mind of this fundamental delusion and achieves a state of nonattachment. Diana Paul has written that:

> ... meditation ... serves the function of introspection of the mind upon itself in its true, instrinsically pure nature. Having meditated upon itself, the mind then awakens to the thought of enlightenment, transforming the ordinary mind (*sattvacitta*) which is extrinsically defiled into the commitment to rediscover the pure, luminous mind (*prabhāsvara-citta*).[41]

This effects the entry into a new world view that understands the conditional nature of things, and yet allows one to continue living a transformed life.

From a psychological perspective, practice requires a paradigm shift, not as a movement within history, but as a radical originary transformation of self-identity. For this to take place, states of conventional awareness and reliance on the cognition of discrete things must be suspended during meditation. The basic function of meditation is not to achieve a lasting state of consciousness but is rather to purify impressions that adversely condition perception. In a sense, the process involves the deconstruction (*asaṃskṛta*) of defiled patterns of *dharmas*. As Rune E.A. Johansson has noted, "the world according to early Buddhism is a perceived, conscious world."[42] Through practice, one awakens to an understanding that one is fundamentally *not* the

---

41. Diana Mary Paul, *The Buddhist Feminine Ideal* (Missoula, Mt.: Scholars Press, 1980), p. 79.
42. Rune E.A. Johansson, *The Dynamic Psychology of Early Buddhism* (London: Curzon Press, 1979), p. 217.
43. Ibid., p. 218.

"distorting elements ... [that] lead to undesirable activities."[43] Neither world nor personality is extolled, both being deemed as impure. Release comes through nonattachment, through a fundamental reorientation away from reification and into the renunciation summarized by the formula "This is not mine; this am I not; this is not the Self of me." With this insight, one becomes free from passion and gains authenticity.

The Meditative No-Self Paradigm in Later Buddhist and Other Traditions

The *Abhidharma* emphasis on radical self-understanding and purgation of all notions of self strikes a chord that resonates with later Buddhist schools as well as other religious traditions that emphasize transformation through meditation. According to Tson Kha Pa, the Tibetan scholar and synthesizer of the twelfth century, the stages of practice found in the so-called Hīnayāna such as *śamatha* and *vipaśyanā* are merely preparations for the study of the Mādhyamika and Yogācāra, which in turn are seen as preparation for tantric practice. In Tantra one ritually assumes another identity in a process called deity yoga. Here, the bodhisattva casts off conventional conditioning (*saṃskāra, vāsanā*) and takes on a new, enlightened identity, literally becoming a Buddha. Tson Kha Pa, quoting the *Vajraḍāka Tantra*, declares that in this highest state of yoga, "oneself is all Buddhas and all Heroes. Though union with one's deity oneself is thoroughly achieved."[44] Christopher S. George explains the process of transformation as follows:

> The transformation of the mundane *ahaṃkāra* or "self—image" of the *sādhaka* or candidate into the transcendent self-image of Caṇḍamahāroṣana [the deity of the text being discussed], such that the candidate ceases to be motivated by his own self-centered value system, and is motivated solely by the Void and Compassion, out of which Caṇḍamahāroṣana materialized..... Thus, for the candidate who has effected this transformation, all his actions become the pure and blameless acts of Caṇḍamahāroṣana, and the world in which he moves is none other than the Vajra-realm, transcending any notion of being or non-being.[45]

44. Jeffrey Hopkins, translator, *Tantra in Tibet: The Great Exposition of Secret Mantra by Tsong-ka-pa* (London: George Allen & Unwin, 1977), p. 137.
45. Christopher S. George, "The Dynamics of the Ahaṃkāra in Vajrayana Buddhism with Special Regard to the Caṇḍamahāroṣana Tantra." The Institute for Advanced Studies World Religions, 1973.

Tantra not only calls for the abandonment and uprooting of ignorantly conceived notions of self, but also provides a new identity for the practitioner, as well as a new, fundamentally restructured world.

The Buddhist concern for nonattachment has obvious parallels in the *Sāṃkhya Kārikā* of Īśvarakrishṇā. In the Sāṃkhya system, as in Buddhism, the intention is to alleviate suffering. The cause of suffering is said to be the mistaking of the compound, active, creative, unconscious *prakṛti* for the inactive, noncreative, pure witness *puruṣa*. Through reflection on the many forms of *prakṛti* and the function of *puruṣa*, one achieves the realization "I am not; naught is mine; this is not I" (*nāsmi, na me, nāhaṃ*).[46] Only then does the compulsive creation cease and one becomes firmly established in the disposition of knowledge (*jñānabhāva*). The body is said to continue "like a potter's wheel" but with a thorough ongoing awareness which prevents a redescent into ignorance. The philosophical differences between Sāṃkhya and Buddhism are well-documented in classical texts and modern studies by Stcherbatsky, Kalupahana, and others. But the culminating experience in Sāṃkhya is the same as that deemed by the Buddha to qualify his disciples for arhat-hood: that one no longer identifies with any particularity whatsoever. For both systems, the key is knowledge accompanied with nonattachment.

It is somewhat more difficult to see the nonattachment paradigm in a Western context, though not impossible. One example is the dialogue between Diotima and Socrates in the *Symposium*, where Socrates is exhorted to overcome attraction to one particular body by seeing the beauty in all bodies. Although an inversion of the Buddhist skeleton meditation, this practice leads from a limited, self-gratifying attachment to a lofty state of mystical vision:

> ... mount ... for that beauty's sake ever upwards, as by a flight of steps, from one to two, and from two to all beautiful bodies, and from beautiful bodies to beautiful pursuits and practices, and from practices to beautiful learnings, so that from learnings he may come at last to that perfect learning which is the learning solely of the beauty itself ... everlasting, and never being born nor perishing, neither increasing nor diminishing ... not beautiful now and ugly then ... not beautiful in one place and ugly in another place. Again, this beauty will not show

46. *Sāṃkhya Kārikā* 64.

> itself to him like a face or hands or any bodily thing at all, not as a discourse or a science, not indeed as residing in anything, as in a living creature or in earth or heaven or anything else, but being by itself with itself away in simplicity ...[47]

Through this process, the faculty of perceiving discrete, objectively real bodies is used as a step in the ascent to the Beautiful, which is beyond all predication. As in Tantra, desire (*eros*) is not suppressed but is used as a spiritual fuel.

From a Christian perspective, St. John of the Cross provides a poem which conveys the sense of a higher knowing, not unlike the *prajñā/jnañā* of Buddhism and Sāṃkhya. This knowing transcends the mundane ways of thinking and discloses a knowing without boundaries which defies all description. The poem contrasts the knowing of things (*saber*) with an undertstanding (*entendir*) which is associated with not-knowing. The experience of this perfect, transcending knowledge (*ciencia perfecto y transcendieno*) brings freedom, ascension, and soaring; it provides a poetic complement for our investigation into Buddhist knowledge and transcendence.

> I entered into unknowing
> Yet when I saw myself there
> Without knowing where I was
> I understood great things;
> I shall not say what I felt
> For I remained in unknowing
> Transcending all knowledge ...
> I was so whelmed,
> So absorbed and withdrawn,
> That my senses were left
> Deprived of all their sensing,
> And my spirit was given
> An understanding while not understanding,
> Transcending all knowledge.
> He who truly arrives there cuts free from himself;
> All that he knew before
> Now seems worthless,
> And his knowledge so soars
> That he is left in unknowing
> Transcending all knowledge...[48]

47. W.H.D. Rouse, translator, *Great Dialogues of Plato* (New York: New American Library, 1956), p. 105.
48. Kieran Kavanaugh and Otilio Rodriguez, translators, "Stanzas Concerning an Ecstasy Experienced in High Contemplation" in *The Collected Works of St. John of the Cross* (Washington, D.C.: Institute of Carmelite Studies, 1979), pp. 718-719.

St. John of the Cross conveys the interiority and exuberance generally associated with mystical experience. However, though he mentions the senses and the process of understanding, he does not explain their function nor does he delineate the path that leads to their transcendence, as do the Buddhists. Christian mysticism is fraught with mystery, shrouded in misty clouds of unkowing. By contrast, the paradigm provided by the *Abhidharma* schools unravels in detail the nature of perceptual experience and provides numerous techniques for its transformation.

Anurādhapura (Sri Lanka) Ratnaprasāda in Abhayagiri complex
Nāga Dvārapāla circa 9th century, Stone
Photograph courtesy of the American Institute of Indian Studies, Varanasi, by way of the Archeological Survey of India. Negative number 338.20.

Section II

INSIDERS' UNDERSTANDINGS

5

The Moral Significance of Buddhist *Nirvāṇa*

The Early Buddhist Model of Perfection

Deegalle Mahinda

Theravāda Buddhists strive to reach *nirvāṇa* (Pāli *nibbāna*)[1] as the goal of their spiritual path.[2] *Nirvāṇa* is a state of happiness and the solution to human unsatisfactoriness (*dukkha*); it is attained within one's lifetime through moral perfection. Buddhism teaches that humanity suffers in two ways: mentally as a result of an internal, psychological process and physically as a consequence of illnesses and one's actions. Furthermore, Buddhism maintains that mental suffering (caused by mental illness — *cetasikaroga*) affects the human being more seriously than physical suffering (caused by physical illness — *kāyikaroga*). Mental, verbal and physical actions together form the *karmic* force which pushes humanity along the infinite cycle of birth and death (*saṃsāra*). while good *kammas* (actions) bring happiness and good birth in future lives, bad *kammas* bring unhappiness and suffering in this life as well as in future lives. Therefore the Buddhist spiritual path always emphasizes the importance of leading a morally righteous life which has the potential to bring happiness to oneself and to humanity as a whole. Moral and skillful (*kusala*) actions ultimately lead to final liberation by freeing

1. Except the Sanskrit term '*nirvāṇa*,' all other foreign language terms in this paper are from the Pāli language.
2. Though the importance of *nirvāṇa* has been emphasized in this paper, the value of *dhamma* for Buddhist spiritual path cannot be ignored. Frank Reynolds has argued very strongly in favor of *dhamma* as a 'center of gravity' in Buddhist ethical action. According to Reynolds, *dhamma* is the 'normative truth' that guides all forms of Theravada action and all other "Theravāda norms for action are expressions of *dhamma*." Frank E. Reynolds, "Ethics and Wealth in Theravāda Buddhism: A study in Comparative Religious Ethics," *Ethics Wealth and Salvation: A Study in Buddhist Social Ethics*, eds. Russell F. Sizemore and Donald K. Swearer (Columbia, SC: University of South Carolina Press, 1990), p. 61.

humanity from suffering, *kamma* and the cycle of birth and death (*saṃsāra*). Thus, for Theravāda Buddhists, *nirvāṇa* is the sole goal, which brings happiness by reso-lving the problems of humanity. This paper will examine the concept of *nirvāṇa* in early Buddhism in order to discern its relationship with morality,[3] and to explore its social implications and its importance as a paradigm for our lives.

The term *nirvāṇa* derives from Sanskrit *nir+vā*, "to blow," which means both "to extinguish" and "to blow out."[4] In Buddhism, *nirvāṇa* is defined as the extinction of the threefold fires--*rāga* (lust), *dosa* (hatred), and *moha* (ignorance).[5] Early Buddhism considers these to be the three roots of all bad or immoral (*akusala mūlāni*) and advises humanity to perform positive actions which generate non-greed (*alobha*), non-hatred (*adosa*), and non-delusion (*amoha*). It further distinguishes right (*sāvajja*) from wrong (*anavajja*), virtue (*sucarita*) from vice (*duccarita*), the wholesome (*kusala*) from the unwholesome (*akusala*), purity (*parisuddha*) from impurity (*aparisuddha*) and *dhamma* (righteousness) from *adhamma* (unrighteousness). Early Buddhism characterizes *nirvāṇa* as moral perfection since the path of liberation involves the perfection of morality and transformation of the individual.

The word *nirvāṇa* has a wide variety of connotations, including the going out of a lamp or fire, health in the sense of bodily well-being since negative qualities such as restlessness are destroyed, security, emancipation, victory and peace, salvation and bliss.[6] The result of quenching the fire (going out) is coolness (*sīta*) and one who has attained the state of coolness is *sītibhūta*.[7] The wide variety of similes used to describe many aspects of *nirvāṇa* include: harbor of refuge, the cool cave, the island amidst the flood, the place of bliss, the medicine for the evil, ambrosia, the further shore, the supreme joy, the ineffable, detachment, the holy city, emancipation and liberation. The most frequent simile is the extinction of the fire of passion

---

3. Damien Keown's *The Nature of Buddhist Ethics* (New York: St. Martin's Press, 1992) is an important recent study which examines the relationship between ethics and Buddhist soteriology. It focuses on *sīla* (morality) and its relationship to the Noble Eightfold Path.
4. Rhys Davids and Stede, *Pali English Dictionary* (London: The Pali Text Society) p. 362.
5. "*yo rāgakkhayo dosakkhayo mohakkhayo* idaṃ *uccati nibbānaṃ*" S.IV.251 Hereafter all the references to Pāli texts are from the Pali Text Society editions.
6. Rhys Davids, p. 362.
7. Vin.I.8;A.II.208;A.V.65; D.III. 233.

(*rāgaggi*). It shows that craving for rebirth is extinguished by not providing fuel for continued existence.[8] This state of perfect serenity is achieved in this life before death.[9] It is realized through concentration of the mind and development of wisdom.[10] One has to depend totally on wisdom to be a saint.[11] The saint is endowed with four qualities (*sīla, indriyaguttadvāratā, bhojanamattaññutā* and *jāgariya*) and is thus assured of the final release.[12] From the Theravāda perspective, the Noble Eightfold Path is the only path (*ekāyano ayaṃ maggo*) which leads to purification of beings.[13] Thus *nirvāṇa* is considered to be a state of perfect happiness (*paramaṃ sukhaṃ*) achievable in this world, within one's lifetime.[14] Although early Buddhism characterizes *nirvāṇa* as undefinable and maintains that there is no criterion to measure the worthy one (*arahant*),[15] its benign quality can be described within the limitations of language as peace, rest and perfect and supreme happiness.

Buddhist morality distinguishes healthy, right and moral actions from those that are unhealthy, wrong and immoral actions: immoral actions lead to the degeneration of humanity and moral ones lead to the upliftment of humanity and ultimately to liberation of the individual. In the Pāli Canon, we find many moral concepts which play an important role in the moral life of a Buddhist even today.[16] The terms *kusala* (wholesome) and *puñña* (merit) are the most important of these. In general, actions which generate peace, harmony, generosity, non-greed, non-hatred and non-delusion, are regarded as *kusala* actions. These *kusala* actions lead to *nirvāṇa*; *akusala* (unwholesome) actions make one deviate from the path of liberation. The Buddha once said that one becomes endowed with right vision (*sammā diṭṭhi*) through the knowledge of both wholesome and

---

8. "*aniccasaññi ... bhikkhu pāpunāti diṭṭh'eva dhamme nibbānaṃ*" A.1V.353.
9. M.1.487.
10. "*bhikkhu panīhitena cittena avijjaṃ bhecchati vijjaṃ uppādessati nibbānaṃ sacchikarissati*" A.1.8.
11. "*idhaññaya parinibbati anāsavo*" A.11.41.
12. A.11.331.
13. "*ekāyano ayaṃ maggo sattānaṃ visuddhiyā ... nibbānassa sacchikiriyā*" D.11.290; S.V.167, 185.
14. S.11.18; 11.115; 111.163; IV.141; M.III.286.
15. Sn. 1076.
16. *Kusula-akusala, puñña-pāpa, karaṇīya-akaraṇiya, samacariya-visamacariya, ariya-anariya, seṭṭha-hīna, sammā-miccā, anāsava-sāsava, sukata-dukkata, sappurisa-asappurisa, kalyāṇa-pāpaka, and sukka-kaṇha* are some ethical terms found in the Pali Canon.

unwholesome actions and their roots.[17] The Buddha recommends the wiping out of unwholesome actions through wholesome ones, since such eradication brings happiness.[18] In early Buddhism, therefore, there is a great emphasis on the causal link between moral actions and the happiness of humanity.

In Buddhism, moral life consists not only in avoiding negative actions, but also cultivating good ones (*kusalassa upasampadā*).[19] For this purpose, Buddhism recommends the five precepts (*pañca sīla*) for lay Buddhists and other morally higher precepts for monks. All these moral virtues, in one way or another, are intended to bring about not only the moral development of the individual but also social harmony and well-being in society.[20] A close examination of the Buddhist ethical system shows that Buddhist moral teachings have certain universal characteristics. The five precepts, for example are common to many religious traditions. Since Buddhism recognizes the worth of all living beings, Buddhist precepts include all living beings within their scope. When one practices the meditation on loving kindness (*mettā*), one has to develop loving kindness to all beings (*sabbē sattā bhavantu sukhitattā*). In the *Metta Sutta* of the *Suttanipāta* this universal loving kindness is highlighted as follows:

> May all beings be happy and secure; may their minds be contented. Whatever living beings there may be—feeble or strong, long (or tall), stout, or medium, short, small, or large, seen or unseen, those dwelling far or near, those who are born and those who are yet to be born—may all beings, without exception, be happy minded! Let not one deceive another nor despise any person whatever in any place. In anger or illwill let not one wish any harm to another. *Just as a mother would protect her only child even at the risk of her own life*, even so let one cultivate a boundless heart towards all beings. Let one's thoughts of boundless love pervade

17. *"yato kho āvuso ariyasāvako akusalaṃ a pajānāti, akusala mūlaṃ ca pajānāti, kusalaṃ ca kusala mūlaṃ ca pajānāti ettāvatāpi kho āvuso ariyasāvako sammadiṭṭhi hoti."* M.1.47.
18. *"yasmā ca kho bhikkhave akusalaṃ pahīnaṃ hitāya sukhāya saṃvattati. Tasmāhaṃ evaṃ vadāmi. 'akusalaṃ bhikkhave pajahathā'ti."* A.1.58
19. Dhp. 183.
20. D.J. Kalupahana, *Buddhist Philosophy: An Historical Introduction* (Honolulu: University of Hawaii Press, 1984), p. 59.

> the whole world—above, below and across—without any obstruction, without any hatred, without any enmity.[21]

Since Buddhist Moral analysis includes all beings *(sabbe sattā)* and cultivates loving kindness towards all beings, visible and invisible, one can consider Buddhist morality has certain universal aspects. The Buddha advises that no one should kill or harm any living being, for every being fears pain and death. One must take into account the preciousness of one's own life (*attānaṃ upamaṃ katvā)* in order to protect the lives of others.[22] Thus, ultimately one's attitude towards one's life is the basic criterion of morality.

This general criterion is explained in more detail in the *Anumāna Sutta,* using two types of inference (*anumāna*). In the first case, one infers from oneself to other, taking one's life as the basis of inference; in the second case, one infers from others to oneself, taking others' experience as the basis.[23] The *Kālāma Sutta* offers a common criterion of morality on the basis of which each individual can determine for himself or herself what is good and bad.[24] The individual's recollection that there is no being in *saṃsāra* who has not been his or her relative, and that all living beings are subject to rebirth, leads the individual to moral and social commitment.[25]

The aim of religious life for the Buddhist is the attainment of liberation (*nirvāṇa)* in this life. The path that leads to liberation is the Noble Eightfold Path, which is known as the Middle Path (*majjhimāpaṭipadā*) since it avoids the two extreme ways of life: self-mortification (*attakilamathānuyoga*) and sensual indulgence (*kāmasukhal- likānuyoga*). This path consists of eight components, each of which is preceded by the ethical characterization "*sammā*" which means right. The path of liberation in early Buddhism is based on righteousness; it gradually (*anukkamena*) leads to *nirvāṇa*, since the moral life in this world is related to the ultimate goal.

The first stage of the gradual path is *sīla* (morality). It includes right speech (*sammā vācā*), right action (*sammā kammanta*) and right living (*samma ājīva*). *Sīla* is the foundation of good living as well as the starting point of the religious and moral life. When one is well

21. *Karaṇiyamettasutta*, Snvv. 145-150.
22. Dhp. 129.
23. *Anumānasutta*, M.1.97.
24. A.1.189; GS.I.172; P.D. Premasiri, "Moral Evaluation in Early Buddhism" *Sri Lanka Journal of the Humanities* 1(1) 1975: 33.
25. Gunapala Dharmasiri, *Fundamentals of Buddhist Ethics* (Singapore: The Buddhist Research Society, 1986), p. 31.

trained in *sīla*, one is in a good position to train one's mind (*citta*). The second stage is *samādhi* (concentration) which includes three components: right effort (*sammā vāyāma*), right mindfulness (*samma sati*) and right concentration (*sammā samādhi*). These three elements train one's mind to a state of *samādhi*. The third stage of the gradual path is wisdom (*paññā*) which includes right view (*sammā diṭṭhi*) and right thoughts (*sammā saṃkappa*). Wisdom enables one to see reality as it is (*yathābhūta*). Wisdom arises only in a concentrated mind (*samādhi citta*). Thus, through a gradual process of training (*anupubbasikkhā*), working out (*anupubbakiriyā*), and practice (*anupubbapaṭipadā*),[26] the spiritual seeker reaches moral perfection.

On one occasion, the Buddha explains how morality leads one to *nirvāṇa*:

> So you see, Ānanda, good conduct has freedom from remorse as object and profit; freedom from remorse has joy; joy has rapture; rapture has calm; calm has happiness; happiness has concentration; concentration has seeing things as they really are; seeing things as they really are has revulsion and fading of interest; revulsion and fading of interest have release by knowing and seeing as their object and profit. So you see, Ānanda, good conduct gradually leads to the summit (*kusalāni sīlāni anupubbena aggāya parentīti*).[27]

In this case the spiritual path in this world and the ultimate goal are interconnected and interrelated within the process of leading the spiritual seeker to moral perfection.

It is important to examine the way Buddhism explains the relationship between moral actions and the nature of the internal mental process. Early Buddhism offers a causal and psychological analysis both of the external behavior of the individual and of his or her internal dispositions. Buddhism views immoral actions such as stealing (*adinnādāna*), killing (*pāṇātipāta*), lying (*musāvāda*), etc., as

---

26. Kalupahana, p. 58.

27. *Iti kho Ānanda kusalāni sīlāni avippaṭisārātthāni avippaṭisārānisaṃsāni avippaṭisāro pāmujjattho pāmujjānisaṃso, pāmujjaṃ pītatthaṃ pītānisaṃsaṃ, pīti passaddhatthā passaddhānisaṃsā, passaddhi sukhatthā sukkhānisaṃsā, sukhaṃ samādhatthaṃ samādhānihsaṃsam, samādhi yathārbhūtañaṇadassanattho yathābhūtañāṇadassanānirsaṃso, yathārbhūtañāṇadassanaṃ nibbidāvirāgatthaṃ nibbidārvirāgāni saṃsaṃ, nibbidāvirāgo vimuttiñaṇadassanattho vimuttiñaṇadassanāinisamso. Iti kho Ānanda kusalāni sīlāni anupubbena aggāya parenti.*" A.V.2; GSV.2-3.

more than expressions of human emotion; it views them also as external manifestations of internal impurity of one's mind. The *Dhammapada* mentions that "all (mental) states have mind as their forerunner, mind as their chief and they are mind made. If one speaks or acts, with a defiled mind, then suffering follows one even as the wheel follows the hoof of the draught-ox."[28] In the same way, the rightly directed mind definitely brings happiness.[29] Early Buddhism emphasizes that external purity depends totally on internal purity. Since evil dispositions are results of perceptions received through the six senses, without transforming internal dispositions of the individual, it is not possible to bring a change in external behavior. Thus all forms of immorality are rooted in the internal dispositions of human beings. The Middle Path, which is based on morality, concentration and wisdom, purifies both internal mental dispositions and external behavior.

Negative dispositions in an individual can be classified into three stages: *anusaya, pariyuṭṭhāna* and *vītikkama*. The term *anusaya* refers to a dormant state (latent disposition)[30] in which evil roots lie dormant or hidden. Rhys Davids translates *pariyuṭṭhāna* as "over-exertion," "a state of being possessed (or hindered)", "possession," "bias" and "outburst."[31] In this stage evil qualities start functioning inside the body in the form of thoughts and emotions. This process exhausts the person psychologically by creating an inner turmoil and an internal pressure which brings unhappiness. *Vītikkama* means "going beyond" or "transgression."[32] This is a stage in which corrupted internal negative dispositions manifest themselves as forms of violence (stealing, murdering, raping, etc.) through human speech and action. Thus, the immoral behavior of humanity is a result of internal impurity of the defiled mind.

The Noble Eightfold Path aims at overcoming negative dispositions of the individual. At the outset of the path, morality (*sīla*) trains and redirects human speech, physical action and livelihood. This prevents the individual from reaching the stage of transgression (*vītikkama*). The individual trains his or her mind in order to disci-

28. Dhp. 1.
29. Dhp. 2.
30. Rhys Davids and Stede, p. 44; S.IV.205; M.111.285.
31. *Ibid.*, p. 433-34; M.1.18.
32. *Ibid.*, p. 644; Vism.11.17; Vin. 111.112; IV.290.

pline emotions and thoughts, and to overcome the stage of over-exertion (*pariyuṭṭhāna*) by attaining concentration (*samādhi*) through meditation. *Anusayas* which can be eliminated through wisdom, exist until one attains enlightenment. At the time of enlightenment one achieves internal purification and integration of one's internal dispositions with physical actions. Thus Buddhist liberation is the process of transforming the internal negative dispositions of the individual in order to uplift and purify the external behavior.

The relationship between morality (*sīla*) and wisdom (*paññā*) is another important aspect of Buddhism. The Buddha points out that morality and wisdom are interrelated and mutually activate each other.[33] "From morality comes wisdom and from wisdom morality ... like washing one hand with another ... so is morality washed round with wisdom and wisdom with morality."[34] This simile of washing hands shows the equal importance of both wisdom and morality in the spiritual path since without one, the other becomes meaningless.

In Buddhism, grounding oneself in *Sīla* is presented as an essential prerequisite for meditational practices,[35] since generating wisdom is a difficult process for a beginner. The great Buddhist commentator Buddhaghosa starts the *Visuddhimagga*, the *Path of Purification*, by presenting the thesis that "after having established oneself in morality one should train the mind and wisdom" (*sīle patiṭṭhāya naro sapañño, cittaṃ paññaṃ ca bhāvayaṃ*).[36] In Early Buddhism a person becomes a great individual by being both moral and wise. Practicing morality is equally possible for both the wise and the ordinary public. Emphasizing the importance of the practice of morality (*sīla*) has been a common theme in Sinhala Buddhisṃ Sinhala texts attempt to make available the understanding of morality to the ordinary public. For example, Dharmasēna Thera's *Saddharmaratnāvaliya*, a thirteenth century Sinhala text, highlights the importance of the practice of morality as follows:

> Sīla, Moral Conduct, is the most important basis for all blessings both in this world and beyond. Whatever adornments one may wear there is none more beautiful than Moral Conduct. There is no perfume more pervasive, no purer water for washing away the impurities of

33. Dharmasiri, p.28.
34. D.1.124.
35. See the concluding section of George D. Bond's paper (pp. 39-40) in this volume where Bond quotes from Michael Carrithers who has explicitly stated the relationship between *sīla* and meditation
36. Bhadantācārya Buddhaghoṣa, *The Path of Purification* (Berkeley: Shambhala, 1976), p.1.

> Defilements, no cooler breeze to calm the heat of passion. There is nothing like Morality to bring one fame. If one requires a ladder to climb to heaven, morality is that ladder. It is the gateway to the city of Enlightenment. Those who seek their own welfare should practice, either the Five Precepts on a daily basis, or the Eight Precepts on full moon days, or, if one has the potential, become a novice and observe the Ten Precepts.[37]

Practicing morality helps one to build up good relations with society and enables one to understand that one is interrelated with the rest of the world. It generates good actions which secure happiness in this world as well as in lives yet to come. Since Buddhism accepts the equality of humanity (*cattārovaṇṇā samāsamā*) despite ethnic, cultural and social differences, a person who is endowed with moral behavior and wisdom becomes a great human being (*vijjācaraṇa sampanno so seṭṭho devamānuse*).

The great human being in early Buddhism is the *arahant* (worthy one). In the descriptions of *arahants* in Buddhist literature, one often finds the expression "*puñña pāpa pahīnassa natthijāgaratobhayaṃ*," which means that arahants have discarded both merit (*puñña*) and demerit (*pāpa*). From this expression some scholars assume that Buddhist saints have gone beyond morality. For instance, Shundo Tachibana, the author of *The Ethics of Buddhism* states:

> The Bhikkhu, the Brahmana, the Buddha (*Sattha, Muni*) are said to be free from such distinctions as good and evil, pleasantness and unpleasantness, purity and impurity, and so on ... when one reaches this state of culture, distinctive ideas will be absolutely abolished, ... He is not immoral, but we may say that he is supermoral. He has reached the mental condition where there is no consciousness of moral, aesthetical, or logical distinction; the relative ideas therefore of good and evil, pleasure and pain, agreeableness and disagreeableness, right and wrong, are all annihilated for him ... he has gone beyond the sphere of morality into that of religion.[38]

37. Dharmasēna Thera, *Jewels of the Doctrine: Stories of the Saddharma Ratnāvaliya, trans. Ranjini Obeyesekere* (Albany, NY: State University of New York Press, 1991), p.12.
38. S. Tachibana, *The Ethics of Buddhism* (London: Curzon Press, 1975), pp. 54-55.

Although the view of Shundo Tachibana that the worthy ones (*arahants*) eliminate merits and demerits is true since the *arahants* have no desire to accumulate merits, there are instances in the Pāli Canon where the *arahants* lead a life endowed with skillful (*kusala*) actions, such as loving kindness and compassion.[39] Therefore, rather than going beyond morality, the *arahants* naturally behave morally since their personalities have been transformed by liberation.

The descriptions of *nirvāṇa* in the Pāli Canon maintain that at the attainment of *nirvāṇa*, the *arahants* discard *puñña* (merit) and *pāpa* (demerit), which function on *karmic* level extending the cycle of birth and death (*saṃsāra*). Since the *arahants* extinguish the *karmic* force and stop accumulation of merits they go beyond *puñña* and *pāpa*. But they are still capable of performing *kusala* (skillful) actions which involve guiding the common worldlings (*puthujjana*) to the path of liberation. These moral actions of the *arahants* do not become meritorious actions since the *arahants* do not have any intention of accumulating merits. In this case, it is important to note the subtle distinction which exists between *puñña* and *kusala*. The term *kusala* means skillful, efficient and wholesome, in contrast to *akusala* which means unskillful, inefficient and unwholesome. Skillful actions (*kusala*) lead to *nirvāṇa* and unskillful actions (*akusala*) make one deviate from the path of *nirvāṇa*. In contrast to *kusala* actions, *puñña* actions lead one in the cycle of rebirth instead of directing one to liberation. After an examination of this distinction between *kusala* and *puñña*, P.D. Premasiri comments on S. Tachibana's statement and observes that it is a mistaken notion caused by considering *kusala* and *puñña* as synonyms.[40] According to Premasiri, though "*pāpa* and *akusala* have been used as synonymous terms," *puñña* and *kusala* have not been used synonymously. The precise and proper understanding of these ethical terms is extremely crucial to the characterization of the moral significance of *nirvāṇa*.[41] Investigating the broader context in the Pāli Canon it is clear that the *arahants* eliminate merits and demerits but they are endowed with *kusala* actions. Furthermore, they perform moral actions without conscious attempt since these are built into their personalities.

After the attainment of *nirvāṇa* the *arahants* lead a life of altruism since they have become moral by nature. Once the Buddha claimed that there is a difference between the actions of the *arahants* and that of the common worldlings (*puthujjana*). The morality of the common

39. *"yāvajīvaṃ arahanto pāṇātipātaṃpahāya pāṇātipātā paṭiviratā nihitadaṇḍā nihitasattha lajjī dayāpannā sabbapāṇabhūtahitānukampino viharati"* A.1. 211f

40. P.D. Premasiri, "Moral Evaluation in Early Buddhism," *Sri Lanka Journal of the Humanities,* 1(1) 1975: 41.

41. P.D. Premasiri, "Interpretation of Two Principle Ethical Terms in Early Buddhism," *Sri Lanka Journal of the Humanities* 2(1) 1976: 67.

worldlings is known as "*sīlamayo*" since their moral actions are conditioned by rules. In contrast, the *arahants* are moral (*sīlavā*) by nature[42] and their actions are not conditioned by rules. They perform moral actions for the well-being of the world without abrogating morality since they are endowed with morality (*kusalasampanna*) and the highest good (*paramakusala*).[43] The Buddha himself claimed that he discarded all *akusala* and was endowed with *kusala* (*sabbākusaladhammapahīno kho ... tathāgato kusaladhammasamannāgato ti*). In fact, the *arahants* who have perfected the eight components of the Middle Path and *sammā ñāṇa* (right knowledge) and *sammā vimutti* (right liberation) are known as *sampannakusala* and *paramakusala*.[44] In this case *kusalasampanna* means being full of sublime qualities such as loving kindness, compassion, equanimity and sympathetic joy.

In early Buddhism the terms *attattha* (egoism) and *parattha* (altruism) lose their superficial distinctions at the deepest (ultimate) level. The *Aṅguttara Nikāya* mentions four categories of people: (1) the one who acts neither for his or her own well-being nor for others' (*na attahitāya ca paṭipanno na parahitāya ca*), (2) the one who acts for others' well-being but not for his or her own (*parahitāya ca paṭipanno no attahitāya ca*), (3) the one who acts for his or her own well-being but not for others' (*attahitāya ca paṭipanno no parahitāya ca*). This last type is highly appreciated as the ideal.[45] One who torments oneself and others (*attantapo ca parantapo ca*) is condemned in Buddhism as inferior,[46] at the same time, however, Buddhism reminds us not to ignore our own well-being for the sake of others.[47] The experience of *nirvāṇa* transcends the superficial distinction between egoism and altruism. Since the person who enters *nirvāṇa* eliminates *atta* (self) and has no identity or individuality to preserve, that person renders an impartial and fruitful service to the whole society. Early Buddhism often emphasizes one's perfectness as a prerequisite for social work. In the *Saṃyutta Nikāya*, the Buddha declares that one safe-guards oneself in safe-guarding others (*attānaṃ rakkhanto paraṃ rakkhati*),

---

42. A.V. 66.
43. P.D. Premasiri, "Moral Evaluation in Early Buddhism," p. 40
44. *"... asekhāya sammādiṭṭhiyā samannāgato hoti. asekhena sammāsaṃkappena ... asekhāya sammāvācāya ... asekhena sammā kammantena ... asekhena sammā ājīvena ... asekhena sammāvāyāmena asekhāya sammāsatiyā ... asekhena sammāsamādhinā ... asekhena sammāñaṇena ... asekhāya sammāvimuttiyā samannāgato hoti." M.11.28-29.*
45. A.1195.
46. D.111.232.
47. Dhp.166.

and one safe-guards others in cultivating loving kindness, *ahiṃsā*, and compassion.[48] The mother's love for the one and only child is a typical example of the transcendent quality which surpasses the superficial distinction between altruism and egoism. In the same way, the experience of the ultimate goal in Buddhism transcends all superficial labels such as egoism and altruism.

Buddhist *nirvāṇa* itself is moral perfection since moral practice gradually leads to liberation by developing moral qualities to the utmost. The realization of *nirvāṇa* is the self-transformation of the individual's personality. Although some scholars, such as Max Weber, view *nirvāṇa* as a selfish ideal,[49] one could see *nirvāṇa* as a goal which brings happiness and peace not only to the individual but also to society at large. Through the path of morality integrated with wisdom and compassion, an individual attains internal purity. After attaining *nirvāṇa*, that person can share the spiritual experience with the world as a 'social worker' in guiding others to the same goal. In fact, *nirvāṇa* is not annihilation but the development of good qualities such as loving kindness, compassion, generosity, equanimity, and sympathetic joy. With perfect mental health and a detached mental attitude, *arahants* lead a life of purity like a lotus without being tainted by the impurities of the world. They extend their personal ideal toward a social ideal by serving the multitudes and unfolding the path of liberation. Being morally perfect and endowed with *kusala* they act as spiritual guides for the society. Since they are endowed with wisdom and moral behavior (*vijjācaraṇasampanno*) they illuminate, with the much needed light of wisdom, the world which is immersed in the darkness of greed for power, material gain, ignorance, hatred and pride.

48. "*Attānaṃ bhikkhave rakkhanto paraṃ rakkhati. Param rakkhanto attānaṃ rakkhati. Kathaṃ ca bhikkhave attānam rakkhanto paraṃ rakkhati?... Āsevanāya, bhāvanāya, bahulīkammena ... Kathañca bhikkhave paraṃ rakkhanto attānaṃ rakkhati? Khantiyā, avihiṃsāya, mettatāya, anuddayatāya.*" S.V.169.

49. Max Weber, *The Religion of India: The Sociology of Hinduism and Buddhism*, (Illinois: The Free Press, 1958), p. 206, 213.

6

Suicide and Emotional Ambivalence: An Early Buddhist Perspective

Padmasiri de Silva

There are three important strands of concern about 'suicide' in the current discussions of the subject across philosophy and religion. First is the concern with 'altruistic suicide,' initially portrayed in the pioneering work of Emile Durkheim.[1] Second, there is the current debate about the unresolved moral problems concerning the 'value of life.' Biomedical technology has made it possible for people to prolong their lives, where in the past they would have died; some times these patients are ill and agonized by suffering and wish that they put and end to their lives.[2] Thirdly, as different from the task of making moral assessments about suicide, there has been a great need to understand its causal matrix, both the psychological forces and the social fabric which may contribute to the emergence of suicidal behavior. The attempt to *understand* suicidal behavior or its prototypes appears to me as important a task as attempting to define and classify or make moral and legal assessments of suicide.[3] It is a characteristic feature of the discourses of the Buddha that reflections on the human mind intertwines closely with reflections concerning the ethical and existential concerns of human beings. Logical boundaries between ethical issues and psychological issues need to be observed when the context demand so, but in this paper, I am exploring the psychological and existential aspects of suicide, and

1. Emile Durkheim, *Suicide* (Glencoe: The Free Press, 1951).
2. see, Jonathan Glover, *Causing Death and Saving Lives* (Penguin Books, 1982).
3. See, Pasmasiri de Silva, "The Logic of Attempted Suicide and Its Linkage with Human Emotions," *Suicide in Sri Lanka*, ed. Padmasiri de Silva (Colombo: Redd Barna, 1989) pp. 25-40.

apart from its intrinsic interest, it may illuminate issues in the adjacent territory.

Suicide in early Buddhism

A basic position that Buddha takes about suicide is that a man or a woman cannot escape the sufferings which are the result of the former deeds by suicide. The image of 'eternal sleep' after death has nourished annihilationist delusions of suicide. It is a false escape route. The following is found in one of the Buddhist texts:[4]

> A monk who preaches suicide, who tells man: "Do away with this wretched life, full of suffering and sin; death is better," in fact preaches murder, is a murderer, is no longer a monk.

The person who attempts to commit suicide or commits suicide fails to see that the tribulations of life to which he is subjected are best understood in terms of the law of dependent origination and *kamma*. One cannot offset by violent means the implications and the consequences of *kamma*. It is the same point which is used by the Buddha for attempts to commit suicide due to religious motives, for example the impatience to attain *nibbāna*. A person who is under the spell off the craving for non-existence (*vibhava-taṇhā*) cannot attain *nibbāna*. A very fitting metaphor, likens this to a person who tries to pluck an unripe fruit:

> He shakes not down the unripe fruit,
> but awaits the full time of its maturity.[5]

The well known *Pāyāsi Sutta* presents the views of a heretical nature that there is no other world after death and that if this truth is well known to wanderers and Brahmins, they would put an end to their lives:

> If these good Wanderers and Brahmins were to know this —'When once we are dead we shall be better off' then these good men would take poison, or stab themselves, or put an end to themselves by hanging, or throw themselves from precipices. And it is because they do not know that, once dead, they will be better off, that they are fond of life, averse from dying[6] ...

4. *Pārājika*, iii; see SBE xiii (1881) 4.
5. *Milinda Pañha*, Part I, 44, S.B.E. XXXV, 1890.
6. *Dialogues of the Buddha*, II, 330, trans. T.W. & C.A.F. Rhys Davids (London: P.T.S., 1951).

Venerable Kumāra Kassapa who responds to this wrong view compares Payāsi to the woman who cuts open her belly to find out whether the child she hopes to have soon is a boy or a girl. The moral of the story is that the virtuous do not force maturity on that which is unripe, one has to lead a virtuous life and the results will follow. One could perhaps hasten ones liberation from suffering by living the Buddhist path with greater vigilance, enthusiasm and persistence. But suicide is no solution.

If these objections were based on a correct understanding of the law of *kamma* and dependent origination, there was a second objection which was made on methodological grounds as asceticism, suicide and self-torture are often attempts to deal at a physical level, issues which need psychological management. The Jains for instance saw in asceticism and physical pain (like the practice of starvation) a way of purifying sin. The Jains accepted that, "vocal sins are destroyed through silence, mental sins through respiratory restraint, bodily sins through starvation and lust crushed through mortification."[7] The Buddha's reply to the Jains is well presented in the *Devadahasutta*.[8] The Buddha's position is clarified with the help of a simile. A man is injured by an arrow which has been smeared with poison. The doctor cuts open the wound, dress it with medicated powder, so that it will heal. In the process of treatment the painful experiences have to be patiently borne by the injured patient. In a similar way bodily and mental hardships are purely incidental to the following of the eightfold noble path, but the hardships do not become an end in itself. The Buddha in fact saw that kind of a masochistic undercurrent can feed such asceticism. That is why asceticism of that type (*tapas*) is regarded as an excess. As L. De La Vallee Poussin comments in his observations on suicide and asceticism, "Buddhism condemns asceticism. Any austerity which is likely to weaken body or mind is forbidden."[9] He also says, "Buddhism had better methods of crushing lust and destroying sin—the realization of the impermanence of pleasure and of the non-substantiality of the Ego ...."[10]

Thirdly, now we may briefly refer to the ethical objections to suicide. During the time of the Buddha moral dilemmas of the kind

7. See the discussion of this point, in L. De La Vallee Poussin, "Suicide: Buddhist," (*Encyclopedia of Religion and Ethics*, James Hastings (ed.), Edinburgh, 1910-27), p. 25.
8. M.III. 214-218.
9. L. De La Vallee Poussin, "Suicide: Buddhist."
10. *Ibid.*,

that exist today were not live issues and for some of the modern ethical conflicts of today, even a context did not exist. In the way that the current concern with euthanasia is conditioned by the progress of technology, issues pertaining to genetic engineering, terrorism or nuclear way were not of concern at the time. Thus the issue of the value of life and sanctity of life as embedded in the first precept (the destruction of life) was introduced as a basis for the social ethics of the community and a pre-requisite for the practice of morality and concentration. I have discussed elsewhere, the Buddhist concept of the value of life in relation to vegetarianism, animal liberation, and even biotic egalitarianism.[11] There has not been very much of the discussion on the Buddhist perspectives on euthanasia and suicide, though there has been a great deal of interest in the subject. A recent discussion by a Buddhist monk who spent a considerable amount of his life as a medical practitioner, (before he became a monk) makes a focussed emphasis about the condition of *consciousness* and *mind* as different from purely physical processes, and the physical functions are important, so long as they support the operation of the brain stem.[12] The meaning of the term 'life' in these 'grey areas' like euthanasia are yet being debated, and may have relevance to the ethical implications of 'suicide proper', but based on the main focus of this article, I wish to shift the discussion to the role of the consciousness and emotions in suicide. In fact the following observation is made by Mettananda Bhikkhu in his discussion of suicide and euthanasia: "The patient who meditates has a very clear understanding of the value of life even in the moments leading up to their death when they must accept that their life is at an end and let go. It is this valuing of life, especially with a view to the next life, that distinguishes the patient who dies happily from the average patient who commits suicide. Excepting a few cases of self-sacrifice that are related in the Pāli Canon, suicide is strongly criticized by the Buddha."[13] He refers to the strong destructive emotions in suicide: "The problem with suicide is the strong self-destructive wish which exists in the mind of a person who wants to kill himself. Usually those intending suicide have a mind full of anger, of recrimination or of envy and this is the negative emotion which they take with them when they die."[14]

11. Padmasiri de Silva, *Environmental Ethics in Buddhism,* (Paris: Unesco).
12. Mettananda Bhikkhu, "Buddhist Ethics in the Practice of Medicine," *Buddhist Ethics and Modern Society,* ed. Charles Wei - hsun Fu and Sandra A. Wawrytko (New York: Greenwood Press, 1991), 195--213.
13. *Ibid.*, p. 12.
14. *Ibid.*,

PART II

We have gone through the Buddhist critique of suicide from the point of view of *kamma* and dependent origination, secondly the critique of method used for liberation and thirdly the ethical aspects of suicide. I did not go into the details of the ethical condemnation of suicide like issues of autonomy and benefit to the community etc, but merely emphasized the importance of the first precept, the respect for life. I have also briefly mentioned the issue of treatment refusal in euthanasia. The main focus of the paper will be the psychological and the existential issues in the study of suicide. It is my contention that one of the most insightful features of the Buddha's understanding of suicide is the peculiar duality of the craving for self-preservation (*bhava taṇhā*) and self-annihilation (*vibhava taṇhā*) which ultimately work within the same framework, in a kind of vicious circle. The *ambivalence* which emerges in the inter-play of these two forms of craving, perhaps, provide a little key to understand some of the puzzling facets of this thicket of suicide. This will also help us to reflexively look at the related human emotions. As I carry through this discussion to the controversial issue of the recorded instances of attempted suicides in the Pāli suttas, the human emotions involved in the attitudes of the suicidal person to the body and the world will receive some pointed analysis. The Buddha advised his son Rahula, "Make Disgust strong in you."[15] But he also condemns the unhealthy emotion of loathing (*jegucchā*) the body, by the one who is scared of the body and wishes to destroy the body."[16]

There is a complex dialectic of emotions or the family of emotions like repugnance, disgust, the loathsome and their relationship to a balanced aspiration towards *nibbāna* and the craving for self-annihilation. There is an intricate pathway where these emotions get filtered down towards the more aggressive and destructive impulses of man, as well as the more purifying routes of equanimity. The debate as to, at what point, the stories of attempted suicide in the Pāli suttas, of those like Sīha, Sappadāsa, Vakkali, Godhika and Channa escaped the narrow ridges of eternalism and annihilationism, is an interesting conceptual issue.[17]

Suicide and the Three Forms of Craving

The five groups of clinging which constitutes man (consciousness,

15. Sn. V. 340.
16. M.III. 232-233.
17. Sīha, *Therīgāthā*, 77; Sappadāsa, *Theragāthā*, 408; Vakkali, S.III.118-124, *Theragāthā*, 350-54; Godhika, S.I.120; Channa M. III.264-267.

feeling, perception, dispositions and the body) constantly generate pressure for recognition as a self. This reckoning to be "I"and "self," while based on clinging is fed by the strong roots of craving. Craving has three forms, the craving for sensuous gratification (*kāma taṇhā*), the craving for egoistic pursuits (*bhava taṇhā*) and the craving for self-annihilation (*vibhava-taṇhā*). While sensual lust is a dominating impulse in human beings and may even provide, at an early stage the muddy waters which can complicate life for a potential suicide, it is the two other forms of craving which are more directly linked to the self notion. Especially when we examine suicides with religious motives, there are types who would visualize a state free of sensual pleasures and the "prison walls of the mutable body,"[18] and attempt suicide, for a possible mystic union with the eternal. Here it is *bhava taṇhā* that is operative, and it is stabilized by the dogma of eternalism and immortality.

If *bhava-taṇhā* is considered as the craving for being and *vibhava taṇhā* as the craving for non-being, it is purely at a very superficial level that they are opposites, as basically they are contrasting attitudes of a man bound to craving.[19] The ordinary worldling gets dissatisfied with what he considers as his 'self,' and looks for a cutting-off or destruction of a not-self, thinking that it is really the destruction of a self. Thus a basic ambiguity is perpetuated. Thus those who attempt to destroy the self are falsely assuming the existence of a self. Thus the annihilationist who "lay down the cutting off, destruction, the disappearance of the essential being" are merely "afraid of their body."[20] The situation a well presented in the form of a graphic simile, of a dog tied to a post by a leash: "Those worthy recluses and brahmans who lay down the cutting off (*ucchedaṃ*), the destruction (*vināsaṃ*) the disappearance of the essential being (*vibhavaṃ*), these afraid of their own body loathing their own body, simply keep running and circling round their own body, loathing their own body."[21] This is compared to a dog running around a post: "Just as a dog that is tied by a leash to a strong post or stake keeps

18. See R.G. de S. Wettimuny, *The Buddha's Teaching and the Ambiguity of Existence* (Colombo : M.D. Gunasena, 1978), p. 153.
19. For a discussion of these themes see Padmasiri de Silva, *Persons and Phantoms*, Gunapala Malalasekera Memorial Lecture (Kandy : Sithumina, 1976).
20. M.III.232-233.
21. Ibid.
22. Ibid.

running and circling round their own body."[22] Men usually "lean upon this duality"[23] of 'existence' and 'non-existence.' The person who is on the path of liberation should not fall a prey to this thicket of *existential ambiguity*. Both persons with annihilationist and eternalist tendencies fall into this thicket. Indeed the same person at different times may shift ground from one end of the pole to the other.

During recent times, the centrality of this basic existential ambiguity has been well emphasized by a few scholars.[24] Wettimuny who has been very much influenced by the venerable Ñāṇavīra[25] points to this existential thrust between the craving for being and non-being as a part of the very structure of our experience: "In this way, we find that in the structure of our experience both craving-for-'being' and craving-for-'unbeing' are present, though one may be more *manifest* than the other depending upon the *nature* of the 'being.'"[26] He also says that it is because the *puthujjana's* existence is based on a false self that the necessity for unbeing presents itself, and a deception must always lead to betrayal. Thus the pendulum swing from being to un-being and un-being to being, the existential ambiguity, accounts for the kind of ambivalence found in cases of attempted suicide.

Edwin Schneidman, one of the foremost suicidologists of recent times, says that the common internal attitude of those suicides known to him may be described as one of ambivalence. He says that though the dichotomous Aristotelian logic does not leave room for ambivalence, in the context of suicide there is a situation which is both A and non-A: "The prototypical suicidal state is one in which an individual cuts his throat and cries for help at the same time, and is genuine in both of these acts. This *non-Aristotelian accommodation to the psychological realities of mental life is called ambivalence*. It is the common internal attitude toward suicide: To feel that one has to do it and, simultaneously, to yearn (and even plan) for rescue and intervention."[27] As Schneidman points out since the writings of

---

23. For a pointed discussion of this duality and the way out, see Ñāṇānanda Thera, *Concept and Reality* (Kandy : B.P.S., 1971), pp. 76-80.
24. R.G. de S. Wettimuny, *The Buddha's Teaching and The Ambiguity of Existence.*
25. Ñāṇavīra Thera, *Clearing the Path* (Colombo : Path Press, 1987).
26. R.G. de S. Wettimuny, *The Buddha's Teaching and the Ambiguity of Existence*, p. 140.
27. Edwin Shneidman, *Definition of Suicide* (New York : John Willey, 1985), p. 135.

Freud came to be known the position that one could both love and hate at the same time and simultaneously could wish to die and entertain fantasies of rescue, came to be intelligible to people. What the Buddha sees behind this ambivalence is a more basic existential ambiguity, which attempts to relate our false sense of the self to the craving for being and non-being.

This existential ambiguity is manifested in the different types of polarities man experiences between pleasure and pain, love and hate, attachment and repulsion and they can be well seen in the attitude towards the body. That such contradictory attitudes like narcissistic self-love and self-hatred, feelings of ego inflation and depression, the desire to live and the desire for annihilation could all stem from an ego-illusion or a fictional sense of self was one of the greatest existential and psychological insights of the Buddha. According to this line of thought, a Buddhist who listens to the message of the Buddha, regarding the nature of suicide, could certainly respond with a great deal of depth to what another famous suicidologist says on the subject. Erwin Stengel, in his well known work, *Suicide and Attempted Suicide*, makes the following observation: "The interplay of life-preserving with life-destroying tendencies, or the love and hate, pervades not only relations to other people but also to the self."[28]

Suicide and the Attainment of Arhatship

I have quite deliberately kept a control over the discussion of suicide so far and kept within the rails. For it was necessary to present what I feel is the Buddhist contribution to the understanding of suicide first, only afterward delve into the controversial areas. In this section, I shall take up for discussion the issue about suicide and arhats, and then in the next section, the question of altrusitic suicides, including a brief reference to some socio-cultural variations.

The Buddha does make clear the reasons why suicide is not a solution to human problems. He also brings out reasons why it is not a technique of spiritual progress. I have discussed the most central of these arguments and then pointed out, what I feel is the Buddha's lasting existential insight on the issue. But there are some cases cited in the suttas which may be considered as exceptions to the rule or as cases which require contextual interpretation.

---

28. Erwin Stengel, *Suicide and Attempted Suicide* (Harmondsworth, Middlesex: Penguin Books, 1983), p. 129.

First, there is the case of the monk Channa who was in great pain and in spite of the fact that Sariputta protested and offered help, food and medicine, the monk Channa committed suicide. But Sariputta says that the monk Channa incurred no blame for this action, as interpreted by the Buddha, the monk "did not grasp after another body:" "But whoever, Sariputta, lays down this body and grasps after another body, of him I say he is to be blamed. The monk Channa did not do this; the monk Channa took the knife (to himself) without incurring blame."[29] In fact, the same point is emphasized in the *sutta, Ānañjasappāyasutta,* where it is said that grasping of any sort is an obstruction to the attainment of *nibbāna,* even grasping after equanimity.[30]

According to the analysis of suicide we have already made, suicide is an expression of craving and grasping. To use the language of Schopenhauer, suicide is a subtle expression of the will, or the most assertive manifestation of the will to live.[31] Thus at the purely conceptual level, the monk Channa's action has transcended and gone beyond this existential ambiguity. What appears to be of great interest in the case of monk Channa and a few other cases to be cited (Godhika, Vakkhali, and Sappadasa) is that, though there is an incipient suicidal impulse which is excited, it is tamed and transformed. Psychologically speaking, grasping of any sort (specially of body) is not present, and there is a sense of equanimity with which death or possible death is faced.

An interesting aside to the case of Channa is found in Puṇṇa's meeting of the Buddha, a context given in the *kindred Sayings,* just following the story of Channa.[32] First the Buddha advises Puṇṇa how one should deal with objects which excites passion and lust, for if one is not lured by them, not enamored by them, and does not cling to them, liberation from ill and suffering is possible. Then Puṇṇa's attention is drawn to the quelling of anger and hatred. After being instructed by the Buddha, Puṇṇa has plans to go and live in the district of Sunāparanta. Then the Buddha says that the people of that district are very fierce and they are bound to abuse and revile Puṇṇa. But

29. *Middle Length Sayings* III.266-67. Trans. I.B. Horner.
30. M.III.265.
31. For some interesting linkages between Schopenhauer and Freud as well as Buddha, see Padmasiri de Silva, *Buddhist and Freudian Psychology* (Colombo: Lake House, 1978).
32. M.III.267-270; S. IV.55-59.

Puṇṇa is prepared to meet this with kindness. Then they may throw clods of earth at him, beat him with a stick and lastly, slay him with a sword. Puṇṇa is prepared to face all this with kindness and about the possible fate of being slain by the people of Sunāparanta, Puṇṇa makes the following comments: "Then, lord, I shall think: 'There are disciples of that Exalted one who, when tormented by, ashamed of, disgusted with, body of life, have resort to stabbing themselves. Now I have come by a stabbing that I never sought.' That is how it will be with me, O Exalted One."[33]

The phrase "tormented by, ashamed of, disgusted with, body and life"[34] is a key phrase. In the *Itivuttaka* there is a reference to two types of views: the eternalist who 'sticks fast' to being and the annihilationist, afflicted by becoming, who goes to an excess and overshoots the mark (*atikhāvanti*).[35] Of the second group it is said, " ... some are afflicted by becoming humiliated thereby, and loathing becoming they take pleasure in not-becoming."[36] Wettimuny makes an interesting comment on the second kind of response. While the degree of repulsion (*paṭigha*) from being can vary from individual to individual, that state of dissatisfaction has a significance: "Now, this dissatisfaction and this looking for an escape from 'being,' by themselves are quite wholesome things. It is in fact the basis of all authenticity; and set in its proper perspective, could become a fruitful approach to the Buddha's teaching."[37] In fact as Wettimuny points out, the *sutta*s indicate an approach of this sort in the *Majjhima Nikāya*.[38] In the conversation that takes place between the Buddha and the wanderer Dīghanaka, three views are cited: (i) Everything pleases me; (ii) Everything does not please me; (iii) Some things pleases me, some things do not please me. Of the view that everything pleases me, it is said that it is close to passion, close to bondage, close to delight .... attachment and grasping. Of the view that nothing pleases me, it is said that it is close to dispassion, to unbinding, not delighting, to detachment and not-grasping.[39]

33. S.IV.60.
34. *Ibid.*,
35. It 43.
36. *Ibid.*,
37. R.G. de S. Wettimuny, *The Buddha's Teaching and the Ambiguity of Existence* p. 143.
38. M.I.497-501.
39. *Ibid.*, 498.

Now the materialist and the pleasure lover,[40] can entertain annihilationism, but here the aim is to drown himself in the pleasures of the senses. But in the one who is loathing becoming, even he may overshoot the mark, there is an authentic turning away, which has to be well directed. If this is so, the very few cases of suicide or attempted suicide of those who at the spur of the moment attained insight, may find some psychological and existential rationale.

This initial discontent is some thing of a philosophical type which has emerged graphically in works like Kierkegaard's depiction of the dissonance and the total breakdown of the aesthetic life.[41] When such discontent and dissonance emerges, a creative metamorphosis is possible, but it can also finds its Nero burning Rome.[42] It is exactly this insight which is articulated, when Ñāṇamoli remarks that "pain of nausea" provides the "backstairs to liberation." He makes a distinction between relative boredom and absolute boredom. The former refer to things like waiting for the railway connections, a long wait at a junction, a rashly accepted week-end with some dull acquaintances who have to be tolerated. Absolute boredom is different: "Absolute boredom is rather the pain of nausea, it is the loss of one's livelihood for the pianist who loses his hands... it is the Great Drought ... the Dark Night of the Soul ... Do not try to turn back now there —here in the desert perhaps there are doors open—in the cool woods they are overgrown, and in the busy cities they have built over them."[43]

"Disgust with the whole world," *sabba-loke anabhirati* is one of the basic notions necessary for the development of contemplative insight: impurity, death, loathing for food, and disgust with the world, as well as impermanence, suffering, renunciation, dispassion and the cessation of the thirst for life.

The meditation on disgust is like a razor's edge, and if not well directed, can lead individuals to "overshoot the mark." In a collection of *sutta* passages translated and edited by Ñāṇamoli Thera, there is good reference to the practitioners who were misled and they went beyond the limit: "They became horrified by their own bodies,

---

40. R.G. de S. Wettimuny, *The Buddha's Teaching and the Ambiguity of Existence.*
41. For a discussion of this Kierkegaardian philosophy in Buddhist perspective, see Padmasiri de Silva, *Tangles and Webs* (Colombo : Lake House Investments, 1976).
42. *Ibid.*,
43. Ñāṇamoli Thera, *A Thinker's Note Book* (Kandy : Nuwaraeliya Printers, 1971), p. 9.

humiliated and revolted by them. Just as a woman or man, young, youthful, fond of ornaments with head washed, would be horrified, humiliated and revolted at having hung round their neck the carcass of a snake ... so were those bhikkhus horrified, humiliated and revolted by their own bodies. And they both took their own lives and took each others' lives."[44] This message reaches the Buddha and he recommends an alternative discourse on the concentration on breathing: "This respiration-mindfulness concentration, bhikkhus, developed and repeatedly practiced, is both peaceful and sublime, unadulterated and of happy life; it causes to vanish at once and suppresses evil and unprofitable thoughts as soon as they arise.

Just as, bhikkhus, in the last month of the hot season, a great rain-cloud causes them to vanish at once and suppress them; so indeed, bhikkhus, respiration-mindfulness concentration, developed and repeatedly practiced, is both peaceful and sublime, unadulterated and of happy life; it causes to vanish at once and suppresses evil and unprofitable thoughts as soon as they arise."[45]

There is a point here that certain types of meditation suits a context and is suitable for a particular type of person. Meditation on the foul and disgust have to be worked on a kind of razor's edge, so that they are filtered through the way of equanimity than, aversion, hatred and revulsion. As Ñyānaponika Thera so clearly observes, "When insight is deepended and strengthened, what has been called "disgust" (in rendering the Pāli term *nibbidā*) has no longer the strong emotional tinge of aversion and revulsion, but manifests itself as a withdrawal, estrangement and turning away from worldliness and from the residue of one's own defilements."[46]

The king of 'disgust' conceptualized in terms of the word *nibbidā* is often translated as weariness, disgust with worldly life, tedium, disenchantment and even with aversion (though the term can be misleading). It is one of the preliminary and conditional states for the attainment of *nibbāna*.[47] The *Uraga Sutta* which has the image of the snake shedding its old skin, is some times used as a simile to describe the kind of 'disgust' conceptualized by the word *nibbidā*:

---

44. D.III.289-290.
45. Ñāṇamoli Thera, *Mindfulness of Breathing* (Kandy : Buddhist Publication Society, 1964.) p. 114.
46. *Ibid.*, p. 116.
47. See, Nyanaponika Thera, *The Worn-Out Skin* (Kandy : Buddhist Publication Society, 1977), p. 16.

> ... the snake feels *disgust* towards its old skin when the sloughing is not yet complete and parts of the old skin still adhere to its body. Similarly, the disgust felt towards residual attachments and defilements will give to the disciple an additional urgency in his struggle for final liberation. Such disgust is a symptom of his growing detachment.[48]

In the *Psalms of the Brethren* we get the story of Sappadāsa, who being overwhelmed by defilements could not get concentration and one pointedness of mind, and this distressed him so much, that he entertained thoughts of self-destruction, that an inward vision gradually expanded and led to the attainment of arahatship :

> ... And now the blade was drawn
> Across my throat to cut the artery...
> When lo in me arise the deeper thought :
> Attention to the fact and to the cause.
> The misery of it all was manifest;
> Distaste, indifference the mind possessed,
> And so my heart was set at liberty.[49]

Like the case of Channa and Sappadāsa to which we have referred to, there are a few more similar citations pertaining to Sīha, Cakkali, Godhika and Mahānāma. The stories are brief and in the case of Vakkali it appears in slightly different forms in two contexts.[50] As potential case studies the material found in the suttas is limited. All of them in general provide us with a *type of suicide* where suicidal impulses get transformed into dispassion and insight into the nature of reality is attained. What I have done in this paper is to describe and examine the psychological and existential background of the more "authentic type of disgust with the world." It is in the background of these reflections, that I may add, reading through the writings of Ñāṇavira Thera, letters and reflections, *Clearing the Path*, is a path that will take you through this narrow ridge which I have taken pains to describe.

When going through the book, I am sure that readers will have a variety of responses, for a work which appears to be very insightful and a little eccentric at the same time. The poignant story of a Buddhist monk who grappled with the thoughts of suicide, while

---

48. Ibid., p. 15.
49. *Psalms of the Brethren*, II, translated by Mrs. Rhys Davids (London: P.T.S.,1951), p. 214.
50. S.III.118-124; *Theragāthā* 349-354.

being so much intensely absorbed in the *dhamma*, naturally presents a great challenge: "I shall not stop here to discuss suicide in the light of the dhamma, except to remark that though it is never encouraged it is not the heinous offence it is some times popularly thought to be, and that the consequences of the act will vary according to circumstances—for the *puthujjana* they can be disastrous but for the *arahant* (the venerable Channa Thera...) they are nil."[51]

PART III

Altruistic Suicide

Emile Durkheim was the first to use the term "altruistic suicide" as a formal concept in the sociological studies of suicide, where he distinguished three types of suicide. First, egoistic suicide, which is the outcome of a lack of integration of the individual to society; second, altruistic suicide, occurs where the individual's life is rigorously governed by custom and habit. Of the latter, it is said, "it results from the individual's taking his own life because of higher commandments, either those of religious sacrifice of unthinking political allegiance."[52] Thirdly, there is anomic suicide, which results due to the lack of regulation of the individual by society, and they get isolated from society. Durkheim held that all societies have a collective tendency towards suicide, depending on its social structure. Today, there is a philosophical issue whether these sacrificial and altruistic suicides, deserve to be called 'suicides' as they are other-regarding than self-regarding.[53] Also today the notion of altruistic suicides have widened from the context in which Durkheim wrote. A typical example may be given from lifeboat ethical situations: suppose a lifeboat will not sustain the number of people who scramble aboard, and some must die in order that others live. A person of advanced years and questionable health, without the ability to swim, voluntarily jumps overboard, drowning immediately. A life has been sacrificed for the welfare of others. Some philosophers do not wish to use the term 'suicide' to describe the situation, as it is regarded as 'other-regarding' than 'self-regarding.'

---

51. Ñāṇavīra Thera, *Clearing the Path*, pp. 219-220.
52. Emile Durkheim, *Suicide* (Editor's Introduction), p. 15.
53. See Tom Regan, ed. *Matters of Life and Death* (New York: Random House), p. 85.

In general, moral dilemmas of this type did not emerge as a pressing issue during the time of the Buddha. I have discussed else where the possible Buddhist perspectives on moral dilemmas.[54] Briefly, ethics is merely a stage on the path to liberation and there is no need to build a kind of heroic ethics in to the system. Working for the welfare of others through compassion, certain types of self-sacrifice and risk taking for the benefit of others, fearlessness of facing the truth and kindred virtues take an important place in Buddhism. Risk to ones life in a certain situation or even accepting death may be understood and declared free of blemish and defilements according to the word of the Buddha, according to context. But the killing of one self for the sake of others is not some thing that the Buddha would build into the system. The work 'altruistic suicide' is a little jarring, as altruistic acts are good and risk taking is merely incidental, and a Buddhist may not convert altruistic suicide into a special creed. Secondly, apart for the Buddhist perspectives on ethical dilemmas, the word 'altruism' also have a unique usage in Buddhism. Firstly, Buddhism does not advocate self-denying altruism associated with suicide, asceticism and self-harm. Secondly, the opposition between egoism and altruism "gets defused" due to the Buddhist analysis of the self.[55] Both of these points have been discussed by scholars. The point has been well described by Steven Collins: "... the rationale for action which acceptance of Buddhism furnishes provide neither for simple self-interest nor for self-denying altruism. The attitude to all 'individualities,' whether past and future 'selves,' past, future, or contemporary 'others' is the same loving-kindness, compassion, sympathetic joy, and equanimity....Buddhism conceives as part of (the qualitative notion of personal identity) a version of rational action which includes necessarily the dimension of altruism."[56]

The action of the Buddhist monks in Vietnam who set fire on themselves to protest against war, even if it defies the descriptions of suicides, may be hard to justify on Buddhist grounds. Even if this is

---

54. See Padmasiri de Silva *Tangles and Webs* (Colombo : Lake House Investments, 1976), pp. 30-45; Padmasiri de Silva, "The Logic of Identity Profiles and the Ethics of Communal Violence: A Buddhist Perspective," in K.M. de Silva ed. *Ethnic Conflict in Buddhist Societies* (London: Pinter Publishers, 1988).
55. See Roy W. Perett, "Egoism, Altruism and Intentionalism is Buddhist Ethics," *Journal of Indian Philosophy* 15 (1987): 71-85.
56. Steven Collins, *Selfless Persons* (Cambridge : Cambridge University Press, 1982), pp 193-194. This citation is well used by Roy Perret in his discussion of altruism.

raised to an ideal state of symbolic act, done with equanimity, does the context bear that description? Basically, one has to be extremely careful in trying to find Buddhist grounds for altruistic suicide.

Buddhism was the philosophy of the middle path in many senses. That is why the Buddha condemned the deliberate infliction of pain on one self as unprofitable.[57] Thus acts of self-sacrifice have to be judged in their own context without converting self-denying altruism into a special creed. To use the terminology of J.C. Flugel, religions which have health and vitality will walk the middle way between narcissism and nemesissism, the narrow ridge between eternalism and annihilationism.

Suicide may have different cultural varieties and ritual expressions as Durkheim pointed out, but the Buddhist focus on suicide is basically from its orientation of the liberation from suffering (*dukkha*). It is because Buddhism is a middle path that as a general philosophy of life and as a way of liberation from suffering suicide is not accepted as a worthy way of responding to the problems of life. As a way of liberation from suffering, the difficult problem emerges, as the struggle for liberation, and the 'disgust' with the world, may not always be blended with dispassion and equanimity. The passion for liberation may get filtered down into an extreme position, of "overshooting the mark." But this overshooting, of it is an authentic turn of mind, may yet have the potential for transformation, dispassion, equanimity and insight. Perhaps our struggle to understand the suicide of the monk Channa and the writings of the Ñāṇavīra Thera point out, that though the practicing Buddhist is well equipped with a good critique of eternalism, he needs a more subtle and complex critique of annihilationism. It was one of our central concerns in this paper to emphasize this point in relation to the problem of suicide.

---

57. M.I.393-396.

7

The Logical Grammar of the Word 'Rebirth' in the Buddhist Paradigm: A Philosophical Sketch

A. D. P. Kalansuriya

> "The human gaze has a power of conferring value on things but it makes things cost more also."
> Ludwig Wittgenstein, *Culture & Value*

I. Introduction

That statements we make in respect of us and the world in which we live appear to be categorized broadly into two: (i) the empirical and (ii) the ethical. All empirical statements, without exception, firstly, are either true or false; and secondly, bring forth knowledge. Ayer highlights the point: "I conclude then that the necessary and sufficient conditions for knowing that something is the case are first that what one is said to know be true, secondly that one be sure of it, and thirdly that one should have the right to be sure."[1] However, ethical statements are neither true nor false factually although the words 'true' or 'truth' or 'Truth' are often ascribed to them. A word about Buddhism is appropriate at this juncture, i.e. the word 'rebirth' has determinate use only within a given paradigm. Paradigms are closed systems of interpretation which have their own inner logic, form of life and form of coherence. What makes sense in one paradigm fails to make sense in another. This implies that there is systematic ambiguity between different ontological paradigms. Let us provisionally say just this much in advance, that the word 'rebirth' in the Buddhist paradigm is ethical and therefore all statements involving it within this closed system (paradigm) are also ethical in nature. Strangely, we tend to

1. A.J. Ayer, *The Problem of Knowledge* (London: Pelican, 1957), p. 35.

forget that these ethical statements are simply value-judgments or value-statements. This is a costly mistake. Besides, categories (i) and (ii) above, cannot be intermixed or intermingled to bring about an alternative category. For clear thinking, this is important. If one fails to understand this point, as Wittgenstein notes, "a wrong pursuit" results.[2]

As regards the word 'rebirth' in the *Buddha-dhamma*, there were some kind of wrong pursuits which led the Buddhist scholars and commentators into a blind-alley. That is to say, various Buddhist scholars and commentators, have attempted to find factual evidence to substantiate conclusively and definitively, a kind of life after death or a kind of life before birth or both.[3] Yet, to date, there was no conclusive proof or definitive substantiation. Why is this the case? Are we not intelligent enough to find conclusive evidence? Alternatively, are we misled into thinking that evidential data could be found, one day, to prove rebirth as a fact?

It is clear that the issue about the Buddhist life after death or life before birth is not an empirical one, and that therefore,the issue of truth or falsity in this context is inappropriate. But often we refuse to accede to this point. Very generally speaking, man has the impulse to run up against the limits of language. Wittgenstein rightly notes the point that misunderstandings concerning the use of words are caused, among other things, by certain analogies, between the forms of expression in different regions of language.[4] Again humans perpetually want to say what cannot be said. This "running-up-against" becomes manifest in amazement. This is an approach which creates great difficulty. All the more so, because it "craves for a solution."[5] Besides, there is no genuine problem as such to solve. The human gaze has a power of conferring value on things (us and the world), but, as Wittgenstein notes, "it makes them cost more also."[6] Our amazement tends to regard all problems as genuine which results

---

2. L. Wittgenstein, *Philosophical Investigations* (Oxford: Basil Blackwell, 1953), p. 43. (See also: Bertrand Russell, *A History of Western Philosophy* (London: Allen and Unwin, 1947), p. 863: "Philosophy throughout its history, has consisted of two parts inharmoniously blended: on the one hand a theory as to the nature of the world, on the other an ethical or political doctrine as to the best way of living."
3. See K.N. Jayatilleke, *Early Buddhist Theory of Knowledge* (London: Allen and Unwin Ltd., 1963).
4. I. Waismann, *Wittgenstein und der Wiener Kreis* ed, B. McGuinness (Oxford: Basil Blackwell, 1967), p. 68.
5. L. Wittgenstein, *The Blue and Brown Books* (Oxford: Basil Blackwell, 1958) p. 18.
6. L. Wittgenstein, *Culture and Value* (Oxford: Basil Blackwell, 1980).

in sending us to sleep again. We are held captive, driven into empty perplexity (Wittgenstein's term is 'metaphysical perplexity') by this amazement. Together with this amazement, the human gaze (as mentioned earlier) has a power of conferring value on things. But we must have determination, vision and courage to distinguish between

(a) things, and
(b) values which we bestow on things.

This means we are now engaged in philosophical activity leading to an ontological analysis to determine a particular paradigm — a given interpretation. That is to say, an exegesis of the *logical grammar* of the word 'rebirth' (*punabbhava*) as appears in the Buddha's *dhamma*-message. In order to facilitate it, some philosophical techniques — Wittgenstein's philosophical techniques — are used here. The key thing is striving after is clarity, order and perspicuity[7]. For they are certainly missing in traditional talks on Buddhist doctrine in which the word 'rebirth' occurs. No solutions by way of substantiation are to be first striven for, but only perspicuity. To put the point yet more explicitly, the *first step* is to *understand the logical nature of statements* involving (a) things, and (b) value. The next step is to *accommodate the word 'rebirth'* in the *Buddha-dhamma* to one of them (a) or (b) of the above, depending on the logical nature of it, and, certainly, not according to our choice. It must be remembered, however, that we are not in search on a solution to a problem for there is no such genuine problem.[8] That is a reallocation of the word 'rebirth' within the language-game in which it has *meaning* and *life*.

II. The Logical grammar of the word 'rebirth'

In the *Dīgha Nikāya* the Buddha expresses the view that when one's mind is concentrated, cleansed, steady and unperturbed — necessarily by the diligent adherence to the Noble Eightfold Path — that retrocognitive knowledge of the past existences is possible. That is, it sounds as if it is a high feat of mental unfolding accomplished by way of one and only one path — (*ariyaṭṭhaṅgikamagga*).[9] The logical grammar of the word 'rebirth' here therefore falls within the precinct of Buddhist language-game which nucleus is but an ethical code —

7. L. Wittgenstein, *Zettel* (Oxford: Basil Blackwell, 1969), section 464.
8. L. Wittgenstein, *Philosophical Remarks* (Oxford: Basil Blackwell, 1975), section 9.
9. D. I. 81. 82.

a procedural guide — *ariyaṭṭhaṅgikamagga*. What makes sense in this paradigm fails to make sense in another paradigm; they are different paradigms coming with very different 'language games.' A specific moral code is implicitly contained in the *ariyaṭṭhaṅgikamagga* which recommends a definitive path leading to the sublime end, but not a probable end or an empirical end.[10] The criteria of truth or falsity applied regarding empirical statements concerning us and the world, are, therefore, out of place pertaining to statements involving the Buddhist word 'rebirth.' All the more so because the statements are value-oriented and not fact oriented. A fact-finding mission in this regard, hence amounts to a wrong-pursuit.

Often amongst Buddhist scholars, a kind of wrong-pursuit is evident. All the more so because of their involvement with the philosophical problem raised as to whether an identity of a person is possible by way of such criteria as spatio-temporality, memory or both. So long as the criteria are clearly debated, the issue is philosophical; but to pass it down to a discourse on Buddhistic rebirth notion makes no sense solely because what is said within the inner logic is the key note in the message rather than what is *meant*. Why is this the case? Because the definitive path and the sublime end are both nonempirical (meaning: ethical) and, as such, it is logically impossible that they are false in any sense. Nowhere do the Canonical texts note any falsity pertaining to the path (*magga*) as well as the end (*nibbāna*). Implicitly contained herein are (a) necessity (*avitathata*), (b) invariably (*anaññathā*) on the one hand;[12] on the other eternally (*sanantana*) certainty and sacrosanctity. If so, the word 'rebirth' contained herein cannot be empirical. Firstly, it is one of the key *ethical* words in the Buddhist conceptual family. Secondly, therefore, this word cannot be uprooted from its conceptual family without making it empty or meaningless. Needless to say that the word 'rebirth' in the *Buddha-dhamma* falls outside the scope of factual evidence.

III. Several usages (non-Buddhistic)

The word 'rebirth,' characteristically, has several usages. What makes sense in one usage fails to make sense in another. That is, different paradigms do not share common meanings of a given word in this

10. M. II. 213.
11. A. III. 35.
12. S. II. 26.

case. Let us pause a while to note a few usages other than the one in the Buddhist paradigm. They are as follows: (i) a usage of such philosophers as Pythagoras, Plato, etc. (ii) a recent usage which is made popular by Ian Stevenson, Gina Cerminara, H.H. Price, C.D. Broad and others; (iii) several mythical and figurative usages in Greek mythology, Hindu mythology, *etc.* (iv) a usage amongst science-fiction writers, etc.

Although the Buddhist usage of the word 'rebirth' is very clear within the logical boundary of the *dhamma*-discourse, unfortunately, Buddhist scholars and thinkers have misconceived its native home, being misled by superficial similarities and analogies. They have bumped up against the limits of the Buddha's exclusive use of this word. The inevitable result being their reflections getting to a whirl-pool, an infinite regress. They say what they like. It takes them no further. Amongst several examples, we suppose the following one would suffice: The veteran Buddhist scholar K.N. Jayatilleke says: "The elite seems to have had an open-minded attitude on the subject and when the Buddhists did accept the theories of rebirth and kamma, they seem to have done so on the ground that their truth was verifiable."[13] But, then, the ethics-oriented 'rebirth' in the Buddhistic paradigm is one which cannot be verified in sense-experience. And, therefore, very generally, such contemporary Buddhist scholars as Jayatilleke have sent the word 'rebirth' on holiday. Accordingly, a pervasive emptiness occurs — not philosophical reflections.

Language, for instance, is not only a labyrinth of paths but also sets everyone the same traps.[14] Characteristically, it is an immense network of easily accessible wrong turnings. Buddhist scholars like Jayatilleke have failed to erect sign posts at all the junctions where there are possible wrong turnings so as to help people past the danger points.[15] The misuse they create is more wrong-headed and half-baked. No wonder Buddhist philosophers find it difficult to know their way about. "Wittgenstein's not" is appropriate: "You approach from one side and know your way about; you approach the same place from another side, and no longer know your way about."[16]

13. K.N. Jayatilleke, *Early Buddhist Theory of Knowledge*, p. 376.
14. L. Wittgenstein, *Philosophical Investigations*, p. 82.
15. *Ibid.*, p. 52e. ("The confusions which occupy us arise when language is like an engine idling, not when it is doing work").
16. *Ibid.*, p. 82e.

If the Buddha's paradigm is understood, the word 'rebirth' in his message does not cause any problem.[17] The reason is that it has a native home. One has to understand it within the native home — the *dhamma* itself — wherein lies its natural use. Characteristically, the Buddha notes: "... there arose in me the knowledge and insight that my emancipation is unshakable, that this is the last birth and that there is no further birth ("*ayaṃ antimā jāti natthi dāni punabbhavo*"). Accordingly, the Buddhist 'rebirth' has its native home embedded in the conceptual structure (logical grammar according to Wittgenstein) of Buddha *dhamma*. It is an ethics-based, ethics-oriented procedural guide with a definitive and an unconditional end, namely, *nibbāna*.[18] If so, no amount of empirical data (evidential data) going to prove or disprove it simply because it is outside the scope of facts. That is to say, it is ethical in nature. To say this is to elucidate the logical grammar of the word 'rebirth' together with its very clear logical place in the Buddhist paradigm.

Failure to conceive its paradigm and the logical place — native home — in the *Buddha-dhamma* disappoints hopes of intuiting its limits. No sooner is it grasped as to its logical place in the *dhamma* than the limited use of it or the paradigm is grasped also. Wittgenstein notes this kind of grasp as characteristically representing a battle against the bewitchment of our intelligence by means of language.[19] This battle has to be won. If not, language keeps tempting us into asking the same basically empty questions. One finds ones' self overloaded with these questions. And what is more, this satisfies a longing for the 'beyond,' because insofar as people think they can see the limits of human understanding, they believe that they can see beyond these. This is a case in which language has trapped oneself or language has misled oneself. One has to overcome this bewitchment, if one yearns for clarity in expression. The only way for us to guard our assertions and statements against distortion is to have a clear view in our reflections as to what a criterion is namely, a yardstick or a criterion in a given paradigm, paradigms being closed systems of interpretation which have their own inner logic, form of life and form of coherence.

---

17. M. I. 69; see also: S. II. 217, 222.
18. A. II. 34.
19. L. Wittgenstein, *Philosophical Investigations*, p. 47e.

IV. Conclusion

In summing up, in the introduction we noted two kinds of category, namely, (i) the empirical and (ii) the ethical. Now we have to take a decision as to the logical nature of the statements involving the Buddhistic use of the word 'rebirth' to limit it to one of the categories noted above. Our philosophical sketch by way of Wittgenstein' techniques makes explicit the view that the word 'rebirth' in the Buddha's ontology takes an exclusive ethical use. That is, the logical grammar of it within the Buddha's paradigm is such that empirical criteria remain logically inappropriate. Admittedly, there is nothing to be proved or disproved as its native home is the Buddhist conceptual structure (grammar) itself which is but ethics-oriented and not empiricism-oriented.[20] Moreover, the Buddhist truths are definitive, unconditional and eternal (*sanantana*).[21] If so, not only empirical criteria of truth and falsity but also evidential data are logically inappropriate in respect of the word 'rebirth' in the *Buddha-dhamma*.[22] I conclude this philosophical sketch by an appropriate statement from Frank Hoffman: "... the fact that what early Buddhism does or might consistently say about the problem of the meaning of 'the same person' across lives amounts to nought is understandable in terms of the texts treating 'there is rebirth' as part of the conceptual background of early Buddhism."[23]

20. Kalansuriya, "On the Notion of Verification in Buddhism and in Logical Positivism, "*Buddhist Western Philosophy* ed. Nathan Katz (Sterling Publishers, 1981), pp. 287-305.
21. A.D.P. Kalansuriya, *A Philosophical Analysis of Buddhist Notions: The Buddha & Wittgenstein* (Delhi: Sri Satguru Publications, 1987), pp. 34-60.
22. See also: Gottfried Rothermundt, *Buddhismus Fur Die Moderne Welt* (Stuttgart, Germany, 1979), pp. 33-37.
23. Frank J. Hoffman, *Rationality and Mind in Early Buddhism* (New Delhi: Motilal Banarasidas, 1987), p. 76.

8
A Buddhist Critique of Theravāda

GUNAPALA DHARMASIRI

Not only out of all the religions of the world, but also out of all the sects of Buddhism, Theravāda can be said to have preserved the most important and crucial message of the Buddha. This message is contained in the *Kālāma Sutta*[1] and it emphasizes that one should be totally critical of all forms of authority. The extraordinary significance of this message should not be undervalued, because it is this message that makes the Buddha an absolutely unique religious teacher in the history of mankind. With regard to this point, the Buddha prominently stands in opposition to all the religious teachers that have appeared on this earth. Because all the other religions are based on the authority of the leaders of those faiths. In every religion, the greatest possible sin is to challenge the leader or the Guru. The Buddha is the only religious leader who encouraged challenging his own authority. The Buddha advises that "an inquiring monk, who cannot read the thoughts of another, should examine the Tathāgata to determine whether he is enlightened or not... the Tathāgata is to be examined in respect of two things, mainly of what can be learned by observation and by inquiring about him...," and one should observe that he does not have nor is reputed to have morally corrupt or mixed modes of conduct but only virtuous conduct. This observation should be done for a long period, not for a short period.[2] This is a result of his unlimited compassion for all beings. He truly wanted to show that the Buddha was not a unique human being, or a unique gift to humanity by God, or by any other supernatural power, and that

1. A.I. 189.
2. M.I. 317.

every human being was able to attain the complete Buddhahood. Buddhism is the only religion where the possibility of going beyond its religious leader or the Buddha, is possible:[3]

> The most sublime feature of the Buddha's message is its absolutely anti-authoritarian attitude. The Buddha respects the intrinsic value and integrity of each and every being, or in other words, the potential omnipotence, omniscience (in the sense of total enlightenment) and benevolence of each and every being. In the ultimate sense, no being is intrinsically superior to another in any sense. Everyone is completely capable of attaining the ultimate supreme perfection exactly as the Buddha did. 'Everyone is a potential Buddha, not different from the original Buddha in any way.'
>
> Most religions, particularly all theistic religions, have followers. The Buddha explicitly and consciously emphasized the fact that no one should follow him, or for that matter, any one else. I think humanity should be grateful to the Buddha for showing this very simple, but profound truth about ourselves. He left the door open to go beyond the Buddha himself. Here it is interesting to note that, although one can go beyond the Buddha, in another sense one cannot, because the Buddha has posited forever the principle of ultimate spiritual (religious) freedom.
>
> In that sense, all religions that follow a religious leader would be seen by the Buddha as slave religions. It is exactly the same situation in authoritarian systems of thinking like Marxism, etc, too. By their dogma they block the whole possibility of the further progress of the human spirit and thought, and we should be constantly aware of this menacing threat to the further evolution of the human psyche. If capitalism exploits man's body, followers' religions and thought systems could be said to be exploiting man's brain or mind.

However, it is unsettling to see that the Theravāda is settling down to be a religion of followers. The Buddha has been transformed into A Great Wise Man (Sinhalese, *Mahadenamuttā*), because no one is traditionally allowed to utter a statement about religiosity without

3. Gunapala Dharmasiri, *A Buddhist Critique of the Christian Concept of God*, (California: Golden Leaves, 1988), pp. 267-8.

referring to the Great Book of the *Tripitaka*. The real tragedy of the contemporary Theravāda, is that the spirit of the teachings of the Buddha has been contradicted by giving prominence to the 'authority of tradition' over the teachings of the Buddha.

But as heirs to the teachings of the Theravāda, we must be aware that Buddhists have the privilege to challenge or criticize their own religion or tradition. In the *Kālāma Sutta*, the Buddha advises that one should not accept any teachings "out of respect for the Teacher, thinking that he is our Guru" (*samano no garu*). No other religion has given this permission to its followers. The Buddha has not only given this permission, but he has also positively encouraged his followers to do so. One becomes a true follower of the Buddha only by not following him blindly. Therefore, as Theravāda Buddhists it is our religious duty to look at and critically examine our own tradition. It is time that we do this because this tradition in its other details seems to be posing some significant problems in our present times. Actually, this type of self-analysis and self-examination is necessary if we want to sustain the spirit of any thought system. We need a permanent (a perpetual) revolution. This is the large scale social parallel of the *Uposathakamma*, which, according to Gokuldas De,[4] was the major factor that kept the community or *Saṅgha* strong for so many centuries.

The reader should be cautioned about some of the sweeping generalizations I make in this paper. We know it is difficult and wrong to make generalizations about human beings. Because all beings have the *Buddha-bīja* or the seed of the Buddhahood within themselves, true religiosity can exist in any social context. Any religion could supply clues to spark off this *Buddha-bīja*.

To clarify a methodology used here: I will be making a distinction between the theory, and practice (of tradition) of Theravāda, Mahāyāna and Tantra. I will be trying to show that very often the tradition contradicts the theory and therefore the tradition has to be critiqued and rehabilitated in terms of the theory. However, when I say that, I do not assert a dogmatic fundamentalist position because this can easily lead to a theoretical dogma. What is important is the spirit of the theory as based on a humane context.

In many ways the Theravāda has been going against the basic teachings of the Buddha. In the Theravāda tradition, the attainment of *nirvāṇa* is always postponed until the advent of the next Buddha. Until then we are encouraged to live as many 'happy' births as

---

4. Gokuldas De, *Democracy in Early Buddhist Sangha*, (Calcutta: Calcutta University Press, 1955), p. 62.

possible in heavens and human worlds as 'very rich people.' That is how the wish-formula (Sin. *Pin Vākya* "statement of merit") of the Theravāda tradition goes. And this is clearly going against the basic Theravāda teaching in the "Discourse on the Establishment of Awareness" (*Satipaṭṭhāna Sutta*) where it says that one can attain *nirvāṇā* in 7 days. Teaching people to beg it from another person like a future Buddha is clearly going against the rationalist approach advocated by the Theravāda teachings; it makes the attainment of *nirvāṇa* (based on *faith*) futuristically oriented.

The widespread view taught by the Theravāda tradition that *nirvāṇa* is unobtainable in the present age, is a highly immoral view in two very important senses. One is that it is factually wrong and therefore misleading. The concept of time does not at all enter the context of realizing *nirvāṇa,* because time is only a derivative of consciousness or mind. *Nirvāṇa* means the rejection of that very mind, by seeing its utter illusoriness. The second reason why that Theravāda view is immoral is that it covertly relished *saṃsāra* and thereby encourages people to do so, as is clearly evident in the *Pin Vākya*: 'After enjoying all the luxuries in heavenly worlds and human worlds for long ages, may I meet the Buddha Maitreya and realize *nirvāṇa'.* This is actually a preaching of the wish of the worldling in the name of the *dhamma.* This is partly a denigration of oneself, and going totally against the true spirit of the teachings of the Buddha. *Nirvāṇa* has no relationship to time at all (*akālika*), and it is something to be realized by the wise through experience (*paccattaṃ veditabbo viññūhi*). Because of its very narrow conception of *nirvāṇa,* Theravāda has to go back nearly two thousand years to find the last *arahant,* Maliyadeva.

An allied belief widely held by the Theravāda tradition is that one has to become a monk if one is to be completely capable of realizing *nirvāṇa.* Their theory goes as follows: "*Nirvāṇic* experience can be contained only in the body of a monk, just as the lion's oil can be contained only in a golden vessel. If a layman realizes the experience of *nirvāṇa,* then he will necessarily have to die within 7 days." This view is clearly contradicted by the Buddha's teachings and example. During the time of the Buddha himself there were many laymen, like Tapassu, Bhallika, Anātha piṇḍika, etc., who had fully realized *nirvāṇa.* Twenty one such persons are mentioned explicitly by name in the *suttas.*[5] The Buddha has never mentioned anything close to this theory, while he has fully accepted the

5. A.III. 148-9. Also, Lal Mani Joshi, *Discerning the Buddha* (Delhi : Munshiram Manoharlal, 1983), p. 22.

possibility of laymen attaining the state of *paccekabuddha*. Therefore, this theory of the Theravada tradition looks more like a political view propounded by the *theras* to keep and buttress their privileged position.

Another serious problem with the Theravāda tradition is its highly patriarchal attitude. Actually, the Theravāda cannot be accused of it directly, because Theravāda being a part of a patriarchal society, there is a social inevitability about it. But this issue has become a major social problem in the contemporary society and the Theravāda can no longer be oblivious to it because glaring social inequities. A religion has to be extra-sensitive to these issues because it is the religion that teaches morality. The problem at issue is exemplified by the Theravāda attitude towards the higher ordination of women (*bhikkhunīs*). Why does the Theravāda tradition try to deny this opportunity to women? They maintain that this cannot be done because the line of succession is not available in Theravāda countries. But the Mahāyāna *Bhikkhunī Sāsana* is available in Korea. Actually this *Sāsana*'s higher ordination was eventually taken to Korea from Sri Lanka, making it all the more a reason. Therefore, the line of succession is clearly there, without any ambiguity.

However, the important point is that, what does Theravāda regard as more important: tradition, or the real suffering, as implied by the request to have higher ordination, of their own mothers ? As explained in the *Metta Sutta,* the epitome of compassion is the mother's love towards her child. If this love is not reciprocated by the sons, a moral imbalance results, and it should be regarded as a heinous crime. Actually if we eliminate our mothers, it will be quite similar to a *Pancanatariya Kamma* because practically it amounts to a kind of spiritual murder: the denial of the spiritual success to the mothers is similar to a mother's denial to feed her child. The important thing for the Theravādins is to question themselves as to why they are finding excuses to deny the most socially significant spiritual request of their own mothers? Does this show a significant moral insensitivity in Theravāda? This is a profound question to ponder upon, in the contemporary context of violence in Sri Lanka.

On the other hand, if we cannot satisfy our mothers' deep requests through it, what is the use of such a religion ? On the other hand, the Buddha has unequivocally stated that women are fully capable of attaining enlightenment. Interestingly enough, the paradigmatic example the Buddha has taken to illustrate the highest possible compassion is the mother's love. Therefore, the Buddhist moral ideal is a matriarchal one. It is important to note that in the general Buddhist tradition, the mother (not the father) is regarded as "the Buddha at home". This idea got explicitly crystalized in Mahāyāna where the absolute reality or the Perfect Wisdom is regarded definitely as feminine as is symbolized by the Goddess *Prajñāpāramitā*. So, does this mean that the Theravāda is insulting the Buddha ?

Does Theravāda regard tradition as more important than a unique moral obligation ? The basic epistemological teaching of the Buddha is not to follow anything as based on "the lines of succession or the tradition of scriptures" (*paraṃparā, piṭakasampadā*). So, this is another instance where Theravāda clearly contradicts the teachings of the Buddha.

An important point to meditate upon is whether there is a relationship between Theravāda and evil. This is clearly seen in the sanctification of the caste system in the Sri Lankan Theravāda order or *Saṅgha*. This shows another instance of moral insensitivity. Before one becomes a Buddhist one has to become a human. Acceptance of the caste system degrades oneself as a member of the human society. When it is seen in the *Saṅgha* it becomes much more than accepted. Actually it becomes sanctified. The Buddha emphasized that the caste system was the most basic and fundamental form of social evil and he fought a sustained social battle, both theoretically as well as practically, against it. Those who believe in the superiority of the high caste should not forget that the Buddha himself did not come from the high caste: the Brahmins, and he often ridiculed at the conception of the high caste. If the caste consciousness has entered into the very soul of the Theravāda, *i.e.* the *Saṅgha*, thus giving it a feudal social structure, then Theravāda has to seriously re-think its own social tradition. That is the strongest social disgrace that Theravāda can do to the Buddha and Buddhism. Many Westerners have pointed this out as the basic evil of the central Theravāda institution.

The most fundamental contradiction in Theravāda is that it has compromised with *saṃsāra*. As the *Pin Vākya* amply illustrates, the immediate goal of the Theravādin is to accumulate as much merit or *pin* as possible. There is a big difference between *pin* (P. *puñña*) and *kusala*. "Although *akusala* and *pāpa* are translated as 'bad' and *kusala* and *puñña* as good and are also often used as synonymous pairs in the Buddhist texts, there are very important subtle differences to be noted among these concepts... the specific Buddhist word used for good is *kusala* which means 'efficient' or 'capable', that is, what is good is what is efficient (or capable of) leading towards *nirvāṇa*. *akusala* is its opposite. *Puñña* is a term common to Hinduism and means merit, and an action that generates *puñña* is called a *puñña kamma*. Here the emphasis is on merit making. Merit making actions have been treated by the Buddha as inferior kinds of moral actions because accumulation of merits can hinder one's spiritual salvation by leading one to births that involve long periods of existence, like those of the *Devas* and *Brahmas*. Therefore, in a sense, a *puñña kamma* could be an *akusala kamma*. Kusala and *akusala kammas* are performed only by persons who have entered into the spiritual path. When an ignorant person kills an animal he is doing a *pāpa kamma*, not an *akusala kamma*, and is consequently accruing *pāpa*. If someone practices charity with a wish to be born in heaven, he is accumulating *Puñña*. One cannot accumulate *kusala*, rather it makes one capable of realizing *nirvāṇa*."[6]

The fact that Theravāda has compromised with *saṃsāra* is highlighted by the absence of a 'practical' tradition of meditation in Theravāda. Monks specialize only on rituals, and preaching the *dhamma* which can again get easily ritualized. Meditation has entered the general Theravāda society only recently, thanks to the tourist industry. Consequently, meditation is functioning more as an industry, either as a drug industry to cure hypertension, or as an industry that earns foreign exchange.

Meditation is, of course, part of the Theravāda tradition, but it is mostly practiced more as another ritual, or a routine drill. There is no practical tradition of meditation in Theravāda as, for example, in Zen Buddhism, where the whole life is permeated with a philosophy of meditation. Meditation becomes proper practice only when it is practiced within the context of proper knowledge and morality. Meditation is a double-edged sword. It can either cut the relationship to *saṃsāra* or the relationship to *nirvāṇa*. Because, meditation can either destroy the ego or it can subtly inflate the ego. One may 'concentrate' on the ego thereby subtly inflating it. Also, if the idea of belonging to an elite or the selected few enters into the meditator's head, that also will lead towards this same direction of ego-inflation and that will lead to deviation from the knowledge or wisdom

6. Gunapala Dharmasiri, *Fundamentals of Buddhist Ethics* (California : Golden Leaves, 1989), p. 24-25.

context. In some meditation centers or concentrations camps, a practice often reserved for locals, is to confer degrees of *Sotāpanna Anāgāmi* in diplomatic confidentiality.

However, the claim of the Theravādin is that the tradition of meditation has been practiced by the forest monks. But what really goes on there is a big mystery. In religions very often mystical criteria are used for deciding sainthood. This is obviously a dangerous criterion simply because it is mysterious. In such a context, a criminal can easily pose as a saint, as it often happened in mystical traditions. Unfortunately, the *arahant* ideal sanctifies this mystery. So, in this context what we need are Bodhisattva criteria.

This, of course, does not mean that genuine meditation, Buddhist or otherwise, is not happening in Sri Lanka. Because every being is a potential Buddha, this can happen in any context of beings. By the same argument, it follows that not everybody here is doing only *pin* (or merit-making activities).

The *arahant* ideal raises some problems which are particularly pertinent to the contemporary social context where intimate interrelationships between the person and the society have come to the forefront of human thinking. It raises the issue whether it is moral to pursue personal salvation exclusively from the society at large. The doctrine of inter-dependence rules out the possibility of a separate person or soul, because nothing can be independent in a world where everything is inter-related to everything else. I cannot think of myself as separate from the rest of the universe. For example, my body is dependent on food which means that my body is dependent on plants, animals, water, oxygen, *etc.* And my growth and existence is inextricably bound up with the rest of the society. A Buddhist's altruistic commitment to others originates from this dependency. Because my existence is dependent on the rest of the universe I owe naturally a debt and an obligation to the rest of the universe. One has to understand that one is a part of a larger whole, and is not a separate person. That is why the ordinary unenlightened man is, in Buddhist terminology, called *puthujjana'* (*puthu* = separate; *jana* = people), or a person who believes that he is separate; *jana* = people, or a person who believes that he is separate. Does this raise the issue whether the *arahant* is a *puthujjana*?

Though many tend to think that the theory of self (*atta*) could be the best foundation for morality, actually the true basis of morality is *anatta* (no-self). It is because of *anatta* that we have to be moral. As we are so obviously interconnected to every thing and every being, how moral, particularly in the Buddhist context, is it to conceive of one's own separate salvation? As the concept of the Arahant forms the ideological foundation of the Theravāda, one could imagine the possible disastrous implications the former can exert on the latter.

In the introduction to the *Jātaka Book,* discussing the decision of the Sumedha ascetic to reject personal liberation for the attainment of the Buddhahood, the idea of personal salvation is looked down upon as follows:

> "It is similar to eating an extremely tasty food in a dark room when beings suffering from intense starvation for a long time, are looking on. It is similar to a mother drinking ambrosia when the children suffering from thirst and hunger are looking on. It is similar to parents running away alone escaping a fire when the children are screaming caught in the fire. Therefore, it is useless going to Nirvana alone and in secrecy."[7]

The Bodhisattva concept signifies the idea of sacrificing one's life for the sake of all beings. Therefore, what is needed is an intense and intelligent aliveness to the problems of the contemporary society and genuine commitment to ameliorate them as much as possible. It is the social relevance that makes a religion meaningful and justified in the society. Otherwise, the society forgets it as irrelevant as it has happened to the Theravāda today. In a religionless society, anything can happen because everything is permitted.

And also, the *arahant* is a *śrāvaka*, 'a follower' of the Buddha. Therefore, the Arahant ideal is not consistent with the basic ideal of the Buddha as portrayed in the *Kālāma Sutta*. This is where the Mahāyāna criticism of Theravāda as Hīnayāna becomes justified. When everybody has the potentiality of becoming a Buddha, it is an inferior path to try to attain the ideal of being 'a follower.'

Another criticism of Theravāda done by Huang Po in his *Zen Teachings* deserves consideration. Attainment of *nirvāṇa* is a result of morality and wisdom which are interdependent, in the sense they wash each other like, as the Buddha said, washing one hand with the other. Morality, practiced alone, can lead to involvement with other beings as one does not have a correct view of Reality as Voidness. Wisdom, practiced alone, can lead to a kind of moral and spiritual alienation from person. Huang Po accuses Theravādins of following

7. *Jātaka Book, Buddha Vaṃsaya* (in Sinhala), ed. Ven. Veragoda Amaramoli (Colombo : Sri Lanka Publishers, 1961), p. 7.

wisdom to the exclusion of compassion, as being portrayed by the Arahant ideal. They cultivate *animittatā* or signlessness only, and therefore, instead of attaining perfect liberation, they really get reborn in Formless Brahma Worlds (*arūpāvacara brahmaloka*). This shows that, of wisdom and morality, if one is cultivated to the exclusion of the other, it can easily lead to perversions.

A very significant point that the Theravāda tradition has to seriously consider is whether there is a relationship between Theravāda and violence, particularly in the contemporary social context. When we see the brutal forms of violence that have taken place recently in three dominantly Theravāda countries, Sri Lanka, Burma and Cambodia, it must make Theravādins wonder and establish awareness on this point. The detailed forms in which the torture was executed in all these three countries show a decidedly well calculated or contemplated manner. Of course, violence in the contemporary world situation is common to many parts of the world. But the Theravādins should be particularly vigilant in this situation for two main reasons. One is the calculated nature of the violence involved. The second is, because Theravāda is strongly committed to non-violence, it has a deep obligation to find out why it has failed in its mission. We should take enough care to explore the possibility of any relationship between Theravāda and violence, and examine whether the religionless world and the moral insensitivity the Theravāda tradition is creating is responsible for such a situation.

It is important to have a look at what is being practiced as Theravāda in the present social context. Theravāda is a technology catering for the smooth running in *saṃsāra* with all its evils. It buttresses the caste system by not only accepting it, but even going to the extent of sanctifying it. Ritualism has assumed a major role within Theravāda. As the ritual of *dāna* functions as an insurance system mainly for the next births, the rituals like *Bodhi Pūjā* and *Pirit* guarantee the safety of the *saṃsāric* undertaking. The Buddha's teachings, as in *Pirit*, can be seen as magic or occult sciences in the service of the mundane. Theravāda uses religion to earn merit to enjoy *saṃsāra* as long as possible. It pays a nominal respect to *nirvāṇa* and the last job of realizing it is handed over to Maitreya Buddha, thus turning Theravāda ultimately into a *religion based on faith*.

There are some urgent social issues the Theravādins should really be concerned about, particularly in the troubled times today.

One is our attitude to the refugees. We must question ourselves whether as Buddhists we made a sustained genuine commitment and effort towards ameliorating their situation in a large and institutional way. Did we do enough? Did we do anything at all? We must compare our stance with that, *e.g.*, of Mother Theresa of Calcutta towards the needy and suffering humans. With all the big talk about charity and compassion, has Theravāda Buddhism recently produced anyone like Mother Theresa? The real problem is: why does Theravāda tend to produce monks that specialize in acquisitions as donations, without even a conception of self-negating sacrifices? When Christain missionaries come to give aid to our needy classes, we are ready to jump up and criticize them. But we forget that through failings to do our duty we ourselves have created those classes, thus supplying the missionaries with fertile pastures. When we criticize them we should not forget that it is the way they genuinely practice their religion. And that is exactly their strength, and Buddhists miss the whole point. Instead of learning a noble lesson from them, we try to assuage our guilt by saying that they, not we, are doing something wrong.

Along with that is the related issue of utilizing the public donations to religious places. The purpose of these donations is that they be used for spiritual or charitable purposes. Instead, what happens is that they are used for material purposes of embellishments of those religious establishments, following the ideals of high class *puthujjanas*. There are untold millions of these funds stored away in banks and other places when the Buddhist compassion should be directing this money for urgent social needs. In a news report it was said that the Śrī Pāda funds in the Treasury exceeds 300 in crores of rupees, while one pilgrim season along brings in around 5 million rupees. However, with all these funds, it was said, the pilgrims are not sufficiently supplied with even basic toilet facilities. (*Divayina*, 12th May 1990, p. 14). So, these funds are not used at least for the devotees who are the very people that contribute to the funds. This is public money and the public has a right to talk about it. And also, it is money generated by Buddhist sentiments and they should be channelled to fulfill these very sentiments. What is needed is a genuine social commitment to Buddhist ideals.

The guardians of the Theravāda are *theras* (Elders) or the *Saṅgha* (Order). There are serious problems here too. One could say that *Saṅgha*, as a social institution, is bound or liable to be conditioned by the society around it. But that is what the *Saṅgha* is supposed to avoid. It is basically a religious organization and therefore its moral duty is to be aware of the evils in the society and react strongly against them educating the society along with it. Like a lotus-born from the water yet totally unafflicted by water the *Saṅgha* is born from the society, yet should be unafflicted by the society. Would there ever be any Buddhism if Prince Siddhārtha left himself to be conditioned by his society? When the spiritual institutions succumb to the evils of the mundane society they cease to be religious any more. Because of the consequent moral degeneration, they cease to have any authority over the society. It is the morality that gives them their real inner strength which, in turn, empowers the *Saṅgha* with authority. One notable feature often seen particularly in the contemporary *Saṅgha* is its secularization and politicization. The acceptance or tolerance of the caste system is one of the best examples. Instead of following the Buddha's ideal of simple life they very often seem to aim towards high class life with its luxuries, and follow the ideals of the secular society. Secular education is given preference over religious education. Often boys are enrolled into *Saṅgha* by some *Pirivena*s (monastic education centers) in order to claim a bigger financial grant from the government. One most shocking feature of the contemporary *Saṅgha* is that there is a new generation of monks that has been brought up without any religious education, who do not know any Pāli at all, cannot preach any *Pirit*, sermons, or any basic rituals. These are alarming signs; if this tradition develops, that would be the end of Theravāda.

In the history of human thinking we have been warned that periods of moral chaos like the present social context will come to pass through humanity in various ages. And they have also warned us that the only solution in such situations is to take refuge in morality. Buddhist social institutions have become totally powerless in the present situation. Institutions are the power centers of the community. When the institutions become immoral the community becomes helpless and powerless, as is well-illustrated by the Buddhist society today.

Another problem is the politicization of the Theravāda. Theravāda institutions are not providing any Buddhist solution to the present social crisis. Buddhism has nothing particularly Sinhalese about it. The Buddhist message is for all beings, including Tamils and terrorists. When human beings are being killed by other human beings, Buddhists must do something about it by exploring the causes and conditions of this malaise in order to find a solution and by contributing to the solution with a sense of real sacrifice. As Buddhists if we identify with the Sinhalese or any group or caste of people, we will be generating anger or dislike toward other groups. As Buddhists we must remember that we have been travelling in *saṃsāra* for long periods and we are at the moment passing through Sri Lanka as Buddhists and/or Sinhalese. If we try to identify ourselves as unique individuals with these groups while we are in Sri Lanka for this very short period of time, we will be generating an enormous amount of anger, hatred and dislike that will seriously endanger our future situation in *saṃsāra*. We must see whether we could help these afflicted people, before we pass on. What is going to help us in the long run is love, not hatred. It may be this same love that will be able to bring about a solution to the present social crisis.

A real tragedy of the Theravāda is its 'closed predicament,' and the unwillingness to consider the significance of the later developments of Buddhism: mainly Mahāyāna and Tantra. The Theravāda treats Mahāyāna as worse than Christianity.

It is interesting to note that the modern Theravāda shows an emphatic reaction against Mahāyāna. Here I am not referring to the recent Theravāda-Mahāyāna controversy in Sri Lanka, since the recent reaction seems to be grounded on the fact that the invasive Mahāyāna effort was more grounded on financial considerations and so deservingly termed *Yen-Yāna*. As their respect was more to the Yen, than to the Mahāyāna teachings, what they were espousing was *Mahāyen*, not Mahāyāna.

It is important to realize that Mahāyāna has been a very important religious and social force in Sri Lanka throughout history. Mahāyāna, not Theravāda, was the most dominant religion in Sri Lanka from the 5th to the 11th centuries. Even after that time, as the archaeological evidence clearly shows, Mahāyāna has been a dominant ethos of Sri Lanka. The cult of Nātha or Bodhisattva Avalokiteśvara, the highest and the most central Mahāyāna Bodhisattva, has been a strong religious force in certain periods.[8] And it is in Sri Lanka that the world's tallest Bodhisattva figure has been found. It is a statue of Avalokiteśvara found in Māligāwila recently. This Nātha tradition has been a strong religious under-current, and in Kandyan times the king was anointed in the Nātha Dēvālē in Kandy Indeed this Nātha Dēvālē is situated within a Buddhist temple, as all the Nātha Dēvālēs more or less are.

8. The magnitude of the impact of Avalokiteśvara of Nātha on the history of Sri Lanka is the theme of John Holt's, *The Buddha in the Crown* (New York: Oxford University Press, 1991).

It seems that the whole practical Buddhist tradition, particularly the folk and village tradition, had been deeply influenced by the Bohisattva concept. The central religious notion of the village Buddhists has been formed not by the teachings of the abstruse Theravāda *Sutta* texts, but by the *Bodhisattva* concept and the *Jātaka Book*. This folk tradition has been mostly receptive to the Mahāyāna concepts. The Bodhisattva concept is such a sophisticated and powerful notion because it perfectly combines the ideals of wisdom and compassion and so that it can effectively generate the enlightened attitude. After all, it is the attitude that really counts. It is interesting to note that in the *Buddhavaṃsa* (or the Introduction to the *Jātaka Book*), the Buddha Dipaṅkara worships the *Bodhisattva Sumedha,* by offering 8 handfuls of jasmine flowers and perambulating him. And then all the *Arahants* that were with the Buddha at the time, worships Sumedha by offering scented flowers.[9] This shows the extreme high esteem in which the Bodhisattva was held in the *Jātaka Book*.

As somewhat different from this village Buddhism, the Theravāda tradition is founded on the establishment of the Theras. Its doctrinal foundation is the early Buddhist teachings.

During its stay in Sri Lanka, Mahāyāna has made a deep impact on the psyche of the masses. One of the most central rites for the dead is the practice of offering of merit through *dāna* on the 7th day after the death of a person. This unanimous and obligatory practice cannot be explained at all through the Theravāda tradition, but only explainable through the Mahāyāna teachings, i.e. through the *Tibetan Book of the Dead* where the crucial significance of the 7th day is explained in great detail. Some of the central religious ceremonies and rites like the *Pirit* ceremony and the tieing of the sacred thread for protection have over Tantric tones though they can also be explained as contained within the Theravāda tradition. However, when their external performances are regarded as ultimate acts they assume a very high magical, and so, Tantric significance. The secularization and politicization of religion have been mainly responsible for this situation.

To consider that Buddhism, or the ultimate possibility of

9. *Jātaka Book, Buddha Vaṃsaya*, p. 8.

human thinking, stopped with a person called Gautama the Buddha is to go against the spirit of the *Kālāma Sutta*. For example, Nāgārjuna's philosophy has often been treated as 'the central philosophy of Buddhism' and in the general Buddhist tradition he has been regarded as the 2nd Buddha. His great contribution was proved that the realization of *nirvāṇa* was mainly an epistemological revolution, and that *saṃsāra* and *nirvāṇa* were identical. And then the Buddhist Tantra came in and to show that, *saṃsāra* could be really treated as *nirvāṇa;* the best response to this world was to enjoy its *nirvāṇic* bliss, rather than reject it outright. The Tantric accusation of the *Theravādins* as escapists deserves serious consideration. While *Mahāyāna* and *Tantra* definitely accept the *Theravāda* stance as a necessary first step in spiritual training, they insist that one must go beyond the first step. The tragedy of the Theravāda is that they are not even willing to consider the possibility of these viewpoints, albeit study and master them. This is particularly important considering the world-denying attitude of the Theravāda. The western world finds this attitude the real big problem of the Theravāda. For Theravāda, 'suffering' is the norm. A prominent English philosopher of religion, referring to this attitude, once remarked that 'only Buddhists suffer!'. In Theravada there is an unconscious attempt to sanctify suffering.

However, there are problems with Mahāyāna too, particularly with regard to its practice. Like Theravāda, Mahayana or any religion, without a permanent revolution, can settle down to a fossilized and secular situation which would contradict with its original teachings. From the Theravāda point of view, the major weakness of Mahāyāna is its cult of *gurus* and the dimension of faith. Though the faith factor has been preached by Mahāyāna teachings only as one of 'skillful means' (*upāya kauśalya*), in practice it has settled down to a blind faith. Practical Mahāyāna believes mostly in ritualism and salvation by faith. The Buddhist Tantra is often understood or practiced as a science of occultism and perverse practices.

In Theravāda, in the name of overcoming desires, they tend to destroy all feelings, ending up being like a dry piece of log. Castrated person becomes holy person. That is why the Theravāda Buddhism tends to be mostly a geriatric religion. The Theravāda goal is to flee, and escape from *Saṃsāra* in forests and caves, seeking release in solitude. What Tantra says is that in ultimate reality there can never be a duality; it should necessarily be one. Therefore, they say that the Theravāda position is logically unsound. If the *Saṃsāra* is only a mental construction, a *māyā,* why should we be scared of our own creations or dreams? Yet the Theravādins are scared of *Saṃsāra* and their method is a form of escapism; and once they go into the retreat, it is of course easy to control one's mind simply because there are no stimulating sense data. What is necessary is to master oneself and get out of the dream. Once we get out of the dream we will wake up to *nirvāṇa* which is this world itself.

Theravāda, Mahāyāna and Tantra traditions will have to go back to their roots and critique themselves, and be rehabilitated in terms of their original teachings. Then these teachings should be compared and properly appreciated. The most imperative thing would be to critique these three types of teaching in terms of each other, because the Mahāyāna teachings will be greatly benefitted by the anti-faith and anti-authoritarian perspective of the Theravāda teachings. Mahāyāna and Tantra will be the best antidote to the negative aspects of Theravāda.

Section III

PHILOSOPHICAL IMPLICATIONS

Anurādhapura (Sri Lanka)   Bodhivṛksha temple   Outer prākāra
Moonstone   circa 8th century, Stone
Photograph courtesy of the American Institute of Indian Studies, Varanasi, by way of the Archeological Survey of India. Negative Number A40.99.

9
Two Dogmas of Buddhism

A.L. Herman

Buddhism, whether Southern Theravāda or Northern Mahāyāna, has been conditioned in large part by two dogmas: one is the dogma of *anitya-duḥkha, viz.*, that the impermanence (*anitya*) of existence is, or inevitably leads to, pain or sorrow (*duḥkha*); and the other is the dogma of *nirvāṇa, viz.*, that impermanence and sorrow, *anitya* and *duḥkha*, can both be ended. Both dogmas, I shall argue, are ill-founded because, first, each is false and, second, they are logically inconsistent in the sense that if one dogma is true then the other dogma cannot be true. The effect of abandoning either or both of these dogmas would call for a radical reconstruction of Buddhism, for it goes without arguing that both dogmas lie at the very foundation of Buddhism.

In what follows I shall, first, state the dogma of *anityaduḥkha* and then argue for its being false; second, state the dogma of *nirvāṇa* and then argue for its being false. By "false" in both instances I simply intend "generating problems of such a magnitude that abandonment of the dogma becomes necessary"; third, I shall conclude by attempting to demonstrate that the two dogmas are logically inconsistent in the sense that if *anitya-duḥkha* is true then *nirvāṇa* cannot be true and if nirvana is true then *anitya-duḥkha* cannot be true.

I. The Dogma of *Anitya-Duḥkha*

In the *Aṅguttara-Nikāya* three apparently independent characteristics (*trilakṣaṇa,* Pāli *tilakkhaṇa*) of existence are cited. Buddha says:

> Monks, . . . *this* causal law of nature [*Dhātudhamm-aṭṭhitatā*] this orderly fixing of things prevails, namely, All phenomena are impermanent. About this a Tathāgata is fully enlightened he fully understands it. So enlightened and understanding he declares, teaches and makes it plain. . . : *this* fact that all phenomena are impermanent.
>
> Monks, *this* causal law of nature, this orderly fixing of things prevails, namely, All phenomena are misery. ...

> Monks, . . . *this* causal law, this orderly fixing of things prevails, namely, All phenomena are not the self.[1]

In a brief space this canonical text of about the first century B.C.E. has stated three of the most central concepts of Buddhism, viz., *anitya* (Pāli *anicca)*, impermanence; *duḥkha* (Pāli *dukkha)*, suffering or anxiety; and *anātman* (Pāli *anatta)* non-self or non-substance. This early text has defined the problem of human existence in its characterization of all existence: human existence is subject to inexorable change, unending misery, and the total absence of an unchanging and eternal Self or Substance that might halt the flow of events, time, and misery.

These three seemingly distinct "causal laws of nature" are in fact logically related such that the latter two, *duḥkha* and *anātman*, are logically entailed by the former, *anitya* and they are in fact, causally dependent on it; in other words, if all existence is characterized by inexorable flux, flow, and change then it follows that there must be both suffering as well as non-Self or non-Being for it is only through the total stoppage or halting of change that non-misery and Self or Being could result: The dogma of *anitya-duḥkha* logically follows from the fact of *anitya*.[2]

1. *Aṅguttara Nikāya* III.134 in *The Book of the Gradual Sayings (Aṅguttara-nikāya)* Translated by F.L. Woodward, Five Volumes (London: Pali Text Society, 1979/1932), Vol. I, pp. 264-265. Emphasis added.
2. I see nothing sinister in the use of the word "dogma" to describe a fundamental precept or authoritative tenet. Many Buddhists like to believe that they are dogma-free. I would suggest that no one is dogma-free, and to believe differently is to believe in at least one dogma.

   Alvin Toffler, in an enormously popular book on change and suffering, nicely illustrates this dogma of anitya-duhkha when he says in his opening sentence, "This is a book about what happens to people when they are overwhelmed by change." Toffler defines change as "the process by which the future invades our lives," (Alvin Toffler, *Future Shock* (New York: Bantam Books, 1971), p. 1), and he uses the term "future shock" to describe "the shattering stress and disorientation that we induce in individuals by subjecting them to too much change in too short a time." (Ibid., p. 2): Future shock, in other words, is *duḥkha*. Summarizing research on what happens to people subjected to repeated change Toffler states: . . . those with high life change scores were more likely than their fellows to be ill in the following year. For the first time, it was possible to show in dramatic form that the rate of change in a person's life - his pace of life - closely tied to the state of his health. [Ibid., p. 330] Toffler concludes, perhaps a bit incautiously (depending on what he means by "established") but certainly enthusiastically: In every case, the correlation between change and illness has held. It has been established that "alternations in life style" that require a great deal of adjustment and coping, correlate with illness. This is so regardless of whether or not these changes are under the individual's own direct control and whether or not he sees

What Buddha discovered was that in life "there is not a moment, not an inkling, not a second when a river does not flow,"[3] and that "what is impermanent, that is not worth delighting in, not worth being impressed by, not worth clinging to."[4] *Anitya* is, consequently, not only a central concept in Buddhism but it can be spoken of as *the* central concept of Buddhism.[5] For it is the discovery of the fact of *anitya* and the problems that it engenders that ultimately lead to the search for the way out of those problems.

The Buddhist attempt to escape the Western version of future shock[6] followed two routes: The first way of ameliorating the effects of *anitya* led to a search for *nitya*, the Unchanging, the Absolute, the way of *nirvāṇa*: let's call this "the way of *nirvāṇa*." The second way of ameliorating the effects of *anitya* led to a search for peace and tranquility in a permanent Self or *Ātman:* let's call this "the way of *Ātman*." The way of *nirvāṇa* and the way of *Ātman* are both ways of meeting the effects of change or *anitya* and the future shock of *duḥkha* to which *anitya led.* The way of *nirvāṇa* is historically prior in Buddhism to the way of *Ātman* and it may, consequently, be more closely associated with Southern or *Theravāda* Buddhism, while the way of *Ātman* may be more easily identified with both Hinduism and

---

them as desirable. Furthermore, the higher the degrees of life change, the higher the risk that subsequent illness will be severe. [Ibid.] The physiological relationship between change (*anitya*) and illness (*duḥkha*) has been known for some time in both the East and West. The experiments that Toffler cites give dramatic reconfirmation to that previous knowledge: when anything changes then stress is sure to follow.

3. *Aṅguttara-nikāya* IV in Edward Conze, *Buddhist Thought in India* (Ann Arbor: The University of Michigan Press, 1967), p. 34.
4. *Majjhima Nikāya* II.263, Ibid.
5. Cf. Th. Stcherbatsky and his discussion of the doctrines of instantaneous being (*kṣaṇika-vāda* from "*kṣaṇika*," "existing for only one moment"), a corollary to the concept of *anitya*. Stcherbatsky notes the singular importance of *kṣaṇika* as a basic concept of Buddhism and the implications of *kṣaṇika*-vada for other philosophic concepts, implications which could apply with equal force to anitya; in the process he quotes the 8th century Mādhyamika philosopher, Kamalasīla:
   Thus their character of being instantaneous, of being split in discrete moments, pervades everything. By proving this one fundamental thesis alone, we could have repudiated at one single stroke the God (of the theists), the eternal matter (of the Sānkhyas) and all the wealth of (metaphysical) entities imagined by our opponents. And Stcherbatsky comments: Such is the leading idea of Buddhism - there is no other ultimate reality than separate, instantaneous bits of existence. . . . Ultimate reality is instantaneous. (Th. Stcherbatsky, *Buddhist Logic*, Two Volumes (New York: Dover Publications, 1962/1930), Volume I, pp. 79-80)
6. See supra Note 2.

later Buddhism, especially Northern or *Mahāyāna* Buddhism. Very briefly, let's examine these two ways before we turn to a critique of *anitya*, itself.

The Way of *Nirvāṇa* and the Way of *Ātman*

The way of *nirvāṇa* is easily identified with one of the central themes of the *Saṃyutta Nikāya* when it announces, "The ceasing of becoming is *nibbāṇa*." In this *Nikāya* one of the chief disciples of the Buddha, Sāriputta, answers the question, "What is *nibbāna*?" by stating that it is "The extinction of desire, the extinction of hatred, the extinction of illusion."[7] In other words, only when all becoming has been stopped will there be *nirvāṇa*. In the *Udāna* (Sayings) of the Pāli *Khuddaka Nikāya* Buddha reiterates:

> O bhikkhus, there is the unborn, ungrown, and unconditioned. Were there not the unborn, ungrown, and unconditioned, there would be no escape for the born, grown and conditioned. Since there is the unborn, ungrown, and unconditioned, so there is escape for the born, grown, and conditioned.[8]

In other words, without *nirvāṇa* as *nitya* there would no escape from *anitya*; that is to say, unless absolute, changeless Being existed there would seem to be no escape from *anitya* and *duḥkha*. Thus the way of *nirvāṇa* leads, one must suppose, to an unchanging Absolute and an Absolute in which all traces of personality and plurality are extinguished. The way of *nirvāṇa*, as a solution to the *duḥkha* brought about by *anitya*, is, finally, remarkably like what has been called "the metaphysical way" of Hinduism, a way which entails absorption into the absolute, Holy Power of the universe, i.e., into *para-* or *nirguṇa* Brahman.[9]

The way of *Ātman*, on the other hand, leads to the stoppage of *duḥkha* through the mystical discovery of a subjective and ultimately real and unchanging Self or *Ātman*. Early Buddhism travelling the way of the *nirvāṇa* to liberation had tried to rid the system of all traces of *Ātman* or Self but without complete success: they removed the concept, but not the need for a passionate and personal self, surviving

7. *Saṁyutta Nikāya* IV in Walpola Rahula, *What the Buddha Taught* (New York: Grove Press, Inc., 1974), p. 37.
8. Ibid.
9. Cf. A.L. Herman, *A Brief Introduction to Hinduism* (Westview Press, 1991), "The Way of Knowledge," pp. 63-87, 111-114.

day to day and into the next life. Early *Theravāda* Buddhism had recognized, as well, the imperativeness to render all vestiges of a real Self nugatory and one must acknowledge and applaud this valiant but vain attempt.

Edward Conze has commented on the historical endeavor by later Buddhists to grapple with and ultimately reject the earlier *anātman* doctrine at the same time that they tried to find an alternative to that plainly unacceptable philosophic tenet:

> In spite of their professions to the contrary, the Buddhists were constantly drawn to the belief in a 'true self,' which would act as a permanent constituent (*dhātu*) behind the ever changing 'continuity.'[10]

This temptation to establish such a 'true self' is clearly illustrated in the early history of Buddhism. The Sautrāntikas, for example, postulated an unchanging "seed of goodness" along with an *āśraya* or permanent substratum; the Mahāsaṃghikas argued for *mūla* or basic consciousness; the Sarvāstivadins propounded *prāpti*, a force that keeps a *saṃtāna*, or pattern of *dharmas* constituting a self, in existence; and the *ālaya-vijñāna*, "store-house consciousness," of a minority of Yogācārins is the wondrous climax of this desperate search for an acceptable "self."

The way of *Ātman* as a solution to the *duḥkha* brought about by *anitya* is, finally, remarkably like what has been called "the religious way" of Hinduism wherein one's Self, following Its liberation from *duḥkha*, survives perpetually as a real but wholly separate entity distinct from other similar Selves.[11]

The way of *nirvāṇa* and the way of *Ātman* approach the dogma of *anitya-duḥkha* from quite opposite directions. The way of *nirvāṇa* attempts to transcend *anitya* in its search for *nitya* and *nirvāṇa*. It seeks to escape from the future shock that *anitya* promises to bring, and in doing so it admits that nothing can be done about *anitya* save to go beyond it. The way of *Ātman*, on the other hand, does not attempt to escape *anitya* so much as it seeks accommodation to it. It admits and accepts *anitya* as a universal metaphysical principle (as does the way of *nirvāṇa*) and then it attempts to live within that acceptance. The devotee can accept or make room for change and change becomes part of reality. The way of *Ātman* optimistically holds that

10. Edward Conze, Op. Cit., p. 133.
11. A.L. Herman, Op. Cit., "The Way of Devotion," pp., 38-49, 107-111.

adaptation to *anitya* is possible and advisable: "*Saṃsāra* is not different from *nirvāṇa* and *nirvāṇa* is not different from *saṃsāra*." Whereas the way of *nirvāṇa* pessimistically holds that successful adaptation to *anitya* is simply not possible: "*Saṃsāra* is not *nirvāṇa* and *nirvāṇa* is not *saṃsāra*."

Conclusion

In conclusion let me say that what I have attempted to show in my remarks about *anitya* is that it is the central concept of Buddhism, lying as it does at the very foundation of Buddhism. *Anitya* is the cause of the problem, *duḥkha*, that sets the Buddhist off in search of a solution, *nirvāṇa*.

I turn next to the analysis of *anitya* wherein I will attempt to show that the dogma of *anitya-duḥkha* is false and consequently ill-founded.

The Critique of *Anitya*

My argument is based largely on the accommodation to *anitya* made by the way of *Ātman*, above, and that argument is this: not all change produces sorrow or *duḥkha* and, in fact, some change produces happiness or *nirvāṇa*; hence, it's false to assume that everything which is transient is *duḥkha* and should be avoided. In other words, if any impermanent state or activity could be shown to be instrumentally happy because it leads to ultimate happiness and the avoidance of all *duḥkha* then it would be false to argue, as the Buddhists do, that "what is impermanent is not worth delighting in, not worth being impressed by, not worth clinging to." The full argument looks like this:

1. If any impermanent state or activity produces happiness then that state or activity is not sorrowful or ill. (This is a statement justified by introspection and pragmatics, by our previous discussion, and the ordinary meanings of "instrumental" and "ultimate" happiness.)
2. The way of *nirvāṇa* and the way of *Ātman* are impermanent states or activities that produce happiness. (The Buddhists seem to admit this but see Note[12].)

---

12. Most Buddhists are extremely careful on this matter, pointing out that *nirvāṇa* is unconditioned and cannot, therefore, be the effect of any cause. If it were conditioned and an effect like any other effect then, given the fact of *anitya*, *nirvāṇa* could come to an end. In other words, unless the Buddhists can protect

3. Therefore, the way of *nirvāṇa* and the way of *Ātman* are impermanent states or activities that are not sorrowful or ill. (This follows from 1 and 2.)
4. Therefore, there are some impermanent states or activities that are not sorrowful or ill. (This follows from 3.)
5. Therefore, it is false to state that everything that is impermanent is ill. (A restatement of 4.)
6. Therefore, it is false to state that *anitya* is always *duḥkha*. (A restatement of 5.)

In other words, if philosophic activity, as defined by the ways of *nirvāṇa* and the *Ātman*, involves and leads to happiness then the dogma of *anitya-duḥkha* is false, i.e., the dogma of *anitya-duḥkha* is illfounded, which is what we set out to prove.

The first and second premises of the previous argument need some explanation. They simply intend that certain activities, certain impermanent states such as pursuing the way of *nirvāṇa*, are not subject to the usual or normal conditions that obtain in the dogma of

---

nirvāṇa in some way, e.g., by calling it unconditioned, one could pop into and out of *nirvāṇa* just as one pops into and out of bed. Walpola Rahula comments on this protective device as follows: "It is incorrect to think that *nirvāṇa* is the natural result of the extinction of craving. *Nirvāṇa* is not the result of anything. If it would be a result, then it would be an effect produced by a cause. It would be saṃkhata 'produced' and 'conditioned'. Nirvāṇa is neither cause nor effect. It is beyond cause and effect." Rahula continues by drawing an analogy with truth: "Truth is not a result nor an effect. It is not produced like a mystic, spiritual, mental state as dhyāna or samādhi. TRUTH IS. NIRVĀṆA IS. The only thing you can do is to see it, to realize it. There is a path leading to the realization of Nirvāṇa. But Nirvāṇa is not the result of this path." (Op. Cit., p. 40)

This is orthodox doctrine but, with all due respect, I find the defense quibbling and obfuscating. "Quibbling" because it flies in the face even of Buddhist common sense where paths that lead to things, if followed, get you to those things; and that's all one wants to claim about *nirvāṇa*, viz., it's what happens after following a certain path. Rahula concludes: "You may get to the mountain along a path, but the mountain is not the result, nor an effect of the path. You may see a light, but the light is not the result of your eyesight." [Ibid.]

I find this "obfuscating" because the analogy is misleading and the point is lost. If one gets to the mountain along a path, then the mountain experience one also gets is the result of following that path. What more could one want? Finally, the light is not the result of my eyesight. It is misleading to assume that is what any one wanted to prove in the first place: all that is needed is to state that my seeing or experiencing the light is the result of my eyesight conjoined with light and several other necessary conditions being present and experienced under so-called standard conditions.

anitya-duḥkha. They point, for example, to the joy that comes from the intellectual activity involved in the study of the Doctrine wherein man is truly happiest and at his best when he is exercising his intellect in solving at least one very important practical problem.[13] Finding joy and liberation in pursuing intellectual solutions to practical problems is found in the tradition in which the Buddha, himself, is described as a physician seeking a practical cure for a flaming fever. Recall that the Four Noble Truths read precisely like a physician's prescription for, or solution to, a medical disease or problem: there is a problem (*duḥkha*); there is a cause (*tṛṣṇā* or *avidyā*); there is a solution (*nirodha* or *nirvāṇa*); there is a way to the solution (the eightfold path). Similarly, it can be noted that the Buddhist philosopher, in general, is dealing constantly with a very practical problem (suffering); its cause (desire, ignorance); its solution (happiness, *nirvāṇa*); and the ways to that solution (desirelessness and knowledge together with the ways of *nirvāṇa* and *Ātman*).

---

13. The Tibetan scholar, Bu-ston (1290-1364) quoting from a Mahāyāna text on the merits of study and philosophy states in a manner that nicely illustrates our point: The *Bodhisattvapiṭaka* says:
    1. He, that studies [the Doctrine], comes to know the Doctrine.
    2. He, that studies, will abstain from sinful deeds,
    3. He, that studies, will reject all that is vain,
    4. He, that studies, attains *nirvāṇa*.

    Bu-ston then states that these verses mean (I quote only the first):
    1. Knowledge of the doctrines to be accepted or rejected through an investigation of orthodox and heretical philosophical systems.
       Acquirement of the right philosophical point of view.

    I omit the other meanings of the verses but add here the five kinds of merit for study:
    1. Study of matters unknown before
    2. Reconsideration of the parts studied
    3. Solution of doubt
    4. Establishment of a correct view
    5. Knowledge of the words and the deepest sense of the climax of wisdom

    Bu-ston then gives the meaning of these five kinds of merit; once again, I omit part of the text:
    1. Extensive study
    2. Elucidation and perfect clearness (of the object studied)
    3. Acquirement of certainty
    4. Consideration of objects form the correct point of view. In other words, philosophy, *i.e.*, the pursuit of study in order to find a rational solution to the problems of life, from what Bu-ston is reporting here, was seen as a way to *nirvāṇa*. (Bu-ston, *The Jewelry of Scripture*, Translated from the Tibetan by E. Obermiller (Heidelberg: Institut für Buddhismus-Kunde, 1931), pp. 9-10).

The activity of thought, whether seen as epistemic, discursive, *prajñā* or *jñāna*, is always an *activity* in which *duḥkha* is absent, for some temporarily, for others permanently. And the point can be proved by introspective examination while engaged in philosophic problem solving: philosophy, in other words, can be seen as a way to happiness and *nirvāṇa*. But the instrumental happiness involved in the very activity of philosophizing is a temporary by-product of thought and should not be confused with the ultimate happiness, *nirvāṇa*, achieved when the philosophic activity or mystical activity has been successfully concluded.

Further, the instrumental and ultimate happiness produced in the philosophic activity of, for example, the way of *nirvāṇa* and the way of *Ātman*, are characterized by an absence of *duḥkha*, a fact which can again be discovered by simple introspection when one is on one or the other of the two paths. Further, it should be clear, given the pragmatic proclivities of the Buddhists themselves, that any activity which successfully leads to the end being sought is right and any statement descriptive of that activity would thereby be true. The first premises of the argument are justified, therefore, on the basis of both introspection and pragmatics. Finally, the activity of thought, itself, is a process, characterized by *anitya*, that need not be *duḥkha* or produce *duḥkha* or lead to *duḥkha*. Therefore, it is false to state that *anitya* is or inevitably leads to *duḥkha*. In other words, the dogma of *anitya-duḥkha* is ill-founded.

II. The Dogma of *Nirvāṇa*

If the dogma of *anitya-duḥkha* defines the cause (*anitya*) and the problem (*duḥkha*) of existence, in general, and of human existence, in particular, then *anātman*, the third characteristic of existence mentioned above in the *Aṅguttara-Nikāya*, points in a sense to the solution of the problem. But the recognition of *anātman* and the intuitive realization that there is no Self or Substance or permanent Being which one can successfully desire, cling to or grasp in order to solve the problem is tantamount to letting go and achieving the liberation known as *nirvāṇa*.[14] "*Nirvāṇa*" means "blown out" and the analogy most frequently employed by the Buddhists to explain it is that of the blowing out of the flame of a candle. The flame is the flame of desire (*tṛṣnā, tanhā*) which, once extinguished, can never be

14. Cf. A.L. Herman, "A Solution to the Paradox of Desire in Buddhism," *Philosophy East & West* 29 (1) 1979: 91-94.

started again (in this body) or passed on to other candles (other bodies): to be "*nirvāṇ*-ed" is to be liberated from desire and it is to solve the problem of *duḥkha*.

In the *Mahāvagga* Buddha preaches his famous "Fire Sermon" on liberation (*nirvāṇa*) that begins, "Everything, brethren, is on fire . . . with the fire of passion, of hate, of illusion, it is on fire, with birth, old age, death, grief, lamentation, suffering, sorrow, and despair." The sermon ends as Buddha recommends indifference or aversion to whatever is on fire:

> And being indifferent he becomes free from passion, by absence of passion he is liberated, and when he is liberated, the knowledge 'I am liberated' arises. Rebirth is destroyed, a religious life is lived, duty is done, and he knows there is nothing more for him in this state.[15]

There is no mention of peace and tranquility in this Pāli text, a point to which we shall recur in our criticism of *nirvāṇa*, below. *Nirvāṇa*, to the author of this text, is essentially a negative state or condition bringing, as it does, an end to suffering and rebirth.

A later text, the *Milindapañha*, also discusses *nirvāṇa* and its implications. A certain Bactrian Greek King, Menander (Pāli Milinda) is questioning a Buddhist monk, Nāgasena, about the Buddhist religion. Among the questions that he asks about *nirvāṇa* are these: "Is it cessation?" ("Yes"), "Do all win *nirvāṇa*?" ("No"), "Is it a happy state?"("Yes"), "How can one known about it without having attained it?" ("By analogy and through metaphor"). Thereupon through analogy and metaphor Nāgasena speaks of the qualities of *nirvāṇa*:

> As the lotus is unstained by water, so is Nirvana unstained by all defilements - As cool water Nirvana is cool and allays the fever of all the passions . . . [and it] removes the craving for sensuous enjoyments, the craving for further becomings, the craving for the cessation of becoming. As medicine protects . . . so Nirvana [protects] from the torments of the poisonous passions [and] puts an end. . . to all sufferings. [Like space] neither is it born, grows old, dies, passes away, or is reborn . . . . Like the wishing jewel, Nirvana grants all one can desire, brings joy, and sheds light . . . .[16]

---

15. *Mahāvagga* I.21 in E.J. Thomas, *Buddhist Scriptures* (London: John Murray, 1931), pp. 54-56.
16. *Milindapañha* in *Buddhist Scriptures* translated by Edward Conze (Baltimore, MD: Penguin Books, Inc., 1959), p. 157.

For the author of this text, *nirvāṇa* is essentially a positive state or condition. And the Bactrian King, a possible convert to Buddhism, responds at this point, "Well said, Nāgasena! So it is, and as such I accept it."

Conclusion

Between the times of these two apparently contradictory texts about *nirvāṇa*, the *Mahāvagga* and the *Milindapañha*, a good deal of philosophic controversy has passed. Each tends to see *nirvāṇa* in a different light and each has come to represent the two quite different attitudes towards *nirvāṇa* as adopted by first, the Theravāda school of Southern Buddhism and, second, the Mahāyāna school of Northern Buddhism.[17] In order to show that the second dogma of Buddhism is false I want to turn to a critique of *nirvāṇa* as that concept is understood by these two schools. I want to argue that no matter which of the two interpretations is accepted, the Theravāda negative view of *nirvāṇa* or the Mahāyāna positive view of *nirvāṇa*, insuperable problems result on either interpretation; and since there are no other interpretations possible, we have a dilemma: call this dilemma "the dilemma of *nirvāṇa*."

---

17. The wrangle over the interpretations of *nirvāṇa* is discussed in Guy Welbon's, The *Buddhist Nirvāṇa and Its Western Interpreters* (University of Chicago Press, 1968). The quarrel centers precisely around the question of the essential nature of *nirvāṇa* as either positive or negative, as bliss or annihilation. One or another view has been adopted by the various interpreters of Buddhism over the decades. The interpreters that Welbon mentions include such distinguished Indologists as H.T. Calebrooke, Eugene Burnouf, Jules Barthelemy Saint Hilare, F. Max Müller, T.W. Rhys Davids, Th. Stcherbatsky, Arthur Berriedale Keith, and Louis de La Vallee Poussin. What the various negative and positive interpretations give us, Welbon observes, is really a measure of each scholar's own insight into Buddhism: ". . . their evaluations, never based exclusively on philological and historico-critical considerations, in every instance reflect the individual scholar's own personal commitment, his sitz im leben, and his understanding of the essence of Buddhism." Welbon concludes: "The response to the question of *nirvāṇa*'s meaning is at the same time an answer more or less complete to all questions about Buddhism." (Op. Cit., p. viii)

I would only remark that if Welbon is correct then *nirvāṇa* can legitimately be seen as either a positive or a negative concept, and whichever concept is chosen becomes an important standard by which to judge any Buddhist's further interpretation of Buddhism.

The Critique of *Nirvāṇa*

The dilemma of *nirvāṇa* holds that if *nirvāṇa* is seen negatively as the total absence of passion and desire and feeling then this is tantamount to being dead, and who wants to pursue a goal that leads to death?[18] *Nirvāṇa* is suicide on this first interpretation. On the other hand, if *nirvāṇa* is seen positively as the presence of peace and tranquility wherein all that I desire is fulfilled then desire is not ended or blown out and the whole intent of *nirvāṇa* is contradicted: *nirvāṇa* is inconsistent on this second interpretation. But, the dilemma of *nirvāṇa* continues, *nirvāṇa* must be seen either negatively or positively; there is no third alternative. The conclusion of the dilemma is then that *nirvāṇa* is either suicidal obliteration or inconsistent continuance.

There are alternatives of course and the Buddhists, particularly the Mādhyamikas, are notorious for seeing alternatives wherever a dialectic of positions occurs. Thus one could, through some sort of Nāgārjunian *śūnya*fication resort to talk about *śūnya* at this point and

---

18. The Hindus, too, have grappled with the problem of liberation where negative *mokṣa* threatens to lead to absorption into Brahman and ultimate suicide. Thus in the *Chandogya Upanisad*, the God Indra comes to Lord Prajāpati for instruction on the true nature of Ātman and how to reach that nature in oneself. Prajāpati teaches that the Self is to be found through three stages of descent: the first stage is waking consciousness, the second state is dreaming consciousness, and the third stage is the negative stage of dreamless sleep. Indra criticizes each of the three as inadequate definitions or stages of reality, and in a panic rejects the third: "if dreamless sleep is to be identified with what his true Self" is like then he would be "like one who has gone to annihilation. I see nothing enjoyable, indeed, where there is no enjoying Self. The goal of this instruction would seem to end in nothingness i.e., it is like suicide, like being dead. To placate Indra Prājapati then instructs him in a fourth stage which carries Indra and Hinduism out of threatened philosophic suicide. The Self in this fourth stage is shown to be capable of experiencing enjoyment, i.e., happiness or *ānanda*. See *Chandogya Upanisad* VIII, 12.5. Therefore, since the essence of Self is enjoyment, the final state of *mokṣa* will be a state that manifests that essence: *mokṣa* is enjoyment. But this *Upanisadic* attempt to solve the problem of liberation and what we earlier called "the dilemma of *nirvāṇa*" simply won't work. For in rejecting negative mokṣa and the first premise of the dilemma of *nirvāṇa* they have thrown themselves into positive *mokṣa* and the second premise. And with that move the new troubles already mentioned have begun wherein liberation and this life, *mokṣa* and *saṃsāra*, become indistinguishable. The Buddhist with his commitment to the dogma of *anātman* is in a still unhappier position for he cannot even claim that the essence of Self is anything at all for, canonically, there is no Self. For more on the Hindu struggle to solve the problem of negative *mokṣa*, see A.L. Herman, "Jivacide, Zombies and Jivanmuktas," *Asian Philosophy, Volume 1 (1) 1991.*

retreat to silence or to metaphors and symbols. But the plain man, our common sense critic here, must feel that such retreats are essentially anti-intellectual and in the worst interests of Buddhism and philosophy. If there is a dilemma here, the thing to do is to recognize it and hunt for a genuine solution rather than to retreat to spurious solutions, anti-intellectual mysticism and obscurantism.

The dilemma of *nirvāṇa* concludes that either *nirvāṇa* is suicide (it's like being dead) or *nirvāṇa* is inconsistent (it's like being alive). The full argument looks like this:

1. If *nirvāṇa* entails the absence of human passion, desire, and feeling then achieving *nirvāṇa* is like being dead. (This seems to be what the *Mahāvagga* was saying above.)
2. If *nirvāṇa* entails the presence of human passion, desire, and feeling then achieving *nirvāṇa* is no different from this life. (This seems to be what the *Milindapañha* was saying above.)
3. Either *nirvāṇa* entails the absence of human passion, desire, and feeling or *nirvāṇa* entails the presence of human passion, desire, and feeling. (This is an assumption that *nirvāṇa* is either a negative or positive condition.[19]
4. Therefore, either *nirvāṇa* is like being dead or *nirvāṇa* is no different from this life. (This follows logically from 1, 2 and 3.)

If the dilemma of *nirvāṇa* is sound, i.e., its premises are true and the argument is valid, then the dogma of *nirvāṇa* is false, i.e., it generates problems of such a magnitude that abandonment of the doctrine becomes necessary. These problems, seeing the end of man

---

19. Some Buddhists might take exception to the characterization of *nirvāṇa* as either negative or positive. Again Walpola Rahula takes to the attack beginning: "Because *Nirvāṇa* is thus expressed in negative terms, there are many who have got a wrong notion that it is negative, and expresses self-annihilation. *Nirvāṇa* is definitely no annihilation of self, because there is no self to annihilate. If at all, it is the annihilation of the illusion, of the false idea of self."
Perhaps that's all true but illusions qua illusions die just as hard as putative veridical interpretations of the world. And any removal of such hard illusions must be seen as negative despite what Rahula goes on to say: "It is incorrect to say that *Nirvāṇa* is negative or positive. The idea of 'negative' and 'positive' are relative, and are within the realm of duality. These terms cannot be applied to *Nirvāṇa*, Absolute Truth, which is beyond duality and relativity." (*Op. Cit.*, pp. 37-38)
'Beyond' or not, people will, Buddhists among them, in their more talkative and communicative moments continue to speak about the unspeakable. All that philosophy can do is to make sure the talk is as consistent and meaningful as possible.

as suicide or seeing the end of man as no different from this life, i.e., as the satisfaction of desire for the sake of enjoyment, appear to be insuperable. Hence, the dogma of *nirvāṇa* that asserts that *anitya* and *duḥkha*, impermanence and suffering, can be satisfactorily ended is false, for there is no satisfaction in suicide nor is there an ending in satisfying desires. In other words, the dogma of *nirvāṇa* is ill-founded.

Conclusion

The general conclusion that we might now draw form our discussion of the dogmas of *anitya-duḥkha* and *nirvāṇa* is that both dogmas appear to violate the very basic standards of reason, i.e., logic and common sense. The dogma of *anitya-duḥkha* that asserted that change and suffering are always connected, either logically or causally, is patently false. We found at least two instances of change, viz., the philosophic activity of the way of *nirvāṇa* and the philosophic activity of the way of *Ātman*, both of which can lead to *nirvāṇa*, that demonstrated the falsity of the claim of the dogma of *anitya-duḥkha*. The dogma of *nirvāṇa* that asserted that *anitya* and *duḥkha* could be satisfactorily ended is also patently false. We found that the dilemma of *nirvāṇa* pointed to two unsatisfactory conclusions neither of which would be acceptable to common sense: for either *nirvāṇa* is suicide or it leads to an existence which is really no different from being alive, *i.e.*, no different from this life. Each of these unsatisfactory conclusions demonstrated the falsity of the dogma of *nirvāṇa*.

Our conclusion to these two parts then is that the dogma of *anitya-duḥkha* and the dogma of *nirvāṇa* are both false, that they violate the philosophic and religious expectations of the plain man, whether Buddhist or not; and that both dogmas are consequently ill-founded.

It remains now to show that the dogmas of *anitya-duḥkha* and *nirvāṇa* are mutually inconsistent and then our task will be complete.

III. The Dogmas of *Anitya-duḥkha* and *Nirvāṇa*

The dogmas of *anitya-duḥkha* and *nirvāṇa* are ill-founded, as I shall try to demonstrate, because if one of the dogmas is true then the other dogma cannot be true. In other words, the two dogmas of Buddhism are mutually inconsistent. The proof of this contention lies in showing that the concepts of *anitya* and *nirvāṇa* are logically incompatible. However, I am going to modify this claim slightly, for from our discussion of *nirvāṇa* in Part II of this paper we have been seen that "*nirvāṇa*" is ambiguous: There is a negative *nirvāna* and there is a positive *nirvāṇa.* I will argue now that the attempt to conjoin the concept of negative *nirvāṇa*, alone, leads to a logical inconsistency; but the attempt to conjoin *anitya* with positive *nirvāṇa* does not lead to a logical inconsistency. Let me explain these conclusions very briefly.

First, in a universe where the dogma of *anitya* accurately describes the way the universe is, there could be no permanent and unchanging state or condition. But negative *nirvāṇa*, *i.e*, the *nirvāṇa* of the Theravāda Buddhist, the *nirvāṇa* of the *Mahāvagga*, and the mokṣa of Prajāpati's third stage of *Ātman* (see Note 18), is, we are led to believe, just such a static and unchanging state or condition. Therefore, the attempt to conjoin *anitya* with negative *nirvāṇa* must fail because the resulting conjunction is plainly inconsistent.

Second, in a universe where the dogma of *anitya* accurately describes the way the universe is, there could be a positive *nirvāṇa* of the sort described by Nāgasena to King Milinda, and the *mokṣa* of Prajāpati's fourth stage of Reality (see Note 18). Such a *nirvāṇa* would envision the magic "wishing jewel" at the heart of the heavenly experience where touching the jewel and wishing would bring whatever the liberated person would desire. The nature of this liberation and the problem with *anātman* that it engendered is bound to crop up again, but our only problem now is to determine whether or not such positive *nirvāṇa* is consistent with a world defined by *anitya*. Again, there seems to be no inconsistency: the heavenly world of positive *nirvāṇa* is a world governed as much by change, it would seem, as is this world.

Conclusion

Our conclusion then is that the dogma of *negative nirvāṇa*, wherein liberation is an unchanging state, and the dogma of *anitya-duḥkha*, wherein change is an unending state, form a logically inconsistent set.

What I have tried to show in this paper on the two dogmas of Buddhism is that both dogmas are ill-founded because, first, each dogma is false and second, because the two dogmas are inconsistent in the sense that if *anitya-duḥkha* is true then negative *nirvāṇa* must be false and vice versa. I have tried to show that the two dogmas fail to meet the philosophic standard of reason, *i.e.*, logic and common sense, and that the inconsistency of *anitya-duḥkha* and negative *nirvāṇa* rests upon their failure to meet the philosophic standard of logical noncontradiction. The effect of retaining these ill-founded dogmas in the face of these philosophic problems would be (has been) to move Buddhism away from empirical truth and reason and closer to either "a questionable pragmatism," where truth is measured by sheer usefulness, or towards "a non-rationalism and mysticism" where truth is abandoned altogether.[20]

20. Our closing remarks intentionally parallel the opening remarks made by Willard Van Orman Quine in his, "Two Dogmas of Empiricism." I would hope that this challenge to Buddhism would parallel Quine's own healthy challenge to empiricism. It might be pointed out that the two alternative routes mentioned here, *viz.*, "a questionable pragmatism" and "a non-rationalism and mysticism," were precisely the routes subsequently taken respectively by Southern or Theravāda Buddhism, on the one hand, and Northern or Mahāyāna, Buddhism, on the other. See K.N. Jayatilleke, *Early Buddhist Theory of Knowledge* (London: George Allen and Unwin, Ltd., 1963), pp. 351-358, for a discussion of the pragmatic nature of Buddhist truth in the older Theravāda tradition; and see David J. Kalupahana, *Buddhist Philosophy: A Historical Analysis* (Honolulu: The University of Hawaii Press, 1976), pp. 163-166, for some conclusions about the hunt for the mystical Absolute in the later Mahāyāna tradition.

10

What is the Status of the Doctrine of Dependent Origination?

RAMAKRISHNA PULIGANDLA

Although the doctrine of dependent origination (*paṭiccasamuppāda*) and its implications and significance have been widely discussed, seldom, if ever, has the question concerning its status been raised. For this reason, I propose to deal with this question in this essay. Is the doctrine an *a priori* truth, an analytic truth, a synthetic truth, or an inductive generalization? I shall examine each of these alternatives and then attempt to assess and clarify the status of the doctrine.

Let us begin with a clear statement of the doctrine of dependent origination. The doctrine may be stated as follows: "This arising, that arises; and this ceasing to be, that ceases to be." Put another way, every phenomenon arises in dependence upon other phenomena, and passes away in dependence upon yet other phenomena. This is to say that no phenomenon arises on its own or passes away on its own. But what is a phenomenon? Here is my definition of "phenomenon:" a phenomenon is anything that is or can, in principle, be an object of consciousness. Let it be immediately noted that all phenomena exist in time, although some phenomena also exist in space. Thus tables, chairs, trees, stars, galaxies, animals, people, *etc.* — the so-called "external phenomena"— can be assigned both spatial and temporal co-ordinates; whereas thoughts, feelings, dreams, mental images, *etc.* — the so-called "internal phenomena"— can be assigned only the temporal co-ordinate. The hallmark of a phenomenon, then, is existence in time; that is, all phenomena are time bound existents. We may thus correctly say that the world of phenomena is time bound existence. Through the doctrine of dependent origination, the Buddha taught that all phenomena, without exception, arise and perish away in dependence upon other phenomena. Let me clarify this point further.

Thus consider, for example, the tree in the yard. How did the tree come to be? Someone planted a seed and the interactions of the seed with the soil, minerals, water, sunshine, and so on are the arising of the tree. It is not as though there were a tree waiting behind the scenes to show up at a certain appointed time. The tree has no existence apart from the interactions among the various phenomena, such as the seed, soil, sunshine, water, etc. That is, the entire being of the tree is constituted of the interactions among other phenomena. Put pointedly, the tree has no self-existence (own-existence); nor does it have a self-nature (own-nature). If something does not have self-existence, how can it have self nature? It is to be emphasized, in order to ward off any misunderstanding, that the Buddha does not deny that the tree has existence and nature; rather, he calls our attention to the fact that its existence and nature are through and through dependent (conditioned). And since "self-existent" means substance, we may express the doctrine of dependent origination by saying that phenomena are not substances; they are insubstantial. And this is precisely what is meant by the declaration that all phenomena are devoid of self-existence and self-nature (*svabhāvaśūnya-dharma*). It is this lack of own-existence and own-nature that is signalled by the teaching that all phenomena are empty. Thus when we take a phenomenon, for example the tree, and analyze it we do not hit upon some inner core as the ultimate residuum; there can be no inner core, no substance, no ultimate residuum dwelling at the heart of the tree. And, according to the doctrine of dependent origination, this observation applies to *all* phenomena, without exception, and thereby uniquely characterizes every phenomenon and hence all phenomenal existence. Thus the doctrine is proclaimed as a universal truth.

Now imagine someone going to the Buddha and saying, "Sir, the doctrine of dependent origination is indeed a very interesting teaching, but how and on what grounds is one to accept or reject this teaching?" The Buddha would ask the person to produce a counter-example to the doctrine; and if one succeeds in producing a counter-example, then surely the doctrine will be shown to be false, in the sense that it is not a universal truth.

The question now is "can one, in principle, find a counter-example?" I submit that no counter-example can ever be found; that is, the doctrine is potentially unfalsifiable. Now, many philosophers, inspired by the Popperian doctrine of falsifiability, would contend that the doctrine of dependent origination, insofar as it is potentially unfalsifiable, is not a scientific but a metaphysical doctrine. It is not necessary for the purpose of this paper to enter into the controversy surrounding science-*versus*-metaphysics. Suffice it to emphasize that the doctrine of dependent origination is not a metaphysical doctrine, in the sense that it does not affirm or deny some super-sensible entities or realities; rather, it is a proposition arrived at through an examination and analysis of the world of phenomena; there is nothing supersensible about the doctrine of dependent origination, in that it has nothing to do with God or gods, the Devil, Heaven and Hell, the mysterious soul, purpose of the world, and so on. It is my contention, which I shall support with arguments, that the doctrine of dependent origination is open to certification by anyone who is willing to conduct inquiry, in which there is no place for any commitment, religious or metaphysical, to anything that is not in principle experienceable.

(1) Is the doctrine of dependent origination an analytic truth? By "analytic truth," I mean, in conformity with its commonly accepted connotation, truth certifiable solely on the basis of an examination of constituent terms. Thus the statement "a father is a parent" is certifiable as analytic truth simply by looking up in the dictionary the meanings of "father" and "parent." We have seen earlier that the doctrine of dependent origination may be stated equivalently in a variety of ways. Let us state is as follows: "No phenomenon arises or passes away on its own." And if by 'phenomenon' we mean anything that presents itself to us, appears to us, is an object of awareness, it is clear that there is nothing in the meaning of 'phenomenon' to suggest that it does not arise or pass away on its own. Thus the statement "no phenomenon arises or passes away on its own" is not an analytic truth. Further, its denial is not self-contradictory; that is, the statement, "some phenomenon arises or passes away on its own" is not self-contradictory, unlike "a father is not a parent."

(2) Is the doctrine a synthetic truth? Again, following the accepted understanding and usage, we shall define "synthetic truth" as truth whose certification requires not only an examination of the constituent terms but also inspection of the world, and hence can be denied without self-contradiction. One is likely to think that the doctrine is a synthetic truth. For, after all, we have seen in (1) that the denial of the doctrine is not self-contradictory; and it certainly says something about the world. There is, however, a serious objection against this way of thinking; any synthetic statement, although false

at a certain time, can conceivably be true (and although true at a certain time, can conceivably be false), and this is precisely what is meant by saying that the denial of a synthetic truth is not self-contradictory. Thus, for example, the statement that there is a tiger in John's bathtub, although false at a certain time, can be true at some other time (can, in principle, be true). And let it be emphasized that the denial of the doctrine of dependent origination, unlike that of a synthetic truth, cannot, in principle, be true. For its denial to be true, one has to point to a phenomenon, actual or possible, which arises out of itself or passes away on its own. And the Buddha resoundingly maintains that one can never, in principle, come up with such an instance.

Ask yourself: What does it mean for a phenomenon to arise out of itself or perish away on its own? It means that phenomena mysteriously appear and disappear—that is, their appearance and disappearance are not related to any other phenomena. Does one understand this? For my part, I humbly confess that I do not. Further, if one were to subscribe to the view that phenomena appear and disappear on their own, one would be opting out of the whole enterprise of rationally comprehending the world and embracing irrationality, mystery and plain hocus-pocus. The Buddha shall have none of these. On the contrary, his exhortation to us is to rationally comprehend the world. The only circumstance under which the Buddha will withdraw the doctrine is that in which one supplies him with a counter-example. And the point here is that there can, in principle, be no counter-examples to the doctrine of dependent origination. Thus it is clear that the doctrine is not a synthetic truth, either.

(3) Is the doctrine an *a priori* truth? I am well aware that the whole notion of *a priori* truth is extremely controversial and there is as yet no clear and universally acceptable clarification of the notion. Nevertheless, for my present purpose, the Kantian meaning of "*a priori*" seems most satisfactory. Thus I shall define "*a priori truth*" as truth that is certifiable without appeal to any *specific* experience, universal and necessary. Before proceeding further, it is to be emphasized that here "necessary" is not to be understood in the sense of logically necessary, but rather in the sense of necessary for the possibility of experience. (Many critics of Kant are guilty precisely of the error of understanding "necessary" in the context of the *a priori* as logically necessary.) Further, the phrase "without appeal to any

specific experience" does not mean having no bearing upon our experience; rather, it means that every experience, actual and possible, conforms to it, not accidentally but ineluctably. And the term "universal" means without exception. In light of this clarification of the meanings of these terms, it is clear that the doctrine of dependent origination is an *a priori* truth. For the doctrine is true of every phenomenon, actual and possible, and the doctrine is necessary in the sense that its denial, although not self-contradictory, cannot, in principle, be exemplified and substantiated (and its denial means the nullification of the very possibility of any experience), and it is universal in the sense that there can, in principle, be no exceptions to it. Thus, from the Kantian standpoint, it is quite reasonable to regard the doctrine of dependent origination as an *a priori* truth (in precisely the sense set forth above).

(4) It is clear from what has been said in (3) that the doctrine of dependent origination is surely not an *a posteriori* truth (whose certification requires appeal to specific experiences and which is not necessary and universal).

(5) Is the doctrine a tautology? We need not, for our purposes, go into any detailed discussion of the notion of tautology. I shall take "tautology" to any statement or formula that is repetitive and non - informative and cannot be denied without self-contradiction. We have seen that the doctrine is not analytic truth, and, given that every analytic truth should be reducible to a law of logic, the doctrine is not a tautology.

(6) Is the doctrine an inductive generalization? We shall define "inductive generalization" as a statement obtained by extending an observation regarding a limited number of instances of a certain kind to all instances of the kind, past, present, and future. An example is the statement that all crows are black. Let us immediately note the following points: an inductive generalization is based on empirical observation — is a synthetic statement, if you will — and therefore can conceivably be false. In short, an inductive generalization is potentially falsifiable; however, the doctrine of dependent origination is not, in principle, falsifiable; for to falsify it one needs to point to a single phenomenon, actual or possible, which arises and passes away on its own, and this one simply cannot do. One does not even know what it is to produce such a counter-example. Thus it is clear that the doctrine of dependent origination is not an inductive generalization.

From the above considerations, it would seem appropriate to characterize the doctrine of dependent origination as a synthetic *a priori* truth (in the Kantian sense). The doctrine, we have seen above, is an *a priori* truth. It is *a priori* truth in that its certification requires no appeal to any specific experiences and it is universal (exceptionless) and necessary for the possibility of experience. Nevertheless, insofar as it is a proclamation of a truth about the way the world is, the doctrine can be classified, in the Kantian sense, as a synthetic *a priori* truth (much like the statements "every event has a cause" and "something cannot arise out of nothing"). But I should confess that this way of regarding the doctrine of dependent origination is not altogether satisfactory, for it sheds no light at all on the question as to how in the first place one has come to grasp it, to see it. It is my considered judgement that in order to answer the above question one needs to uncover certain phenomenological facts. It is to this task I shall now turn.

We have pointed out earlier that all phenomena exist in time. But what does it mean to exist in time? To exist in time is to be subject to change—to arise and perish away. This is to say that nothing that does not change can exist in time. In short, substances cannot exist in time. But whence arises our sense of time? Our sense of time is grounded in our perception of change. That is, perception of change is the necessary condition for our sense of time. And it should be clear that perception of change is also the sufficient condition for our sense of time. All this can be expressed by saying that if x exists in time, then x is subject to change and if x is subject to change, then x exists in time. Or, equivalently, we may say that x exists in time if and only if x is subject to change. It is of the utmost importance to note that we can have absolutely no sense of time if we are the kind of beings that cannot perceive change. This is to emphasize that it is not as though we perceive time on the one hand and perceive change on the other and then conclude that time and perception of change are identical, one and the same; quite to the contrary, there can be no such thing as "perceiving time," for time is not some *entity* to be perceived, is not any *thing* to be perceived; rather, perception of change *is* the perception of time—the sense of time.

What is the point of all these observations, one might wonder. The point is that the doctrine of dependent origination is the most profound *phenomenological* observation, not to be confused with an *empirical* one. It is the articulation of the deepest insight into what is, for anything, to exist. I want to insist that the term "insight" not be understood in the sense of the *a priori*, or, for that matter, identified with any of the plethora of truths. Rather, it is to be understood in the sense of pure phenomenological datum—that existence is change, including the arising and passing away of any phenomenon; existence is sheer dynamism, if you will. That is, the coming to be and passing away of *any* phenomenon is none other than—no more and no less than—the nexus of change involving a multiplicity of phenomena. Hence the doctrine of dependent origination.

In the light of this, I suggest that the doctrine be classified as *phenomenological* truth, not as *a priori* truth, whose very conception is vague, unclear and fraught with severe controversies and serious disagreements. It would be positively misleading to classify the doctrine of dependent origination as an *a priori* truth in the Kantian sense, because for Kant the *a priori* is a contribution of the mind to the enterprise of knowledge; in sharp contrast, for the Buddha, the heart of the doctrine is not some abstract intellectual construction, but is experienced directly and purely phenomenologically; for there is here no talk of categories, the contribution of the mind, conditions for the possibility of experience, the transcendental method, and so on.

I am not hereby saying that the Buddha does not engage in subtle and profound *analyses* of the doctrine. My point is simply that the Buddha did not arrive at the doctrine by categorial, philosophical activities; rather, the insight, of which the doctrine is the articulation, is purely phenomenological, in a primordial sense. The insight is available to anyone who is phenomenologically astute, and, needless to say, one can be taught and enabled to command the insight oneself. There is nothing mysterious, metaphysical, theological or supersensible about the insight. It is through and through phenomenological. And once it is clearly understood as to what is for anything to exist— to be a phenomenon — the doctrine becomes an analytic truth, but not in the trivial sense. Rigorously speaking, the doctrine becomes a tautology.

For consider the following line of thought: things exist in time. What kind of things exist in time? Well, things that exist in time. This means, things that exist in time exist in time, a tautology. But it would be the height of ignorance and un-wisdom to dismiss the doctrine as a tautology. For what is important here is not making the obvious remark that the statement of the doctrine is really a tautology, but to ask whether it is true that things exist in time. If the answer is, Yes, then it makes not a whit of difference whether the statement is a tautology. When one comprehends truth the things exist in time (that is, are ineluctably subject to change), then one comprehends the truth of the doctrine of dependent origination. Let it be emphasized that there can be no other kind of things, for to be a thing, a phenomenon, is to be subject to change and that is just what it means to say that things exist in time. And to understand that things arise and pass away in dependence upon other things is to understand that no things (phenomena) are substances; that is, they are devoid of own being and own-nature—*svabhāvaśūnya-dharma*. All phenomena are empty. In light of these observations, the doctrine of dependent origination is most faithfully and correctly classified as "phenomenological-analytical truth."

Before bringing this essay to a close, I wish to make a few salient observations concerning the doctrine of non-self (*anatta*) in the Buddha and Hume. We ask the questions, how did the Buddha arrive at the teaching of non-self? How did Hume arrive at it? In answering these questions, we gain clarity of fundamental differences. Hume's claim that there are no mental substances, substantial, enduring selves is based upon phenomenological inquiry. For, as is well-known, Hume says that when he withdrew into his innermost recesses to discover himself, he only came upon an idea, a feeling, an impulse, an image *etc.*, but not a substantial self to which these belong. And of course the guiding dictum of his inquiry is, "no impression, no idea." That is, an idea that is not eventually traceable to an impression is not admissible into any reliable body of knowledge but is to be committed to the flames. And Hume's phenomenological discovery is in full harmony with his dictum because his claim that there is no substantial self is based on the fact that he could not trace this idea to any impression. And how did the Buddha arrive at his teaching of *anatta*, non-self? Before proceeding further, it is important to note that the Buddha's doctrine of non-self is not the denial of a self (a changing self, composed solely of the *skandha*s) but the denial of a substantial, permanent self—of substances.

Now to the doctrine of *anatta*. The doctrine of *anatta* is a direct corollary of the doctrine of dependent origination. If there can exist no substances, there can exist no *substantial* selves, either. In other words, the doctrine of *anatta* is a logical consequence of the doctrine of dependent origination. And since, as I have argued above, the doctrine of dependent origination is a phenomenological truth, any logical consequence of it, for example the doctrine of *anatta*, must also be a phenomenological truth, and Hume confirms this. That Hume did not come to the claim of non-self in the same way the Buddha did is clear from the fact that Hume, by making impressions independent of each other, treated them as if they were substances. And of course Hume was not aware that he was so treating them. Reason? Hume did not have the doctrine of dependent origination in any of the versions. For the Buddha, impressions, like all else, are through and through governed by the doctrine of dependent origination. They too are empty, insubstantial.

To conclude, the doctrine of dependent origination does not fit any of the standard categories of truth. It is grounded in a primordial phenomenological insight into what it is to exist, to be a phenomenon; and once this insight is articulated and analyzed, the statement of it is but the doctrine of dependent origination, and hence the doctrine is a phenomenological-analytical truth.

11

Process Philosophy and Theravāda Buddhism

SHANTA RATNAYAKA

The leading process philosopher, Alfred North Whitehead, studied Buddhism in the 1920's and thereafter referred to Buddhist metaphysics with high respect. In accordance with his process philosophy Whitehead advocated "becoming" and thereby rejected the dominant Western world view of "being." His exposition of process of becoming looks very much like a neo-Buddhistic view of life. Following Whitehead, other process philosophers like Charles Hartshorne, John B. Cobb, and Steve Odin, hold Buddhism in high esteem. All these scholars have been more acquainted (not because of any philosophical reasons but because of some international political developments) with the Mahāyāna Buddhist tradition and less acquainted with the Theravāda Buddhist tradition.

Along with their appreciation of Buddhism, they have posed some philosophical questions for Buddhist metaphysics. Especially, Charles Hartshorne and Steve Odin have raised many questions regarding the Buddhist theory of causality.[1] The thrust of the question goes into the nature of Dependent Origination. Gradually, the questioning has extended to several other aspects of Buddhism such as its ontology, ethics, and soteriology as well; thus the question has grown into a serious one. The present essay argues that the answer to this philosophical question is found in the early school of Buddhism, namely, Theravāda.

In order to present the Theravāda viewpoint, some of the process criticisms will be stated. These criticisms are quoted here only as stepping stones so that the criticisms will be dealt with adequately. In addition, the relevant discussions will open certain avenues to reach a common ground for Process Philosophy and Theravāda Buddhism. All these criticisms have been made by process philosophers themselves.[1]

As the theory of Karma is widely known, process criticism of karma has been made here the point of departure. Immediately after that, the criticism of causality will be introduced and discussed. Then, further ramifications of the problem will be taken into consideration. The natural outcome of this rebuttle, is none other than the proof of a deep and close relationship between Process Philosophy and Theravada Buddhism. That itself is the goal of this study.

Process Criticism of *Karma*

The philosophical terms of the following quotation will become clear gradually in the discussion:

> "The doctrine of karma is clearly cumulative in structure and becomes meaningless unless causality means `conditioning by antecedents...'[2]
>
> "Another consideration here is that if the Hua-yen doctrine of simultaneous-mutual-causation and unhindered interpenetration is applied uncritically to the level of physical actuality, then one of the most profound and central doctrines of Buddhism — Hīnayāna, Mahāyāna and Vajrayāna alike — becomes wholly invalidated; namely the inexorable law of karma."[3]

This is a valid argument. *Karma* brings result, therefore, *karma* is the cause, and result is the effect. In order to bring result, *karma* has to be an antecedent or prior to the result. *Karma* must be cumulative too, otherwise, there is no possibility of producing results later. Without these characteristics, the doctrine of *karma* has no meaning. *Karma* operates in the course of time as the past *karmas* produce the present results, and both past and present *karmas* produce future results. If causality does not run through the time, from the past to the present and into the future, theory of *karma* becomes invalidated.

Although critics have said that *karma* is an inexorable law, *karma* has never been considered inexorable. With regard to the time-bound (i.e. running through the past, present, and future) nature of *karma*, Theravāda Buddhism has never taught otherwise.

1. The present author has no intention of criticizing any Buddhist school—Mahāyāna, Vajrayāna, Hīnayāna, Hua-yen, or Kegon—but offers a Theravāda rebuttal to the criticisms of the process philosophers.
2. Steve Odin, *Process Metaphysics and Hua-yen Buddhism*: A Critical Study of Cumulative Penetration vs. Interpenetration (Albany: State University of New York Press, 1982), p. 101.
3. *Ibid.*, p. 100.

According to Theravāda, *karma* is cumulative, and is antecedent to the result. Such temporal nature of *karma* has always been well accepted in the ancient Buddhist tradition. The following stanza exemplifies this traditional theory of *karma*: (Note that "*karma*" and "*kamma*" are the same as the former is Sanskrit and the latter is Pāli).

> *Kamma*-result proceeds from *kamma*,
> Result has *kamma* for its source,
> Future becoming springs from *kamma*,
> And this is how the world goes round.[4]

Thus, the above mentioned two features of Process Philosophy, namely cumulative and antecedent nature of causality, are present in the theory of *karma*. Seen from this philosophical viewpoint, the doctrine of *karma* remains valid and meaningful. Both the argument and theory of *karma* above are related to the next point of criticism, i.e., causality. Therefore, we will have another look at them in the following discussion.

Process Criticism of Dependent Origination and Hua-yen Buddhism

> Thus, whereas both Whitehead and Hua-yen grasp co-causation and cosmic togetherness as being at the very heart of actuality, for Whitehead causal origination is a creative process resulting in an emergent togetherness or novel togetherness, as opposed to the total togetherness established by *śūnyatā* (universal relativity) and *pratītyasamutpāda* (dependent coorgination).[5]

The doctrine of Dependent Origination is common to all Buddhist schools; it is known in Sanskrit as *pratītya samutpāda* and in Pāli as *paṭicca samuppāda*. In the above passage it has been rendered into English as "dependent co-origination." The critic has placed Whitehead's causal origination "as opposed to" Dependent Origination. The reason for him to see such opposition is, of course, the particular manner that Hua-yen has interpreted the Dependent Origination. Although other interpretations are possible in Hua-yen Buddhism, their primary interpretation is based upon the simultaneity of cause and effect. In the whole of the Hartshornean

4. Bhadantācāriya Buddhaghoṣa, *The Path of Purification (Visuddhimagga)*, trans. Bhikkhu Nyanamoli (Berkeley: Shambhala Publications Inc., 1976), p. 699.
5. Odin, *Process Metaphysics and Hua-yen Buddhism*, p. 74.

process view and in some interpretations of Whiteheadian process view, causality runs through time such as from the past to the present. Therefore, a discrepancy between Hua-yen theory and process theory is inevitable.

Hua-yen interpretation of Dependent Origination can be easily understood through the demonstration give by Fa-Tsang (643-712) at the Hall of Mirrors. He placed an image of the Buddha at the center, and fixed mirrors on all four walls, the ceiling, as well as the floor. When he placed a torch beside the image, reflections of the Buddha image were seen from all directions *ad infinitum*. As the mirrors interreflected upon each other, Fa-Tsang succeeded in demonstrating the principle of interpenetration, co-causation, or dependent coarising to his congregation. Especially, the Empress Wu Tse-Tien, for whom he did this demonstration, was thoroughly convinced of the doctrine.[6] This is the interpretation meant by the above mentioned "simultaneous mutual causation and unhindered interpenetration."

Theravāda interpretation of the Dependent Origination differs remarkably from that of Hua-yen. Simultaneous causality is not the prominant doctrine in Theravāda. Instead, cumulative causality is the common phenomenon throughout the Pāli *Tipiṭaka*. There are several long and short formulas of Dependent Origination; the most common of them is the twelve linked causation as follows:

> Because of ignorance activities arise, because of activities consciousness arises, because of consciousness mind and matter arise, because of mind and matter six bases arise, because of six bases contact arises, because of contact feeling arises, because of feeling craving arises, because of craving attachment arises, because of attachment becoming arises, because of becoming birth arises, because of birth ageing-death-sorrow-lamentation-pain (physical) - mental pain-despair arise.[7]

In this teaching the effect follows the cause. For instance, contact takes place first, then as a result of contact and many other causes, feeling arises; then, as a result of feeling and its accompanied

---

6. Garma C.C. Chang, *The Buddhist Teaching of Totality: The Philosophy of Hwa Yen Buddhism* (University Park: The Pennsylvania State University Press, 1971), p. 24.
7. *The Book of Analysis (Vibhaṅga): The Second Book of The Abhidhamma Piṭaka*, trans. by Aggamahāpaṇḍita Pathamakyaw Ashin Thittila (Setthila) (London: Pali Text Society, 1969), 180.

causes craving arises, which means feeling comes first and craving next; so process goes on. A hall of mirrors will not demonstrate the Thervāda doctrine of Dependent Origination. A contact, feeling, or craving emerges anew; therefore, in the fullest sense of the word, there is "emergent togetherness or novel togetherness" in the Theravadin's process view; and it is quite consonant with the Hartshornean Process Philosophy.

The previously discussed *karma* theory can be cited here for further clarification. *Karma* and result do not function like two mirrors that reflect upon one another simultaneously. A result can take place today or at this present moment, although its cause, which is a particular *karma,* occurred several million years ago. In the process of *karma* there is cause and effect; *karma* is the cause and its result is the effect, but the two are not co-arising. The following stanza from the Theravada tradition also testifies to the same effect:

> There is no *kamma* in result,
> Nor does result exist in *kamma;*
> Though they are void of one another,
> There is no fruit without the *kamma.*[8]

Now we have seen that causality in Theravāda maintains, in the main, cumulative penetration but not interpenetration, successive fusion but not mutual fusion, and asymmetrical causality but not symmetrical causality. Causality is asymṃetrical as the process of causality is going on from the present end, but not so at the past end; one end is open but not the other end. Here the similarity between the causal theories of Theravāda and Hartshornean Process Philosophy becomes vivid. The same criticism has been extended to Mahāyāna Buddhism as we now see in the following argument.

Process Criticism of Nāgārjuna and Mahāyāna Buddhism

> Let us go back eighteen centuries, to Nāgārjuna the Mahāyāna Buddhist, a man at least comparable to Bradley or Hume in subtlety, and a man who, like them, wishes to show that there is no rationale for the idea of real connectedness. An exhaustive division is proposed. Effects are one of the following: different from their causes, not different, both different and not different, neither different nor not different. Each of the four

8. Buddhaghoṣa, *The Path of Purification,* p. 700.

> cases is then shown to be irrational. But all four are couched in symmetrical terms! Since intuitively the cause-effect relation has a direction, is not symmetrical, the analysis cannot be correct.[9]

Although Charles Hartshorne often admires Buddhist process thinking, here he criticizes Nāgārjuna who is the greatest logician of Mahāyāna Mādhyamika tradition. Nāgārjuna presented himself as an interpreter of Dependent Origination. Nevertheless, in Hartshorne's view, Nāgārjuna's interpretation is not correct because his exposition is based on symmetrical causality.

In the Theravāda tradition there exists a great respect for Nāgārjuna, yet his interpretations are not accepted at all. His theory of causality has not gained any place in the Theravāda commentaries or in their later writings. Instead, asymmetrical causality has been the Theravādin's interpretation of Dependent Origination, as seen in the previous section of the present study. In this manner, Theravādin's view is analogous to the Hartshornean process view, though some Mahāyāna views may not be.

Process Criticism of Vajrayāna (Tantric Buddhism)

> At once, the Tantric notion of *sahaja* or "togetherness-awareness" recalls the conception of experiential togetherness in Whitehead's metaphysics, which propounds that the whole universe stands indivisibly together as an aesthetic harmony of feelings within the awareness of each perspectival occasion of experience. However, the mode of togetherness is by no manner of speaking the total togetherness assumed in the Hua-yen or Tantric metaphysics, but the 'production of novel togetherness' whereby the (antecedent) many become one and are increased by one in the course of creative advance. To repeat Whitehead's words: 'Creativity' is the principle of novelty .... the 'production of novel togetherness' is an ultimate notion embodied in the term 'concrescence'."[10]

Here *Sahaja* (total togetherness) of Tantric or Vajrayāna Buddhism has been contrasted to novel togetherness of process meta-

9. Charles Hartshorne, *Creative Syntheses and Philosophic Method* (La Salle: The Open Court Publishing Co., 1970), p. 213.
10. Odin, *Process Metaphysics and Hua-yen Buddhism*, pp. 151-152.

physics. "Concrescence" is a Whiteheadean term for the new entity or the new becoming in the process of existence. And each entity is produced by many causes, and thereby many are increased by one. But, in the view of total togetherness there is no increase, therefore, Tantric metaphysics differs from the above discussed process metaphysics.

Total togetherness can be illustrated with the metaphor of ocean. "There is no wave that differs from the water — the wave itself is the self-same revelation of the water; there is no water that differs from the waves — it is water itself that makes the waves."[11] According to this theory, an individual manifestation or "concrescence" is like a wave of the ocean, there is neither increase nor decrease in the totality.

Turning to Theravāda Buddhism, one can see a different explanation. A process of perception (series of experiences of consciousness) from the *Abhidhamma* can be cited, for an example. When one sees, hears, tastes, or in such other experiential occasions, one comes in contact with some object, sound, food, etc. Then the event of seeing, hearing, tasting, etc., take place. One single event of seeing itself is, in fact, a series of subtle occasions of experience. When the eye comes in contact with the object, there is unconscious continuum (*bhavaṅga*) because of the present event of contact, it is followed by vibrating subconsciousness (*bhavaṅga calana*), and that is followed by awakening subconsciousness (*bhavaṅga upaccheda*). After this awakening, there comes the intensive part of the event which includes inquisitive subconsciousness (*avajjana*), eye consciousness (*cakkhu viññāṇa*), receptive consciousness (*sampaṭiccana*), investigative consciousness (*santīraṇa*), determinative consciousness (*votthapana*), exertive consciousness (*javana* or *karma*), and retentive consciousness (*tadālambana*).[12] These come into being or "become" one after the other, but the whole process takes place within a moment. If one keeps on seeing the same object, similar processes of seeing will recur.

If the event is an act of hearing then ear consciousness (*sota viññāṇa*) occurs instead of eye consciousness. Throughout one's life these processes take place; in other words, living is altogether a

11. Chang, *The Buddhist Teaching of Totality*, p. 139.
12. The Venerable Anuruddha Thera, *Abhidhammattha Saṅgaha*, ed. H. Siri Dewamitta (Colombo : Maha Bodhi Press, 1929), p. 17.

process. Here, unlike the ocean and wave theory, each event is a new event, each event is a product of innumerable causes, and as Whitehead says, many are increased by one because of that event. This example should show that although a disagreement between Vajrayāna and Process Philosophy can be seen, a very close resemblance between Theravāda and Process Philosophy does exist.

Process Criticism of Hīnayāna Buddhism and Yogācāra Buddhism

> Early Hīnayāna Buddhism applied the formula of dependent coorigination with great tenacity to the conception of a separate independently existing ego or self (*ātman*), factoring it into a multiplicity of *dharmas*. However, these *dharmas* were the ultimate moments, irreducible elements or ontological absolutes of existence. Thus, the Madhyamika school of Nāgārjuna charged the Hīnayāna theorists with having constructed a pluralistic realism wherein only the reality of the self (*ātman*) is negated, while the *dharmas* themselves are wholly reified as having some sort of absolute, irreducible and independent existence of their own. At the other extreme, the Madhyamika school charged the Yogācāra Buddhists with having constructed a monistic idealism wherein such notions as consciousness (*vijñāṇa*), one mind (*ekacitta*) and the storehouse (*ālaya*) are all hypostatized as the ontological ultimates... The Hīnayana and Yogācāra schools both go astray by conferring absolute validity on concepts having their place only on the level of pragmatic truth.[13]

None of the above charges would fall upon the Theravādins because they have adhered from the beginning to the no-soul doctrine. Pāli *Dhammapada,* for instance, teaches that all *dharmas* including *nirvāṇa* are soulless.[14] As Theravādins meditate daily, the three characteristics of the world are impermanence, suffering, and soullessness. One aim of learning the very doctrine of Dependent Origination is to understand soullessness. Therefore, the Theravādins have never applied the Dependent Origination to establish a theory of self (*ātman*). On the Theravadin view, nothing in the mundane

13. Odin, *Process Metaphysics and Hua-yen Buddhism*, p. 129.
14. Dhp. 279.

existence is independent. Only *nirvāṇa* is independent, ultimate, and absolute.

It has been a repeated mistake to identify Hīnayāna with Theravāda. But at this juncture the denial of the absolute and independent *dharmas* itself testifies to the fact that Theravāda is neither Yogācāra nor Hīnayāna. Some scholars continue to make the mistake of identifying Hīnayāna with Theravāda. The Theravadins themselves never call their religion "Hīnayāna." Therefore, it is inappropriate for anyone to dub them with derogatory names. A few Buddhist schools, such as Sarvāstivādins, claimed the existence of independent *dharmas* and maintained the pluralistic realism in the early history of Buddhism. Theravādins were not among them. All in all, Theravāda is not Hīnayāna, and Hīnayāna is not Theravāda; therefore, the criticism of Hīnayāna does not fall upon the Theravāda.

Process Criticism of Creativity

The polemic here is that the Hua-yen Buddhist theory of total non-obstructed interpenetration and unhindered mutual containment with its underlying symmetrical infrastructure has accounted for complete ontological togetherness, cohesiveness and solidarity, but at the expense of all creativeness, novelty and freedom. Each *dharma* can be exhaustively factored or reductively analyzed into its causal relations and supportive conditions without remainder. By definition, total determinism is entailed by such a view in that each *dharma* is simply an effect of its manifold of causes: there is no creativity, freedom or novelty.[15]

In our explanation of *karma*, Dependent Origination, and stream of consciousness, we have observed how causality is productive, originative, or creative of novel entities in the process of existence. In addition, we have noted how that causality, philosophically speaking, is asymmetrical.

The above criticism shows that the other type of causality, namely symmetrical causality, is not creative of novel entities. On the other hand, creativity of novel entities is an essential characteristic in the causality of Process Philosophy. Once again, the fact that Theravāda is compatible with Process Philosophy becomes evident. Next, criticism from the same metaphysical view is directed to universal compassion (*karuṇā*) or loving kindness (*mettā*).

---

15. Odin, *Process Metaphysics and Hua-yen Buddhism*, pp. 77-78.

Process Criticism of Universal Compassion

However, again reflecting their divergent metaphysical commitments of symmetry as over against asymmetry, whereas the Chinese Buddhist concept of compassion or sympathy (*tz'u*) represents the total interpenetration and mutual fusion of subject and object or one and many, Whitehead's notions of sympathy and concern represent a cumulative fusion or one-way penetration....[16]

In all branches of Buddhism wisdom and compassion or universal lovingkindness are major teachings. However, a serious philosophical question is raised here about the possibility of feeling compassionate if only simultaneous penetration is what there is ontologically. Whitehead's "feeling of feeling" or "sympathetic concernedness" is one way penetration, as is the pattern of causality in process theory. Thus, as the above quotation states, a difference between the Chinese Mahāyāna view of compassion and Whitehead's sympathetic feeling can be discerned. In order to compare the same with Theravāda, here is an example:

> Now it is by means of one of these *jhāna*s beginning with the first that he dwells pervading (intent upon) one direction with his heart endued with loving kindness, likewise the second direction, likewise the third direction, likewise the fourth direction and so above, below, and around; everywhere and equally he dwells pervading the entire world with his heart endued with lovingkindness, abundant, exalted, measureless, free from enmity, and free from affliction. For this versatility comes about only in one whose consciousness has reached absorption in the first *jhāna* and the rest.[17]

A compassionate person "dwells pervading one direction with his heart endued with lovingkindness" means that the meditator radiates his love upon all the beings of that direction. It does not mean that all the beings of that direction radiate love back upon the meditator. In that particular act neither does the meditator himself radiate his love upon the beings dwelling in other directions. Clearly, in such a feeling of love, asymmetrical causality functions, but not symmetrical causality. This ethical issue, just as the metaphysical ones, should illustrate how much Theravāda parallels process views.

16. *Ibid.*, pp. 144-145.
17. Buddhaghoṣa, *The Path of Purification*, pp. 333-334.

From this ethical problem we can move into the final point of this paper, i.e., soteriology.

Process Criticism of Englightenment or *Nirvāṇa*

> Thus, the picture of Whitehead's concept of peace which unfolds from his writing is that of a deep, harmonious, oceanic, transpersonal dimension of felt immediacy—ecstatic, final, and wholly released from the tragic suffering and affliction inherent in creative advance as perpetual perishing...
> However, in contradistinction to the Hua-yen doctrine of li-shih-wu-ai, Whitehead's identification of appearance with reality in the experience of final peace does not involve the realization of a static totality wherein past, present and future events all simultaneously interpenetrate into a single thought-instant....[18]

Process Metaphysics and Hua-yen Buddhism vividly shows how Process Philosophy of Whitehead, like Buddhism, teaches that suffering is intrinsic to the process of existence, and that transition and perpetual perishing are essential characteristics of the process. Further, Whitehead states: "That the suffering attains its end in a Harmony of Harmonies. The immediate experience of this Final Fact ... is the sense of Peace."[19]

However, this enlightening experience, as argued from process viewpoint, cannot be come upon by a simultaneous interpenetration into a single thought moment. For instance, all the unenlightened thought moments of the past cannot be interpenetrated simultaneously. Such an event or statement is essentially self-contradictory. This way Tantric, Hua-yen, (and Japanese Kegon) interpretation of *nirvāṇic* experience is incompatible with Whitehead's "Final Fact" or "Peace".

Theravāda, on this "Final Fact" also, is at one with Whitehead. At this point, Steve Odin very appropriately turns to Theravāda Buddhism in order to compare Whiteheadian "Peace" with Buddhist teaching of *nirvāṇa* and says: "In the classic Pāli text entitled The Questions of King Milinda it has thus been written: If you ask: 'How is *nirvāṇa* to be known?' It is by its freedom from distress and and

18. Odin, *Process Metaphysics and Hua-yen Buddhism*, pp. 154-155.
19. *Ibid.*, p. 154.

danger, by confidence, by peace, by calm, by bliss, by happiness."[20] Therefore, here we all — King Milinda, his discussant Nāgasena, Whitehead, Hartshorne, Odin, and the reader as well as the writer of this essay — can come to a common ground of understanding where Process Philosophy and Theravāda Buddhism nest together in peace and harmony!

20. *Ibid.*, p. 153.

12

Theravāda and Processes: *Nirvāṇa* as a Meta-process

NINIAN SMART

The supposition that the Buddha banned certain questions because they are not conducive to liberation does not get to the root of the matter, for a very obvious reason: a merely pragmatic discouragement of speculation would be ineffective. It is true that the simile of the person struck by an arrow might favor the pragmatic interpretation, but the simile of the fire going out points in quite a different direction. I would like here to recast a discussion I first expressed in 1964, and then to suggest a way of looking at *nibbāna* (Skt. *nirvāṇa*) which is somewhat novel and might produce reverberations both with the thinking of Schopenhauer and with some Mahāyāna notions, not to mention with process thought.

In my 1964 discussion I took a position not unlike that of K. N. Jayatilleke in his famous *Early Buddhist Theory of Knowledge,* namely a kind of Wittgensteinian interpretation of the undetermined questions or *avyākatāni.* The Theravādin list of these includes, of course, questions about the finitude of the cosmos as to space and time, about the identity or otherwise of the *jīva* or soul and the body, and about the existence or otherwise of the *Tathāgata.* It appears to me that all these issues are secretly or overtly about the same thing, namely *nibbāna.* How so? First, the finitude of the cosmos is not just a physical or astronomical question. Its deeper meaning is about whether there is something beyond or outside the cosmos. There is in a sense an end to the cosmos, when the *arhant* deceases, for then the cosmos ends (for him at least). But that sort of end of the cosmos is not some literal boundary. Then second, the question about the *jīva* cannot be fully explicated without taking *nibbāna* into account. What the Buddha did in effect was to jettison the permanent self or *ātman* in favor of the possibility of *nibbāna.* In other words, he kept to a main function of the self namely to be a liberated entity in due course. But he cut out the entity. A living being in capable of liberation. In other ways the notion of a permanent self is both useless and pernicious: useless because what does not change cannot be a factor in changes; and pernicious because it may conduce to egocentrism. Regarding its uselessness, one can spell this out by thinking of an unchanging S underlying a series of events, e1, e2 and so on. Since it is assumed that S is the same during both e1 and e2 it cannot account for e3.

To use an informal example: if I burst into song at e3, this can hardly be due to my skull which is unchanged all through (relatively speaking). It must be due to some other factor (my remembering my beloved, say). But in substituting *nibbāna*'s possibility for the unchanging self, the Buddha rendered the question of the *jīva* and the body puzzling. The intent of the question is to ascertain whether the soul can be separated from the body. It can't really: but yet there is the possibility of *nibbāna*, that is of a kind of liberation (and attaining that is a main function of the self or soul). Finally, and third, the question about the Tathāgata is more obviously about *nibbāna*. The Tathāgata has attained *nibbāna* in this life, but is not going to be reborn at death. What should we say, then, about survival?

The example of the going out of the flame points to the unanswerability of questions about *nibbāna* because they are wrongly posed. You can ask when a flame went out but not where it went. We may treat the *avyākatāni* in a Wittgensteinian manner as being radically senseless. They are worse than the question "Is the king of France bald?" because, while it is merely contingent that there is a king of France (and we might also joke that Mitterand is the king of France), it is not *contingent* that *nibbāna* 'transcends' events in time and space. Given the Buddha's analysis of the nature of the cosmos, *nibbāna* is *necessarily* non-cosmic, is *necessarily* not in time and space. So questions about it are intrinsically unanswerable, if unanswerable at all. Those questions resemble more "Is the letter F in love?" than "Is the king of France bald?"

Let me lay alongside this observation the fact that the Theravādin writings ascribe omniscience to the Buddha. Maybe there was an element of one-up-man-ship in this, to counter claims that Māhavīra was omniscient. But even so there were other beliefs, such as that giving the Buddha special cognitive powers (the *dasabala*), which implied that he had preternatural insight. It would be assumed therefore that he knew the true nature of *nibbāna*. But of course the incapacity to answer a wrongly formed question is not a defect in knowledge. No one could know whether the letter F is in love or not. Had the Buddha merely been warning people not to waste their time with 'metaphysical' questions he would have known the true answers to the undetermined questions, and withheld these. Yet he is not supposed to have had the closed fist of the teacher. It is more logical to think of the questions as being radically unanswerable, so that even a Buddha could not make sense of them. His failure to know the answers would not be a defect in his knowledge.

But he might know something else: namely, *why* the questions were unanswerable. No doubt *arhants* could grasp this too. And possibly we might know that. Now, above I have suggested that there is *necessity* about the senselessness of the questions because it is necessary that *nibbāna* does not exist (or occur) as an empirical state. More explicitly the Buddha says in *Suttanipāta* v. 1076: there is no measuring the individual who has ended the process of rebirth.

The key terminology here is: *na pamānamatthi.* There is no way of estimating the liberated individual, and no perceptual access. For that matter, there is no access through reasoning. We can also reverse our perspective and look to the analysis of the individual and her world in the Theravāda. The person is a mere conditioned process in interaction with her environment and involving the concurrence of the *khandhas*. There was thus no individual to refer to when she was no longer reborn. In short the individual was radically non-existent in *nibbāna*: so her absence is something of necessity rather than contingency. But yet there is something mysterious about individuals which so to speak lies beyond the complex of processes which makes each of them. That extra is the possibility of *nibbāna*. But it is not as if this possibility is a something, even if in the Mahāyāna the concept of the Buddha-nature sounds as if it is a kind of ingredient in the individual's make-up or constitution. The possibility merely signifies that in certain circumstances there is no more rebirth and the conditioned processes are replaced by some X which is unthinkable, indefinable.

Parenthetically, there is a question which we need to deal with to tidy up our account. Attaining *nibbāna* is of course something the saint does in this life: so perhaps someone attains it at the age of thirty and then lives to eighty. During his fifty years of emancipated life (a form of *jīvanmukti* or living liberation) a person retains his 'substrate' — his bodily and mental constituents. We have hitherto been talking of *nibbāna* without substrate, when the saint passes away. This-life *nibbāna* might be said to involve the perception of or insight into 'the' X.

At death, then, the individual stream of processes which has had as a part of itself the perception of or insight into the X is replaced by the X. This, roughly, is the schema presented in the Theravādin context.

Now, there is perhaps for some readers the issue as to whether a transcendent X can be more like a process than a being. Let me briefly explore this issue. The concept of transcendence in the Western tradition has been typically interwoven with the notion of an ultimate being (God, the Creator). And so there has been a picture presented: the cosmos of beings over against the one Being which or who created the cosmos. Therefore it has been natural to write of a transcendent being. There have been those however, notably Paul Tillich, who have wished to indicate that God as transcendent is not a being, and so have used some other locution: "being itself." Being is by analogy with a being, but is not in space (or time). In the West there has been little interest in the notion of a transcendent which is not a being. What about a transcendent process or event? The first reaction could be negative: how can you have a Process in itself, or an event beyond time? After all, processes and events presuppose time. Well, does not a being presuppose space? If you escape upwards into being, why could the Buddhist not similarly ascend to Process or Event? Perhaps that is what *nibbāna* is—a process beyond processes or maybe, better, process beyond processes. (There is an extra complication to the comparison: God is usually conceived as not being-itself only but as a person, but we can leave this point on one side here.)

It does not seem to me more contradictory to think of process than of being as transcendent. And so we could think of the Buddha's message as claiming that there is process-in-itself beyond the impermanent processes of this world. Or, as Buddhist philosophy developed into the thesis of momentariness, then there is, so to speak, the ultimate moment which lies beyond the moments of *saṃsāra*. This might be a way of bringing out the radical anti-substantialism of the Buddha. For we can imagine various dispositions of the notions of substance and non-substance in various systems of metaphysics. We can have the Aristotelian substance-substances dualism, contrasting God as the ultimate substance with a cosmos itself made up of substances. Or we could have a substance to non-substance dualism, contrasting God as the ultimate substance with a cosmos itself made up of substances. Or we could have a substance to non-substance dualism, in which God is contrasted with the world seems as a congeries of non-substances, that is events. This is found in, for instance, Islamic occasionalism. In a rather different mode, there is the notion of one substance and the rest mirage. Or again there is the possibility of a non-substance underlying a non-substantial world. Usually this has been expressed in the Buddhist case by recourse to the idea of the *śūnyatā* underlying or making up the 'real' nature of events, etc.

Now let us return to the undetermined questions. If my analysis is correct they are all unanswerable because they involve a component in the reply which is indefinable, the unknowable X which is *nibbāna*. There is not an answer to the question whether the cosmos has an end, because such end as it does have (namely the attainment of *nibbāna*) cannot be expressed. If a series of events, for instance the events making up the life of the Tathāgata, is capped by an ultimate Event, then it is neither correct to affirm that the Buddha lives on nor that he does not. Of course, ordinary and ignorant speech can take over. It became customary to think of Buddha as being 'there' in some mysterious and confused sense, so that he could be reverenced and concretized into statues, *etc.* The function of Buddhist dialectics in its many forms is to explode this ever-recurrent substantializing tendency and deconstruct the ultimate (as well as this world). If the characteristic of the Mahāyāna was to move from the emptiness of the *skandha*s or groups of events making up the individual to the emptiness of all *dharma*s or constituent elements of the cosmos, then the dialectic could move from the undetermined questions as confined to the list

To expand this point further, we could think of the Theravāda as essentially *skandha*-oriented and of the Mahāyāna as *dharma*-oriented. The undetermined questions in the Theravāda relate to the individual, even when they are ostensibly about the *loka* or cosmos. This explains why the scope of the question is not universalized. On the other hand, once one gets the idea that it is not just from the point of the individuals that there is emptiness, but that the indeterminacy of language applies to the inner nature of everything, then *nibbāna* becomes, so to speak, pervasive (which it is not in the Theravāda). And because this is so then the ultimate nature of everything is indefinable.

It might still be asked as to whether we can do anything to render the idea of process-itself more intelligible. It is supposedly a transcendent 'event' or 'series of events' by analogy with *saṃsāric* processes. Now when we try to explain how it is that the transcendent being is non-spatial, we can use the analogy of the mind — thoughts, for example, cannot be strictly located. The thought of the battle of Waterloo is not to the left of my right ear. It is not reasonable to apply lateral spatial predicates to thoughts and a lot else besides. Is there an analogous non-temporal 'event' which does not take temporal predicates? Perhaps we could use the parallel of the specious present: a holistic 'stretch' of consciousness might be seen as having internally no before or after. Likewise, the momentary flicker of consciousness postulated in the *Abhidhamma* and post-canonical literature. (Between each flicker, by the way, momentary death is thought to occur: if only one could stop the onward march of instants, one would attain a momentary state which would be deathless, *amata*.) In such a way one might begin to think of a timeless process, as being-itself is a non-spatial 'thing.' The substitution in a sequence of a timeless process for temporal processes would be a way of analyzing *nibbāna*. All this is a deduction from Buddhist non-substantialism. I shall go on to elaborate some consequences we might draw from this.

But here let us digress a moment, in relation to the motives for desubstantialization. One main motive no doubt was conceptual or philosophical. This had at least two roots. First, there was the Buddhist critique of language, in opposition to the way brahmins reified and even divinized the sacred Vedic tongue. Conventionalism raises the possibility — and for Buddhism the actuality — of the systematically misleading character of language. There was no question of some primordial fit between words and things. It was but a short step to saying that language errantly pushes us towards belief in substances, because of the lordly way of nouns. Second, the Buddhist emphasis on causality, and its flowering in *asatkāryavāda*, left no great place for substances. If a substance is unchanging then it cannot explain anything. And if it changes it can be boiled down into its episodes. Beyond these philosophical thoughts there lay a distrust of substance, no doubt, as being the typical language of ritual. One thing is transubstantiated into another. Brahmins liked the sticky talk of substance: after all, holy power was a kind of thing residing in the brahmin himself, not to mention the Holy Power of Brahman itself. Early Buddhism has a perception of the Brahmanical *āstika* religion analogous to McKim Marriott's modern theory of Hindu substance. (The fact that Buddhism was such a vital ingredient, sometimes dominant in Indian classical civilization, such Hinduizing theories as that of Dumont have to be treated skeptically.) Substantialism encourages also collectivist thinking, and Buddhism has a remarkably individualistic coloration. And so the Buddhist espousal of processes and conventionalism has a religious as well as a philosophical meaning.

What are the more general implications of thinking of the transcendent as being more like a process than a thing? First, it is easier to think of it as neither singular nor plural. The fault with Kant's noumena is that they are plural, and yet by Kantian doctrine that is an absurdity. Second, when coupled with Buddhist critique of language it suggests that there does indeed lie something beyond both our perceptions and our theories of reality. Nevertheless, Buddhism has not, I believe, thought through a major point concerning the distinction between phenomena and 'noumena' or the beyond. Before we get to that, a point can be made about the very idea of phenomena. The assumption of some philosophical literature is that phenomena do not have intellectual content (so to speak). The fact is that the way we look at the world is often suffused with concepts: there is a table, there a mountain, here the color red, here my friend. Perception is typically propositional. Further, though some physical entities are beyond direct perception they can be seen by the means of instrumentation. Galaxies invisible to the naked eye can be seen through the telescope. So when we talk about what is perceptible we really mean technologically-enhanced-perception-accessible. But not only that: even such enhanced perception does not perceive all the theories which clothe the phenomena, so to speak. In short, this-worldly phenomena are more than phenomena in the old-fashioned sense, as intended by Kant. So we can say that phenomena in the way in which we ought to be using the idea are not strictly perceptual phenomena. Perhaps we should use another term: maybe, the graspable.

But we recognize that there is always a hinterland to the graspable. On the other hand, the frontier between what we grasp and what lies beyond is forever shifting. We have, in a dialectic with nature, extended our grasping from the atom downwards to the quark, and who knows what beyond that? If we take a Mahāyāna perspective, we could interpret Buddhist philosophy in a quasi-Kantian sense, as affirming that beyond graspable processes there lies process in itself, always eluding our theories, concepts and perceptions, even if retreating along an advancing frontier of knowledge. There could be analogies here with Schopenhauer. The world could be described as process and representation (rather than will, in my view a badly chosen analogy).

We might view mainstream Mahāyāna philosophy from this point of view as postulating an empty and indescribable process underlying or pervading the graspable cosmos (*loka*). This seems an apt account of how we might view that which is scientifically and otherwise accessible on the one hand and what lies 'beyond' on the other. The indescribable challenges us, and turns up problems of unforeseen kinds to refute or modify our theories. The concept of nature sometimes serves in the West to comprise both process in itself and the graspable phenomena.

However, this notion of a wider application of the transcendent in Mayāyāna seems indeed different from the more limited scope of the idea in the Theravāda. Before I come to that, it is important to see that the notion of the transcendent as I have used it does not significantly differ from that of the immanent. This is a thesis not often grasped in Western thinking. After all, both *transcendent* and *immanent* are bits of jargon relying on spatial metaphors, that is those contained in the prefixes *trans*- or beyond and im - or within. It is clear that if we say (for instance) that God transcends the cosmos we do not literally mean that she is in a different part of space beyond space. Nor if we say that he or she is within all things that by cutting open the cheese you will find God in there. So neither beyond nor in is a literal direction. Do analogical directions point differently? The fact is that both the transcendent and the immanent are non-spatial in a literal sense. But the use of the different terms does point to something. One could put this in the Buddhist context as follows.

In the Theravādin context *nibbāna* is transcendent. It is beyond events. But it does not pervade. It is not a Theravādin idea at all that *nibbāna* is 'behind' events or that *samsāra* equals *nibbāna*. It is not as though every event is 'secretly' *śūnyatā*. Of course in a suitably defined sense of emptiness every event is empty. But the Theravāda does not extend its transcendental minimalism the way that the Great Vehicle does. There is no tendency to see *nibbāna* 'in' everything (that is in all processes or events). On the other hand, even if *within* taken analogically has no intrinsic difference of placement to *outside* or *beyond*, the Mahāyāna thinks of the characteristics of *nibbāna* as pervasive. The reason is as stated earlier that the Theravāda is more subjective, more psychological, more focussed on the individual and his or her experience. Passage through the world is a lone pilgrimage, with, however, help and advice from others, down a kind of *karmic* tunnel with light at the other end, namely *nibbāna*, which is a kind of transcendental event or process. The Mahāyāna picture is somewhat diverse: all events ultimately exhibit liberation, and the liberating experience is seeing that this is so. To put it another way: the Theravādin theory is not so dependent on the idea of realization, even if the forces which bind us to the world have at their root *avijjā*. A sort of ontology dominates over saving epistemology. But of course I recoil at the word 'ontology' in so far as Buddhism rejects both being and beings.

There are no doubt religious reasons for the philosophical position of the Mahāyāna as against the Theravāda. Let me put it this way: the Theravāda was centrally concerned with meditation. Meditation and analysis were the keys to liberation. Can there be doubt of that? It might be that emphasis would swing, so that sometimes monastic communities could think that analysis (therefore scholarship) was their primary concern. And of course, obviously enough, monastic communities can easily forget their primary concerns anyway: witness some of the politics of monkhood over the last thirty-five years in Sri Lanka. On the other hand, the Mahāyāna was increasingly inclined towards some of the main values of Hinduism (so called). And so the sentiments of *bhakti*, itself in origin maybe owing much to Buddhist influence, came to be directed towards the ultimate. Devotional Buddhism personalized the character of transcendent Buddhas. But it also contributed to the idea that the ultimate is somehow *pervasive*. The notion of *nibbāna* as pervasive could encourage the idea that the Buddha pervades, control everything from within (but not in a literal sense). So for these reasons the Mahāyāna went for a more substantive and pervasive role for the concept of *nibbāna*. These shadowy substantialized tendencies in the Indian Mahāyāna were reinforced by Tantra. The more magical and ritualistic phases of Buddhism (which I would regard ultimately as a betrayal of Buddhist conventionalism and the early moralization of Brahmin religious values, etc.) reinforced the 'ontological' tendencies of the religion, taking it very far from the Therāvāda. So both *bhakti* and *tantra* contained forces which underlined what may be called the 'pervasionism' of the Great Vehicle.

The net result of the foregoing discussion is that the Therāvādin's pointing to transcendent process helps to explain the force of the undetermined questions. If the Buddha knew everything, then he knew what was knowable. But the transcendent *nibbāna* which was the light at the end of the tunnel of individual existence was unknowable and without the possibility of exposition. Consequently all those undetermined questions, each of which involves direct or indirect reference to *nibbāna*, are intrinsically unanswerable. Whether the Buddha himself had any glimpse of the Mahāyāna extension of this idea is also for us (but contingently, because of the sparsity of reliable historical data) unknowable.

But there are ideas which could emerge from the thoughts I have sketched, for future philosophers to take up. We could easily adopt the model of the universe as having, in addition to the conceptually-impregnated and technology-extended phenomena, a hinterland of process which is as yet unknowable to us, because theories have not yet caught up with it, or penetrated more deeply into it. Whether the world (cosmos) is 'infinite' in this respect is worth thinking about. Could it be that we could never completely occupy the hinterland and understand everything? It seems to me doubtful for various reasons. How could we ever know that the 'edge' of the universe was without its own hinterland?

In brief it seems to me that the questions raised by the undetermined questioned are fertile today, and need to be corralled within the fences of historical scholarship.

13

"Orientalism" in Buddhology

Western Preunderstandings in Understanding Buddhism

Frank J. Hoffman

Introduction

> The colonial conquest of the mind lasts much longer than the political domination.
>
> Gombrich and Obeyesekere[1]

This is a paper about Orientalism and the philosophical study of Buddhism.[2] In it the "philosophy of Buddhist religion" is discussed in relation to the problem of "Orientalism" as expressed in Said (1978).[3] Herein I intend to explore with reference to Buddhism the question of whether, and if so to what extent, Said's critique of Orientalism places methodological limits on what the philosophy of Buddhist religion can do; on what limits or *lacunae* obtain for Said's own critique; and, finally to conclude with some suggestions about one way forward against the background of critique's like Said's that are broadly deconstructionist in tone.[4]

---

1. Richard F. Gombrich and Gananath Obeyesekere, *Buddhism Transformed: Religious Change in Sri Lanka* (Princeton, NJ : Princeton University Press, 1988), p. 290.
2. Edward W. Said, *Orientalism* New York: Vintage Books, 1979. (1st edition, New York : Pantheon Books, 1978.)
3. I do not concern myself here with the complex question of whether and to what extent Said may have modified his position since the publication of the first edition of *Orientalism* in 1978, and am interested in the position expressed in *Orientalism* — the ideas expressed rather than the personality of Said or the development of his thought.
4. An earlier version of this paper was presented to The Buddhist Forum at Harvard University on December 3, 1991. I am grateful to Professor Masatoshi Nagatomi, other faculty members, and the graduate students for critical feedback on that occasion. I am also indebted to Professor Vidya Dehejia, NEH institute partici-

In a recent article I defended an approach to the philosophy of religion which would pluralize it while retaining the traditional emphasis on conceptual analysis. In distinguishing my approach from those of Steven Collins and Don Cupitt, it emerged that a philosophy of Buddhist religion should:[5]

(a) take its material with philosophical seriousness : be critical and evaluative;
(b) raise problems against the background of the Buddhist texts themselves: be textually based;
(c) treat Buddhism as a religion with philosophical implications;
(d) take a comparative approach when necessary to illuminate a specific problem (the comparative approach may relate ideas of Eastern or Western thinkers in both philosophy and religion);
(e) analyse conceptual problems rather than put forth religious beliefs.

Rather than a monolithic Philosophy of Religion which is really Philosophy of Christian Religion (as is prominent in so many textbooks on philosophy of religion), one would find Philosophy of Buddhist Religion in addition to the latter alongside philosophies of other major religions. The intellectual antecedents for the self-conscious recognition of a plurality of philosophies of religion have been in place for some time, but few have cared to draw the obvious conclusion in favor of pluralizing philosophy of religion.[6] Specifically, the range of abilities manifested in the historial and philosophical approach of Ninian Smart, the conceptual analytic approach of John

this paper when it was presented in the summer of 1992 during the NEH Summer Institute, "Indian art: Sacred and Secular" in which I was pleased to be a participant. It was interesting to see that the students and faculty in art history are quite attuned to the Orientalism issue, having been informed by an earlier generation of art historians that this or that Asian art work is a "monstrosity"—and to see even now how Western assumptions may sometimes lurk behind the claim that there is a "pan-Indian style" or that some artworks are "unfinished."

5. Frank J. Hoffman, "Towards a Philosophy of Buddhist Religion" in *Asian Philosophy* 1 (1) March 1991, p. 26.

6. Arvind Sharma, *A Hindu Perspective on the Philosophy of Religion* (New York: St. Martin's Press, 1990). Aside from the fact that he attends to Hinduism rather than Buddhism for the most part, Sharma's treatment is structurally rather similar to, but briefer, less textured, and more schematic than the approach I have in mind. My review of this work appears in a recent issue of *International Journal of Philosophy of Religion* 34 (1993).

Hick, and the valuing of the insider's perspective characteristic of Wilfred C. Smith, have all moved the field of philosophy of religion in pluralistic directions.

One of those who encouraged the pluralizing of philosophy of religion is the late B. K. Matilal. He writes: "With such a study of comparative religion as the basis we can develop the philosophy of religion having a character distinct from the current western philosophy of religion yet complementary to it ... Philosophers, while developing Indian philosophy of religion, should be able to take a stance, for professional purposes, of philosophical neutrality."[7] It is this *sort* of approach I wish to extend and develop in arguing for the pluralizing of philosophy of religion, *e.g.,* in the philosophy of Buddhist religion. Only thereafter will one have "philosophy of religions" in any full sense which reveals the possibilities of philosophy of religion.

Much that I will have to say has to do with methodology for philosophy of religion. Concerning methodology the words of a contemporary Sri Lankan Wittgensteinian interpreter of Buddhism, A.D.P. Kalansuriya, are memorable ones. He writes: "If one wishes to look at the Dhammic discourse piously or faithfully, one may not get interested in an issue about methodology. For issues pertaining to the nature of the Dhammic statements are not raised and discussed in popular Dhammic discussion in Buddhist lands. Likewise, issues pertaining to methodology are not raised also. However, both issues are significant ones in Buddhist philosophy."[8]

But there are some who will say, mainly from Marxist and deconstructionist perspectives, that the type of approach I favour must be brought "up-to-date" by a recognition of the political dimension of attempts to know the philosophies of other cultures. "All knowledge is political" is the slogan one hears, usually without careful analysis of the various things this might be taken to mean. Nevertheless, this is an important challenge to philosophy of religion, and deserves to be taken seriously.

Some might think that whereas Said's critique of "Orientalism" was topical in the 70's, it is by now passe, but I do not think that the issues he raises have ever been clearly resolved. Those who think the

---

7. B.K. Matilal, *Logical and Ethical Issues of Religious Belief* (Calcutta, India: University of Calcutta, 1982), p. 172.
8. A.D.P. Kalansuriya, *A Philosophical Analysis of Buddhist Notions* (Delhi: Sri Satguru Publications, 1987), p. 163.

topic is passé are likely not to have looked at Said's work, or to think, narrowly, that what he says applies only to Islamic material or comparative literature. Occurrences in both learned publications and the politics of academia suggest that re-reading Edward Said's *Orientalism* may be appropriate in the 90s. Tartakov's 1986 article and events in the Philadelphia area during 1991-92 suggest that the issues which Said poses are still very much with us.[9] Specifically, Tartakov shows how a critique of "Orientalism" is necessary for a right understanding of art history. Also the University of Pennsylvania's Oriental Studies Dept. was renamed Asian and Middle Eastern Studies, largely because of input from a vocal minority of Asian students (who consider themselves Japanese, Korean, Chinese, Indian *etc.* but not "Orientals"). Newer universities may not carry the baggage of such nomenclature, but even there (say, in California) the issues Said raises are thinly buried under discussions of student "quotas."

Since once this paper is published it attains a finality which is really incommensurable with the thinking and rethinking of Said's critique in relation to various disciplines I suppose is desirable, I would like to say in advance that one should not see this paper as definitive. Even the exploration of a sub-problem of the possible application of Said's critique to "Buddhology" may take more exploration and development than it can be given here. It will be enough if the issue is raised to the surface in this connection with Buddhology.[10]

Ronald Inden applies Said's thesis to Indology, but hardly at all to Buddhology.[11] Although he sees the loosely unifying role of Buddhism within one sector of academe,[12] he treats Buddhism only in passing here and there. Finally in the concluding remarks, Inden comments that there is a difficulty in including Buddhism in his "substituting the notion of a theophantic polity for that of divine kingship" because, in contrast to Vaishnava and Shaiva gods, the gods in Buddhism lack the same "ontological status" and the Buddha's own role is not "cosmic overlord."[13] To some extent it seems that

9. Gary Michael Tartakov, "Changing Views of Orientalism" in *Dimensions of Indian Art* Pupul Jayakar Seventy (Delhi : Agam Kala Prakashan, 1986), vol. I, text.
10. A recent work on Orientalism of interest to South Asianists is Carol Breckenridge and Peter Van der Veer (eds.), *Orientalism and the Postcolonial Predicament* (Philadelphia : University of Pennsylvania Press, 1993).
11. Ronald Inden, *Imagining India* (Oxford, Basil Blackwell, 1990).
12. Inden (1990), p. 37.
13. Inden (1990), p. 269.

Buddhism represents anomalous data within Inden's work. It is therefore clear that there is room for further treatment of Said in relation to Buddhology. (See the forthcoming Donald Lopez (ed.) volume on Orientalism when available.)

I would like to make a comment about the tone of this article. The tone is in places one of irony, but not of sarcasm. It cannot legitimately be one of sarcasm, for Said's critique of "Orientalism" is important in the reassessment of one's own Buddhological practice. The intention is to provide a balanced account. Where there are criticisms of Said, this is not intended merely as criticism for its own sake, but to try to avoid the left/right polarizing tendency which informs politically driven accounts of Said's critique of Orientalism on both sides.

I. Discussion of Terminology

"The colonial conquest of the mind lasts much longer than the political domination."[14] Said observes "from 1815-1914 European direct colonial dominion expanded from about 35% of the earth's surface to about 85% of it."[15] Explicating Orientalism Said quotes Lord Curzon's dictum that Oriental Studies is "the necessary furniture of Empire."[16]

Concerning the complex relations which obtain between power, salvation, and truth-claims, Paul J. Griffiths more recently writes: "So, for example, when Christians represented a dominant colonial power vis-a-vis Buddhists it is not surprising that Christian thinking about Buddhists tended to be fairly uncritical in its assumptions of superiority and the desirability of converting Buddhists to Christianity. And now, with the reassertion of national, ethnic, and religious, identity that has followed upon the independence of Asian countries, the position is often reversed: Christian theologians suffer from post-colonialist guilt, while Buddhist, Christian, and Islamic assertions of superiority are intimately connected with quasi-nationalistic resurgence."[17]

---

14. Richard F. Gombrich and Gananath Obeyesekere, *Buddhism Transformed: Religious Change in Sri Lanka* (Princeton NJ: Princeton University Press, 1988). 290.
15. Said (1979), p. 41.
16. Said (1979), p. 215.
17. Paul J. Griffiths, *Christianity Through Non-Christian Eyes* (Maryknoll NY: Orbis Books, 1990), p. 11.

Inundated by ethical relativism, people today may find moral courage hard to come by. Whatever its other drawbacks, Griffiths' inclusion of apologetics within theology appears to promote moral courage in the strength of one's convictions.[18] Buddhist scholars also criticize each other's approaches. It is interesting, for example, to notice a contemporary Sri Lankan philosopher, A.D.P. Kalansuriya criticizing what he calls "Buddhist modernists" (such as Kalupahana and Jayatilleke) from a Wittgensteinian point of view[19]. Such arguments are important, and, not being mere squabbling, deserve to be taken seriously.

The term "colonialization" is more strongly pejorative than the more neutral "colonizing"— to express the phenomenon in its more provocative form, suggestive of moral blindness rather than just the alleged or real neutrality of social science, colonialization is the term of choice. I do not presume the alleged neutrality of a social scientist, but write as a philosopher who draws by turns both inspiration and conceptual puzzles from studying Asian thought, especially Buddhism. My bias is with those who, like Inden, have the courage to say: "I am claiming that it is wrong to see Indian thought as essentially dreamlike and to view Indian civilization as essentially irrational."[20] But only after a comprehensive historiography of Buddhism is written will one have a detailed and right understanding of the profound underpinnings of Inden's brief sentence just quoted.

It might seem odd that the term "Buddhalands" in the title* is plural, whereas the paper itself focuses on making the case in Sri Lankan context. But to speak of "the Buddhaland" in this case would privilege the Sri Lankan understanding of Buddhism in a way which might be offensive to Buddhists of other lands. Let others extrapolate to other country foci as they deem it appropriate.

The term "preunderstandings" refers to those presuppositions (not necessarily at the conscious level of axioms) which mold western thinking about Buddhism, which in turn may be relearned understandings of Buddhism by indigenous people. Although shirking Buddhism somewhat in his book-length treatment of "Indian thought," Inden alerts one to problematic preunderstandings in Hinduism for which parallels in Buddhism may be found. For

18. Paul J. Griffiths, "An Apology for Apologetics" in *Faith and Philosophy* 5 (4) October 1988.
19. Kalansuriya (1987), pp. ix and 78 passim.
20. Inden (1990), p. 48.
* This paper was originally presented at Harvard under the title, "The Colonialization of Buddhalands", and a discussion of the terms in it is retained here.

example, Inden speaks of the unfortunate presupposition of orientalist discourse of "equating Indian thought with Hinduism and equating Hinduism with the monistic pantheism and Idealism attributed to Advaita Vedanta."[21] Although there is no exact parity, the reductionistic process is similar in the tendency to equate Buddhist thought *in toto* with the Pali Canon and the Pali Canon with the very words of Sakyamuni Buddha *simpliciter*. Some phrases in writings of those in the tradition of K.N. Jayatilleke (to whom all Pali scholars nevertheless owe a debt) unfortunately exemplify this tendency. Especially when one is concerned with Vedanta on the one hand or the Pali Canon on the other, one should guard against such reductionistic thinking. Issues about "canon" are treated in Jan Gorak.[22]

Understanding might also be achieved through ritual participation, through both use and contemplation of art works, *etc.*, so that propositional belief of which credal belief is one species is not the only vehicle for "understanding."

Credal beliefs should not be thought to provide logical underpinning for religious practices or rituals — as if there were first some rational structure and secondly the practice or ritual came along. Excessive emphasis on the epistemological aspect of early Buddhism is the sort of approach I wish to reject. What is more credible is that ritual and symbolic meaning develop in tandem, but that symbolic meaning is not always reducible to cognitive proposition. Credal beliefs are important to philosophers, who are interested in the logical relations between statements in a system of statements and between parts of concepts alleged to form a coherent concept. But philosophers should not ignore the ritual dimension of religious experience, as if ritual were merely icing on the philosophical cake. As Wittgenstein observes in *Lectures and Conversations on Aesthetics, Psychology and Religious Belief*: "If I have to say what is the main mistake made by philosophers of the present generation, including Moore, I would say that it is that when language is looked at, what is looked at is a form of words and not the use made of the form of words."[23]

---

21. Inden (1990), p. 130.
22. Jan Gorak, *The Making of the Modern Canon* (London and Atlantic Highlands NJ: Athlone), 1991.
23. Fergus Kerr, *Theology after Wittgenstein* (Oxford and New York : Basil Blackwell, 1986), p. 152.

It would be a simplistic and inaccurate view of Wittgenstein to say that he is thought to value language for its own sake. In fact he makes clear that language is connected to practices of everyday life, including religious practices. "Language games" and "forms of life" interpenetrate so that in paying attention to language one is by that fact paying attention to how life is lived. As Kerr says, "Wittgenstein reminds the reader that all meaning, even the very gesture of pointing something out, must have conceptual links with the whole system of the human way of doing things together."[24] Meaning emerges from natural reactions of people together in human community, it does not exist in the form of free-floating ethereal propositions (*pace* Platonic idealists). As to the creed of the Buddha it has been perceptively pointed out that it is not reducible to theism, polytheism, monism, or dualism.[25]

II. Edward Said's *Orientalism* : a Controversial Book

Said raises important issues about the nature of "representation" (when other cultures are described), alterity, the uses of distinguishing between "us" and "other", which categories matter most for analysis, how "canon formation" takes place, and the role of the intellectual *vis a vis* the state.[26] Said distinguishes four main dogmas of the Orientalism he subjects to vigorous deconstructive criticism: (1) the East is sharply distinguished from the West; (2) texts are emphasized; (3) Western vocabulary is necessary in order to understand the East; and (4) the Orient is to be feared or controlled.[27]

On (3) one surely needs Western vocabulary to communicate to Western-educated audiences, but the danger of distortion is evident. As Kalansuriya says speaking of Kalupahana's notion of Buddhist empiricism in relation to the idea of verification: "A main characteristic of modernism, however, appears to be an *isolation* of the notions from their normal context, namely, the Dhammic one."[28] If "Buddhist empiricists," with apparent sympathy, interpret logical positivists such as A.J. Ayer as speaking in one voice with Buddhism, they effectively isolate one strand of Buddhist talk from the textured

24. Kerr (1936), p. 76.
25. J.H. Bateson, "Creed (Buddhist)" in *Encyclopaedia of Religion and Ethics* ed. by James Hastings (New York: Charles Scribner's Sons, 1951). Reprint of 1910 edition, pp. 232-233.
26. Said (1979), pp. 325-326.
27. Said (1979), p. 301.
28. Kalansuriya (1987), p. 80.

fabric of Buddhism with the result of overall distortion.

One might ask what has Said to do with the interpretation of Buddhism? Much of what he asserts about Orientalists and Orientalism may be asserted of Buddhologists and Buddhism (e.g., unwarranted assumptions of synchronic essentialism and ontological stability).[29] The first three of the four dogmas of the Orientalism he discredits are characteristic of philosophical approaches to Buddhism and, more generally, to Asian thought.

How do the defining features of Orientalism (1) through (4) above as given by Said compare with alternative accounts ? Here it is interesting to compare Said's account with that of Bryan S. Turner. "By 'Orientalism' I mean a syndrome of beliefs, attitudes and theories which infects, not only the classical works of Islamic studies, but also extensive areas of geography, economics and sociology. This syndrome consists of a number of basic arguments: (i) social development is caused by characteristics which are internal to society; (ii) the historical development of a society is either an evolutionary progress or a gradual decline; (iii) society is an 'expressive totality' in the sense that all the institutions of a society are the expression of a primary essence. These arguments allow Orientalists to establish their dichotomous ideal type of Western society whose inner essence unfolds in a dynamic progress towards democratic industrialism, and Islamic society which is either timelessly stagnant or declines from its inception. The societies of the Middle East are consequently defined by reference to a cluster of absences — the missing middle class, the missing city, the absence of political rights, the absence of revolutions. These missing features of Middle East society serve to explain why Islamic civilisation failed to produce capitalism, to generate modern personalities or to convert itself into a secular, radical culture."[30]

---

29. In a philosophical essay of this kind the varying administrative policies in such different colonial administrations as the Dutch, Portugese, and British in Sri Lanka cannot be discussed in detail. It should be noted, however, that the variances among these policies would make the application of Said's description of what happens in "Orientalism" more or less applicable under a particular colonial administration. This raises the question as to whether Said has essentialized the colonialists. Regarding variances, the reader is referred, in the first place, to Walpola Rahula, *The Heritage of the Bhikkhu* (New York: Grove Press, 1974).
30. Bryan S. Turner, *Marx and the End of Orientalism* (London: George Allen & Unwin, 1978), p. 81. Controversies in Sociology # 7 edited by T.B. Bottomore and M.J. Mulkay.

None of (i) through (iii) are generally assumed by philosophers, and so on this characterization of "Orientalism" it does not provide a philosopher with the same problem as in Said's characterization of "Orientalism" as defined by (1) through (4) above. There may indeed be other ways of defining "Orientalism," but my intention is not to survey them all but to confine attention to the *locus classicus* statement as given in Said (1978) and in Turner (1978). The latter is included because, as will become evident in reviewing Griffiths (1989), there are cases in which the philosopher does characterize Asian concepts by way of an absence which might be viewed from a Western perspective as a deficiency.

Has Said provided a view of how we could get at the reality of the other ?

"What is given on the page and in the museum case is a truncated exaggeration, like many of Stacy's Oriental extracts, whose purpose is to exhibit a relationship between the science (or scientist) and the object, not one between the object and nature."[31] Part of this is right, and yet the suggestion that there is something left over to be had consistent with Said's own approach is dubious — what would this latter be? Said has not provided even a sketch of a theory as to how one *could* get at the relation between the object and nature. But so far as his vision goes — he sees only one side of the coin, *viz.* "Orientalism" and not Wixted's "Reverse Orientalism"[32] — Said is an expert debunker of the pretentions of power-driven Orientalist describer/despisers such as either indeed have existed or exist on Said's construction of them. However, on his own operating strategy, which is broadly in line with deconstructionist tendencies, it is not clear how he might proceed to a positive view of a reality which scholarship might uncover. This point is particularly important — and unclear in Said — where he observes that the Orientalist Saint-Hilaire articulates a view of scientist, object, and nature according to which "nature itself can be reperceived as continuous, harmoniously coherent, and fundamentally intelligible."[33] But what is Said's own view about the possibility of understanding nature — is nature just a "surd" incapable of any explication? If, as seems likely, Said would say that Marxism is the underlying framework within which Said's

31. Said (1979), p. 142.
32. John Timothy Wixted, "Reverse Orientalism" *Sino-Japanese Studies* 2(1) December 1989.
33. Said (1979), p. 145.

critique of "Orientalism" is formulated, is the framework any longer tenable in what appears to be shift towards "free market economies" all around?

III. Lingering Colonialization

As Ninian Smart observes in his paper, "India, Sri Lanka and Religion" it is not easy for Buddhism to ascribe to Smart's "theory of the ultimate unity of religions ... For Buddhism — at least Theravada Buddhism — such a transcendental unity of which the gods are manifestations just does not work."[34] This is a rather curious way of putting it — as if it is the Buddhists' responsibility to fit themselves into Smart's theory, rather than the responsibility of the theoretician to formulate a theory which takes into account all the known data. However, the positive point from Smart's quotation which one may draw from in the present context is the recognition that attempts to transcendentalize Theravada are doomed to failure.

But if attempts to "transcendentalize Buddhism" and bring it in line with other religious under a theory of their unity are doomed to failure, what of the important residual question Smart proposes, *i.e.* how to formulate a theory of interrelations relations? Smart argues that it is precisely the lack of such a theory of other religions and other world views in Sri Lankan Theravada Buddhism which is politically dangerous.[35]

There is thus a need to construct inter-religious models for global understanding (and offer critical attention to problems of establishing criteria by which other religions may be viewed) as John Hick sees in having hosted a conference at Claremont Graduate School on the subject.[36] Kalansuriya also speaks models but understands these as internal to particular religions as in: "the model — suffering — explains the vacillating world of human existence; his eventual emancipation from that existence."[37]

Griffiths would not agree with Smart's point above. For Griffiths states, in effect, that Sri Lankan Theravada has a theory of the other.

---

34. Gustavo Benavides and M.W. Daly (eds.), *Religion and Political Power* (Albany: SUNY Press, 1989), p. 18-19.
35. Smart in Benevides (1989), p. 18.
36. The papers from John Hick's 1992 conference appear in James Kellenberger (ed.), *Interreligious Models and Criteria* (London: Macmillan, 1993). See also Hick, John (1988). "A Concluding Comment" *Faith and Philosophy* 5(4) October.
37. Kalansuriya (1987), p. 97.

He says of the historically significant interpreter of Sri Lankan Theravada, K.N. Jayatilleke: "Jayatilleke sees Buddhism as tolerant and pragmatic but not relativistic in its attitude to non-Buddhist religious communities."[38] The resolution between this implicit conflict between Smart and Griffiths may well be to say that, although Theravada Buddhism has no highly developed theory of interreligious relations, it does have the outlines of such a theory. Jayatilleke observes that one of the planks of Buddhist tolerance is compassionate action in the belief that hatred does not cease by hatred but by love.[39] Even Smart says — not that Buddhism has the outlines of a theory of interreligious relations in general — but: "This was Buddhism's 'theory of Christianity' in effect: Christianity was good for generating fine ethical attitudes, so it was good for Christians to live up to their faith; hence the less tolerant missionary response to Buddhism was a matter of some initial surprise."[40] Clearly, a detailed Buddhist theory of interreligious relations remains a *desideratum*, and Smart has quite rightly called attention to this fact.[41]

If we slice it synchronically in a certain way, Buddhism becomes a perverse mirror image of our (Western) selves and of our concerns. Probably unintentionally, for all his conceptual sophistication and "Buddhalogical" expertise, Paul Griffiths paper "Buddha and God: A Contrastive Study in Maximal Greatness" seems to exemplify this.[42] Therein what emerges is a picture of the Christian God for whom agency is a great-making property, in contrast to the Buddha for whom non-agency is a great making property. This is the result of taking one slice of Buddhism compared to another slice of Christianity, adopting a synchronic essentialist analysis. Acceptance of a religious Westerner's childhood adage "an idle mind is the devil's workshop" would permit the inference that Buddha-mind is demonic. Since this inference is evidently absurd, the premise that leads to it should be vigorously questioned. As Said observes of the figures of speech used by Orientalists to describe the Orient from its

38. Griffiths (1990), p. 141.
39. Griffiths (1990), p. 152.
40. Smart in Benevides (1989), p. 21.
41. In my paper on the concept of focal point for a forthcoming Claremont conference proceedings volume, *Interreligious Models and Criteria* I address the theoretical issue of interreligious relations in such a way as to make room for non-theistic religions such as Buddhism.
42. Paul J. Griffiths, "Buddha and God : A Contrastive Study in Ideas about Maximal Greatness," *Journal of Religion* 69 (4) 1989.

philosophical vantage point of "radical realism:" "they are always symmetrical to, and yet diametrically inferior to, a European equivalent, which is sometimes specified, sometimes not."[43]

When finally some of the Asians themselves reunderstand their own traditions (*e.g.*, as in (1) (2) and (3) above), it perversely turns out that the same odd thing said by said of the modern Western Orientalist holds true: "His Orient is not the Orient as it is, but the Orient as it has been Orientalized."[44] Philosophers of religion, too, must be on guard against the possibility of this sort of criticism. Otherwise one may find that, as W.D. Hudson says of Arvind Sharma, the Asian material "was being laid upon a bed of Procrustes to make it fit the categories in terms of which it was being discussed."[45]

IV. Resultant Problems for Philosophy of Buddhist Religion

It is sometimes difficult to determine exactly when a view is *emic* (to use terminology appropriated by Frank Reynolds from Marvin Harris). But that the *emic/etic* distinction is generally useful there should be no doubt. Within the on-going Buddhist tradition as well as amongst Western scholars who are not Buddhist, the interpretation of Buddhist *nirvana* in fact occurs, at least sometimes, appropriately. Reflectively asking, "What is one doing *in* interpreting Buddhist *nirvana*?" takes the discussion to a deeper level.[46]

On readership and audience, to whom is one communicating and for what purpose? This is a problem any philosophy of Buddhist religion must face. Peter Gaeffke raises the problem of the audience for writers on Asia in projecting "... an increasing crowd of deconstructionists may soon claim exclusive rights to explain the Orient to us."[47] Gaeffke's approach contrasts markedly with that of Peter van der Veer, wherein one worry is the tendency "to essentialize Sanskrit civilization."[48] I prefer to understand the audience for

43. Said (1979), p. 72.
44. Said (1979), p. 104.
45. W.D. Hudson, Review of Arvind Sharma, *"A Hindu Perspective on the Philosophy of Religion," Asian Philosophy* 1 (1) March 1991: 96.
46. If I understand him rightly, on this point I must part company with Kalanuriya. For he seems to think that within *dhamma* an interpretation of Buddhist *nibbana* is inappropriate, where this comment is supposed to silence all discussion. Kalansuriya (1987), p. 231.
47. Peter Gaeffke, "A Rock in the Tides of Time: Oriental Studies Then and Now," *Academic Questions*, Spring 1990:73.
48. Peter van der Veer and Steven Vertovec, "Brahmanism Abroad: On Caribbean

philosophy of Buddhist religion as anyone exercised by the problems of philosophy who is engaged in the study of Buddhist texts regardless of political orientation.

One issue under the general rubric of self and audience is how one is to understand the self. Fergus Kerr (1986) mounts a sustained attack on dualism of spiritual self and physical world, a picture which results in antipathy toward the body. His recommendation for the way forward in Christian theology is, with help from Wittgenstein, to elimate these notions and to be vigilant about their reappearance in different guises, such as in theologian Don Cupitt's divinization of the self *via* a sort of self-realization theology. Writes Kerr: "The person at the centre of modern theology has acquired the attributes of the God of classical theology."[49] Interestingly for students of Buddhism, Kerr's program, which is directed as much against self-conceit as against self as a metaphysical doctrine, reunderstands the way forward for Christian theology in terms which would appeal to Buddhists mindful of the *anatta* (no self or nonsubstantiality) doctrine.

On texts and interpretation Said speaks of "the textual attitude"[50] and of the Orientalist's "disappointment that the modern Orient is not at all like the texts".[51] He asserts: "... the advances made by a 'science' of Orientalism in its academic form are less objectively true than we often like to think."[52] The question remains as to how a sensitive appropriation of the texts can result from the conditions Said outlines.

One thing is clear, that from the point of view of scholarship aimed at understanding it will not do to trod the path of epistemological fundamentalism, as Fergus Kerr nicely brings out in the following quotation: "... the very idea of a personal experience that would be infallible, self-authenticated, unprejudiced etc., because it was the result of sloughing off all received opinion, tradition, authority etc., in fact the very idea with which Descartes opens the *Meditations*, is remarkably reminiscent of certain tendencies in the history of Christianity that would put the individual believer directly and inwardly into a relationship with God which excluded in advance all mediation

Hinduism as an Ethnic Religion" in *Ethnology*, 30 (2) April 1991: 157.

49. Fergus Kerr, *Theology After Wittgenstein* (Oxford and New York : Basil Blackwell, 1986), p. 17.
50. Said (1979), p. 92-92.
51. Said (1979), p. 100.
52. Said (1979), p. 202.

by a historical community with authoritative tradition, rituals and the like. The desire of philosophers like Russell and Moore, at the dawn of modern analytic philosophy in Cambridge, to get down to the primitive sense-data in order to find a level of experience that would supposedly be free of all interpretation, subjective distortion *etc.*, is fundamentalism transposed into an adjacent discourse."[53]

Under the rubric of texts and their interpretation comes the problem of literary "canon." Jan Gorak devotes an entire book chapter, "Edward Said and the Open Canon," to the canon issue in its connection with Said's thought.[54] There Gorak observes: "We can blame the canon, Said suggests, for the fact that the tacit acceptance of Western domination persists long after its most militant prosecution ends. In the modern world canons operate as highly paid servants of still-expanding postcolonial empires; they reinforce the dominance of Western economies and Western values. Canons play a major part in the tragedy which has left Western intellectuals without the will to disseminate new knowledge of cultures the popular media still consider as alien worlds."[55]

But as Gorak points out Said himself sometimes uses a language of power he elsewhere attacks as canonical.[56] Indeed it seems neither necessary nor desirable to eliminate canons altogether (at least in a weak sense of recommended reading lists as starting points).

On diachronic v. synchronic if philosophy is, at least in part, the critical analysis of arguments and the clarification of concepts ("conceptual analysis"), then it lends itself to synchronic analysis. In that case how does one take into account conceptual change and diachronic perspective? Is not the philosophical view amenable to Said's criticisms about the snychronic slicing and stereotyping of the Orient?[57] Said writes: "Knowledge of the Oriental, because generated out of strength, in a sense creates the Orient, the Oriental, and his world"; "synchronic essentialism" does not take into account the potential of reality for change.[58]

This problem is especially clear in what is called, for lack of a better term, "comparative philosophy." As I see it, with very few

53. Kerr (1986), p. 24.
54. Jan Gorak, *The Making of the Modern Canon* (London: Athlone, 1991).
55. Gorak (1991), p. 209.
56. Gorak (1991), p. 212.
57. Said (1979), p. 40.
58. Said (1979), p. 240.

exceptions (*e.g.*, E. Deutsch, *Studies in Comparative Aesthetics*) this term is not a precise designation of any particular methodology, but a pragmatically useful unifying term for philosophers studying both Eastern and Western texts who find value in so doing.

The danger of rampant and superficial comparisons in "comparative philosophy" was clearly recognized by Kalansuriya, who, while presenting Buddha-*dharma* through Wittgensteinian eyes, endeavors assiduously to avoid doing violence to the Buddha's message.[59] My own view, arrived at independently, is similar to Kalansuriya's on this point.[60] Perhaps, as John Koller suggests without stating verbatim, the best use of comparative philosophy may be made by those who are most skeptical of its wholesale programatic employment while being in awe of its laser-like power when directed to piecemeal investigations.[61]

On knowledge Said observes "far from being merely additive or cumulative, the growth of knowledge is a process of selective accumulation, displacement, deletion, rearrangement, and insistence within what has been called a research consensus." (Said, 176) This is true so far as it goes, but is there any alternative ? But Said has not made plain just how he thinks the "citationary way" Orientalists treat each others work be jettisoned in favor of getting at the thing-in-itself ? What precisely has one not got that might possibly be had here? Clearly, the experience of interpreting texts as well as experience in cultures which value a given text is nevertheless experience mediated through cultural filters. For instance, the relearned understandings of Sri Lankan Buddhists accustomed by what Gananath

59. Kalansuriya (1987), p. 248.
60. Frank J. Hoffman, *Rationality and Mind in Early Buddhism* (Delhi : Motilal Banarsidass, 1987), pp. 1-9.
61. John Koller's comments on comparative philosophy are perspicacious. In his review of my *Rationality and Mind in Early Buddhism* in *Journal of Indian Philosophy* vol 17 no. 4 December 1989 Koller writes: "Although he disavows any comparative program, by bringing together insights of the *Nikayas* with those of recent philosophy of religion and Buddhalogical studies, Hoffman has provided us with a good example of how comparative philosophical thought can simultaneously deepen our understanding of contemporary philosophical issues and our understanding of contemporary philosophical issues and our understanding of traditional texts." (p. 431) Roger Jackson's finely detailed and critical but appreciative review of the same work in *The Journal of the International Association of Buddhist Studies* vol 12 no. 2, 1989 shows by contrasting British and French contributions of Indology how an issue such as whether Buddhism is a form of empiricism could arise (p. 111-112).

Obeyesekere calls "Protestant Buddhism" is a case in point.

Said's *positive* view of the antidote to "Orientalism" is that it helps "refine knowledge and reduces the scholar's conceit" and "dispense with racial, ideological, and imperialist stereotypes."[62] Thus, after the clouds of rhetoric have dispersed, the positive view Said offers appears rather bland and nondescript — almost as though he has told his audience what they wanted to hear. Said is surely right that scholars should be modest in their claims and be sensitive to the occurrence of stereotypes. But beyond this, overall, Said (1987) does not place any insurmountable methodological obstacles for constructing a philosophy of Buddhist religion. The following cautionary observations which are in line with Said's critique of "Orientalism" may, however, be helpfully carried into practice by philosophers of Buddhist religion.

V. Methodological Recommendations for Philosophers of Buddhist Religion

"Neither an apologist nor a despiser be''— avoid Said's Orientalist explainer/exploiter trap. Said speaks of the "absence of sympathy covered by professional knowledge."[63] "The main issue for them was preserving the Orient and Islam under control of the White Man."[64] Recognize "the will to power" over the Orient that figures, directly or indirectly, in Orientalism.[65] Cultivate "imaginative sympathy" and utilize both *emic* and *etic* categories, seen not as mutually exclusive but as complimentary. As Said sees it, "only an exaggerated sense of cultural duty drives a scholar to study what he does not think well of."[66]

"Avoid apologetics" — despite critiques of fundamental scholarship the goal of which is *understanding*, I wish to reassert the value of what I regard as this more traditional job. Griffiths is right that apologetics has an appropriate home in theology, wherein representative intellectuals are responsible for presenting and defending their traditions. But theology is distinct from philosophy of religion (from which it follows that it is distinct from the "comparative philosophy

---

62. Said (1979), p. 328.
63. Said (1979), p. 104.
64. Said (1979), p. 238.
65. Said (1979), p. 222.
66. Said (1979), pp. 289-290.

of religion" — a field which Griffiths' present post requires that he profess — and one would hope that Griffiths does not wish to extend it here. Once apologetics is admitted into philosophy of religion (outside its proper home of theology), then there is no sector of philosophy of religion which can any longer be a reservoir of learning where one can find comparatively unbiased descriptions of conceptual pros and cons of a particular religion. This is not to suppose that philosophy of religion can ever yield a complete and entirely unbiased perspective. Compared to apologetical theology, however, philosophy of religion can provide a seeker with a *comparatively* unbiased statement of pros and cons of particular religions. It is also true that some types of writing are on the borderline between these two approaches. Without saying that borderline writing should never be allowed, one can affirm the value of keeping a clear distinction between the two sorts even in examining work of this borderline type.

"Be not a shunner of experiencing, but of relativism" — Although there is no guarantee that, even *with* relevant experience of Asia one will roughly get things right in doing research, Said quite properly warns of the dire consequences of "the almost total absence in Contemporary Western culture of the Orient as a genuinely felt and experienced force."[67] Experiencing the Orient need not, however, lead to relativism. As B.K. Matilal observes : "When a well-meaning Western man says to Indians that the Indian culture has uniqueness which it should never lose, for it is holistic, it is futuristic, it is ecological and so on, I believe we must check the temptation. For this might lead us back to the unjust societies of the past, unjust but impeccably justified by the logic of relativism, which is somewhat mistakenly called the law of *karma*. Justification of inequalities by a reference to God's will seems to be less subversive than justification by the law of karma. For the latter seems more rational and hence paradoxically more dangerous: it legitimizes inequalities!''[68]

"Thou shalt not slight truth" — do not fall into the facile sophomorism that "truths are illusions" quoted uneasily by Said who appears to take it back while stating what he takes to be a Nietzschean "insight."[69]

---

67. Said (1979), p. 208.
68. B.K. Matilal, *Confrontation of Cultures* (Calcutta and New Delhi: K.P. Bagchi, 1988), p. 28.
69. Said (1979), p. 203.

In another passage he is less equivocal: "... the real issue is whether indeed there can be a true representation of anything, or whether any and all representations, because they *are* representations, are embedded first in the language and then in the culture, institutions, and political ambience of the representor. If the latter alternative is the correct one (as I believe it is), then we must be prepared to accept the fact that a representation is *eo ipso* implicated, intertwined, imbedded, interwoven with a great many other things besides 'the truth' which is itself a representation."[70]

"Is this a false dichotomy?" one might ask. Does it understand the nature of "a true representation" in such an apparently rigorous way such that nothing can count as an example of it?

If there is no truth apart from representation, how then can there be "deformations?" Said claims that Orientalism is not a deviation from some imagined "Oriental essence." All operations of language are "deformations", and although never absent, the role of positive knowledge is far from absolute.[71]

As Hendrik Vroom has asserted: "An enquiry by the philosophy of religion is itself also motivated by the question of truth."[72] It is not easy to give a philosophical account of "truth" in general or of "religious truth," in particular, and yet truth remains a postulate of academic inquiry. Without the postulate of truth, which dangles like the carrot on a stick before the proverbial rabbit, academic inquiry becomes pointless.

VI. Conclusion

In conclusion, it is necessary to summarize a view of the way forward against the background of the possible objections to the approach to the philosophy of Buddhist religion approach I advocate. The favored approach is maintained despite Said's cautionary reminders and chastisements which Western text scholars would do well to consider.

In so doing it is appropriate to paraphrase the thoughts of the late distinguished scholar, B.K. Matilal, who thought deeply about philosophical matters from a dual perspective both Indian and

---

70. Said (1979), p. 272.
71. Said (1979), p. 273.
72. Hendrick M. Vroom, *Religions and the Truth* (Grand Rapids MI : Eerdmans, 1989), p. 386.

Western. His obituary in *Journal of Indian Philosophy* brings out something of his great importance to the field. Among the intellectual tendencies found notable in the West recently:[73]

> There has been increased effort to assess and evaluate the consequences of moral and cultural relativism. The distinction between history and fiction has been seriously challenged. Orientalism, discourse-analysis and deconstruction have punctuated many writings on Indian history or anthropology. It has been in this context widely recognised that the past Western perceptions of Indian art, literature, religion, philosophy, ethic, cultures, were all distorted through imposition of Western categories. But wherefrom the new perceptions will come? The received doctrine is that it will come if we can only *see* the phenomena, and not *perceive* them. The new ethnography is phenomenological, not interpretive.

If the sort of approach I favor is correct, then we cannot make do with just the phenomenological study of Buddhism but do need the philosophically interpretive study of Buddhism. This does not mean that philosophers of religion should be apologists, but that in the quest to *understand* other religions interpretation is unavoidable. "Neither an apologist nor a despiser be!" is a motto for the philosophy of Buddhist religion which marks the way forward.

---

73. Matilal (1988), pp. 26-27.

Appendix

THE FORTY-SIX *CITTA DHARMAS*

Impurities

1 *Moha* - ignorance
2 *pramāda* - carelessness
3 *kausīdya* - heaviness
4 *aśraddha* - no faith
5 *styāna* - sloth
6 *auddhatya* - addiction to pleasure

Unfavorable elements

1 *ahrī* - lack of self-respect
2 *anapatrapya* - inconsideration of others

Vicious elements

1 *krodha* - anger
2 *mrakṣa* - deceit, hypocrisy
3 *mātsarya* - envy
4 *īrṣyā* - jealousy
5 *pradāsa* - approving objectionable things
6 *vihiṃsā* - violence
7 *apanāha* - breaking friendship
8 *māyā* - deceit
9 *śātya* - trickery
10 *mada* - vanity

General mind functions

1 *samādhi* - concentration
2 *adhimokṣa* - inclination
3 *manasikāra* - attention
4 *smṛti* - memory
5 *prajñā* - insight
6 *chanda* - desire
7 *sparśa* - sensation
8 *cetanā* - volition
9 *saṃjñā* - conception
10 *vedanā* - feeling

Aspects of Goodness

1 *śraddhā* - faith
2 *vīrya* - strength
3 *upekṣā* - equanimity
4 *hrī* - self-respect
5 *apatrapā* - decorum
6 *alobha* - no cupidity
7 *adveṣa* - no hatred
8 *ahiṃsā* - non-violence
9 *prasrabdhi* - dexterity
10 *apramāda* - acquiring & preserving good qualities

Miscellaneous mind-states

1 *kaukṛtya* - repenting
2 *middha* - absent-mindedness
3 *vitarka* - searching mind
4 *vicāra* - fixed mind
5 *rāga* - love
6 *dveṣa* - hatred
7 *māna* - pride
8 *vicikitsā* - doubting

Index

abhidhamma (Skt. *abhidharma*), 35-36, 79 fl., 190
  and *putthujanas*, 24
abhisamācārika, 24
  and *sikkhāpadas*, 25
  as *lokiya*, 31
ādibrahmacariyaka, 24
  and *sekhas*, 24
ahimsa, 115-116
altruism (*parattha*), 114
  transcended in *nibbāna*, 115
amata, 201
ambivalence, 123
anatta, 160, 181-182, 220
a priori/a posteriori truths, 178-179
analytic/synthetic distinction, 177
anātman, 160, 173, 180
Aṅguttara Nikāya, 20, 24, 27, 115, 159-160
anitya, 160-161, 164-167, 173
annihilationism, 48, 132
  subtle critique needed, 132
anusaya, 111
apologetics, 223-224
arahant, 21, 27, 42, 113-114, 116, 148
aṟam (good life), 69
  as instrumental, 69
  as ethical regulative, 69-70
ātman, 162, 196
Avalokiteśvara (Nātha), 153
avijjā, 61
ayatana, 83

Bateson, J.H., 73
bodhisattva, 153
Bond, George, 8, 17 fl.
Brahman, 201
brahmins, 201
Buddha, 44, 59 fl., 115, 182
  anti-authoritarian, 142
Buddhaghosa, 21, 25, 35, 37, 94, 186
Buddhavaṃsa, 21
Buddhist Publication Society, v

Carr, Brian, 12
Carrithers, Michael, 39-40
causality, 159-160, 175 fl., 201
  asymetrical, 188-189, 191-192
  as phenomenological truth, 181
  as synthetic *a priori* truth, 179-180
  cumulative, 187
  simultaneous, 187
  symmetrical, 189, 192-193
  twelve linked, 187
cetanā, 37-38
Chapple, Christopher Key, 8, 79 fl.
Christian mysticism, 100-101
citta dharmas, Appendix
Cobb, John B., 184
cognitive proposition, 213
Collins, Steven, 2-3, 208
comparative philosophy, 4, 10-11, 57, 221-222
compassion (see also *metta*), 151
Confucius, 94
Conze, Edward, 163
creativity, 192
credal beliefs, 213
criteria (standards), 3, 148, 173
Crossin, John, 42
Cupitt, Don, 5, 208
Curzon, Lord, 211

dana, 27-28
dasabala, 197
dasa sīla, 17-19
Deegalle, Mahinda, 9, 1 fl., 105 fl.
dependent origination (see also causality and *paticcasamuppada*), 175-183, 186-188

and analytic truth, 176
and synthetic truth, 176
as an *a priori* truth, 178-179
as a phenomenological truth, 181
not *a posteriori*, 179
not a tautology, 179, 181
unfalsifiability of, 176-177
De Silva, Padmasiri, 8, 117 fl.
Descartes, Rene, 220
Deutsch, Eliot, 11, 222
Dhammapada, 24, 57 fl, 191
dhamma (Skt., *dharma*), 66-67
dharmas (elements), 79, 81, 83
citta -, 85-90, Appendix
Dharmasena, Thera, 112
Dharmasiri, Gunapala, 5, 8, 97, 141 fl.
diachronic/synchronic distinction, 221
Dīgha Nikāya, 20-21, 135
commentary on, 31
dispositions
three types of negative -, 111
diṭṭhi, 23
three categories of, 23
division of this work, 5-6
dukkha, 24, 49, 160, 167
destruction of, 38
liberation from, 132
Durkheim, Emile, 117, 130, 132

ego, 68, 147
egoism (*attattha*), 115, 147
transcended in *nibbana*, 115
emic/etic distinction, 219, 223
empiricism, 136, 174, 176-177
not in Buddhism, 136, 139, 176-177
emptiness (*sūnyatā*), 183, 200
enlightenment (see also *nibbana*)
gradual, 20
Ergardt, Jan T., v, 12
eternalism, 132
and annihilationism, 132
ethics, 17, 26-27, 29, 40, 105 fl.
Buddhism as ethics-oriented, 139
European Society for Asian Philosophy, 12

falsification (see also verification), 136
Fa-Tsang, 186
features of this work, 5-6
fire sermon, 168
five precepts, 27
Flugal, J.C., 132
forest monks, 148
forms of life, 214
four noble truths, 166

Gaeffke, Peter, 219
good life, 63-64, 69
Buddhist and Tamil views of, 64
God, 199
Gombrich, Richard, 12, 207
Gopalan, Subramania, 8, 57 fl.
Gorak, Jan, 213, 221
gradual path, 109-110
Griffiths, Paul J., 211, 216-218
guru, 141

Hartshorne, Charles, 184, 186, 188-189
Herman, Arthur L., 5, 9-10, 159 fl.
Hick, John, 5, 217
Hoffman, Frank J., 1 fl, 9-10, 139, 207 fl.
Holt, John, 29
Hua-yen, 186, 192
Huang Po, 149
Hudson, W.D., 219
Hume, 40, 182-183

inbam, 69
imaginative sympathy, 223
impermanence, 159
Inden, Ronald, 210, 212
inductive generalization, 179
Islam, 200, 215, 223

Jātaka, 21, 149
Jayatilleke, K.N., 4, 11, 137, 174, 196, 218
jīva, 197
John of the Cross, Saint, 100-101
Johansson, Rune E.A., 97-98

Kālāma Sutta, 141, 149
Kalansuriya, A.D.P., 8-9, 133 fl., 209, 212, 214, 217, 222
Kalupahana, David J., 11, 174, 214
kamma (Skt. *karma*), 67, 184, 188
  criticism of, 185
kusala and *akusala*, 36, 105-106, 108, 114
  and process thought, 185-186
  and virtue, 40
  and Buddha, 115
kammapathas, 33
  two forms of, 33
  connection to path, 35
  three categories of, 38
  as positive qualities, 41
Kandy, 153
Kant, 178, 180-181, 202, 178-179, 202
Kerr, Fergus, 214, 220
Koller, John, 224
Khuddaka Nikāya, 162

language games, 214
Lopez, Donald, 211

Mahācattārīsaka Sutta, 23, 34
Mahalingam, Indira, 12
Mahāsāṃghikas, 163
Mahāvagga, 168-169, 171
Mahāvīra, 197
Mahāyāna, 159, 162, 198, 200, 202, 204
  criticism of Theravāda, 149-150
  in Sri Lanka, 153
"*Mahāyen*," 153
Majjhima Nikāya, 126
Milinda Pañha, 25, 168-169, 171
Marxism
  and capitalism, 142, 217
  and deconstructionism, 209
  critique of, 142, 217
Matilal, B.K., 4, 209, 224-226
meditation, 91-97, 147
method, 3-5, 7-10, 209
metta, 34, 68, 113, 115-116, 192-193
Mettananda, Bhikkhu, 120
Metta Sutta, 108, 145

middle way, 132
model of liberation, 49, 55-56
  and *paticcasamuppada*, 51, 55-56, 175
Mohanty, J.N., 4
Moore, Charles A., 11
Moore, G.E., 221
Mother Theresa, 151
morality (see also ethics), 105 fl.
  as leading to *nibbana*, 110
  as matriarchal, 145-146
mūlā, 36-37
  and virtues, 41
  and wisdom, 112
  kusala/akusala forms, 36
mysticism, 100-101, 174

Nāgārjuna, 96, 170-171, 188-189
Ṇāgasena, 168
Ñāṇamoli, Thera, 127
Netti Pakaraṇa, 21-22, 37
nibbāna (Skt. *nirvāṇa*), 21, 43 fl., 105 fl, 162, 170-173, 194, 196, 204
  and cessation (*nirodha*), 48
  and *paṭiccasamuppāda*, 49-50
  as a meta-process, 196-205
  as negative state, 169
  as positive state, 169
  as psychological change, 43, 62-63
  as transcendent, 203-204
  and *śunyatā*, 170-171, 175, 183
  dilemma of, 169, 171
  etymology of, 167-168
  two phases of, 45-46
  need for model of, 49
noble eightfold path, 23, 34-35, 107, 111-112, 135
nonattachment, 99
nonviolence, 34, 115-116
Norman, K.R., 1-3
Ñyānaponika, Thera, 128
Ñyāṇavira, Thera, 129, 132

Obeyesekere, Gananath, 207, 222-223
Odin, Steve, 184, 186
Olendzki, Andrew, 8, 43 fl.

omniscience, 197
Orientalism, 209-210
  four dogmas of, 214

pabbajita, 25
Pachow, W., 29
Pali Canon, 213
Pali Text Society, 1-2, 7
pañca sīla (see also *sila*), 30
pāpa (demerit), 113-114, 146-147
paradigm, 133 fl.
  - shift, 96-97
  definition of, 133
pariyutthana, 111
path (*magga*), 29, 35
  and *kammapathas*, 36
  and virtue, 36, 42
  language as labyrinth of-s, 137
  nonempirical, 136
paṭiccasamuppāda, 49-50, 52-53, 175 fl.
  as synthetic *a priori* truth, 179-180
  bifurcation in, 55
Patimokkha, 29
  Parajika in, 29
Patisamhidamagga, 21
patriarchy, 145
permanence, 162
phenomena, definition of, 175
phenomenological truth, 181
philosophy of religion, 5, 209
philosophy of Buddhist religion, 208, 225-226
pluralism, 208-209
poruḷ, 69
practice, 91-96
pragmatism, 174, 196
precepts of abstention, 26
Premasiri, P. Don, 11, 114
process philosophy, 184 fl.
  and compassion, 193
  and creativity, 192
  and *Hinayāna*, 191
  and *Madhyamika*, 191
  and *Mahayāna*, 188-189
  and *Yogācāra*, 191
"Protestant Buddhism," 1
Protestant Reformation, 7
Psalms of the Brethren, 129
Puligandla, Ramakrishna, 9-10, 175 fl.
puñña (merit), 32, 107, 114, 146-148
puthujjana, 22, 114, 123, 148

questions,
  about being Buddhist in society, 148, 151
  about *nibbana*, 43, 205
  about ordination of women, 145
  about virtue, 42
  about impermanence and suffering, 159 fl.
  undetermined (*avyakatani*), 196-197, 205
Quine, W.V.O., 174

rāga (or lobha), dosa, and moha, 37, 106
Ratnayaka, Shanta, 9-10, 184 fl.
rebirth, 39, 133 fl.
  among the rich, 143
  and *kammapathas*, 39
  as background, 139
  logical grammar of, 135 fl.
  not a factual matter, 136
  uses of the term, 136-138
reductionistic process, 213
  bhava -, 121-122

Tantrayana (Vajrayana), 156, 189-191
Tartakov, Gary, 210
Tathāgata, 141, 159, 200
  questions about, 197
tautology, 179
Theravāda, 34, 159, 161, 198-200, 203-204
  and process thought, 184 fl.
  critique of, 141 fl., 143
three refuges, 27
Tillich, Paul, 199
time and change, 180
Tipiṭaka, 187
Tirukkuraḷ, 57 fl.
Tiruvaḷḷuvar, 59 fl.

transcendent/immanent distinction, 203
truth, 174 fl., 177-179, 225
Turner, Bryan, S., 215

Udāna, 162
uposatha day, 27
Uraga Sutta, 128

Van der Veer, Peter, 219
Vasubandhu, 91-96
verification (see also falsification), 136-137
vīdu, 69
Vinaya Piṭaka, 29
violence (see also nonviolence), 150
vipaśyanā, (Pali, *vipassanā*) 95
virtues, 34, 36, 40-42
  and action, 41
  as integral to path, 42
Visuddhimagga, 21, 25, 91, 112
  four kinds of *sila* in, 25
vītikkama, 111

Warren, Henry Clark, 79
way of *Ātman*, 161-163
way of Hinduism, 162
way of *Nirvana*, 161-163
Wettimuny, R.G. de S., 126
wheel of life (*bhavacakra*), 51
Whitehead, Alfred North, 184, 193-194
Wittgenstein, Ludwig, 9, 133 fl., 137-139, 213-214
Wixted, John T., 216
women in Buddhism, 145
  ordination of, 145

Yearley, Lee, 40
Yogācāra, 163

Zen, 147, 149-150